Günter Leypoldt, Manfred Berg (eds.)
Authority and Trust in US Culture and Society

Günter Leypoldt is a professor of American literature and culture at Heidelberg University, the author of *Cultural Authority in the Age of Whitman: A Transatlantic Perspective* (2009), and editor of *Intellectual Authority and Literary Culture in the US, 1790-1900* (2013) and *Reading Practices* (2015).

Manfred Berg is the Curt Engelhorn Professor of American History at Heidelberg University. He is the author and editor of nineteen books, including *The Ticket to Freedom: The NAACP and the Struggle for Black Political Integration* (2005); *Popular Justice: A History of Lynching in America* (2011); *Woodrow Wilson. Amerika und die Neuordnung der Welt. Eine Biographie* (2017).

Günter Leypoldt, Manfred Berg (eds.)

Authority and Trust in US Culture and Society

Interdisciplinary Approaches and Perspectives

This publication was funded by the German Research Association (Deutsche For-schungsgemeinschaft)

Bibliographic information published by the Deutsche Nationalbibliothek
The Deutsche Nationalbibliothek lists this publication in the Deutsche Nation-albibliografie; detailed bibliographic data are available in the Internet at http://dnb.d-nb.de

Cover layout: Maria Arndt, Bielefeld
Printed by Majuskel Medienproduktion GmbH, Wetzlar

PDF-ISBN 978-3-8394-5189-2
https://doi.org/10.14361/9783839451892

Contents

Preface

This book argues that looking at authority and trust in interrelation can elucidate crucial aspects of culture and society, in the United States and elsewhere. The essays assembled here have emerged from a collaborative research training group (Graduiertenkolleg 2244) entitled "Authority and Trust in American Culture, Society, History, and Politics," funded by the German Research Foundation (DFG) and based at the Heidelberg Center for American Studies (HCA). Since its inception in 2017, this research initiative has brought together scholars and graduate students working in American Studies from a variety of disciplines across the humanities and social sciences (historiography, religious studies/church history, urban geography, political science, international relations, linguistics, and literary and cultural studies).

The essays reflect the vibrant discussion culture among this group of authors, the first cohort of graduate researchers (Kristin Berberich, Florian Böller, Louis Butcher, Elizabeth Corrao-Billeter, David Eisler, Claudia Jetter, Aleksandra Polińska, Maren Schäfer, Aline Schmidt, Tim Sommer, Sebastian Tants, Cosima Werner, Georg Wolff), and the people at the HCA. All of us have profited greatly from the generous input of scholars who visited our lecture series in the past three years to present their latest work and engage in conversation with us (in order of appearance, Juliet Kaarbo, David Alworth, Donald Pease, Peter Schneck, Alan Partington, Andreas Reckwitz, Hans Joas, Jeffrey Alexander, Claire Squires, Heike Paul, Guido Möllering, David Wilson, Omar Lizardo, Amy Hungerford, Kameshwari Pothukuchi, Laura Dassow Walls, Caroline Levine, James English, Sandra Gustafson, Hugh Ryan, Merve Emre, Hartmut Rosa, Michèlle Mendelssohn, Gisèle Sapiro, Alexander Starre, Barbara Buchenau, Kai Sina, and Cameron Thies). We are also grateful to the large number of people who helped us bring this collection together: Thanks to Hannes Nagl, Lena Pfeifer, Williams Rothvoss-Buchheimer, and Styles Sass for getting the manuscript into shape; to the editorial team at transcript for making this publication possible; to the German Research foundation for their funding, and to Knowledge Unlatched for including this collection in their open access program.

Günter Leypoldt
Manfred Berg
Heidelberg, October 2020

Introduction
Authority and Trust in the United States

Günter Leypoldt

> "A 'crisis of authority' has overtaken America and the West generally"
> *New York Times, July 1st, 1979*

> "Trust Is Collapsing in America"
> *The Atlantic, January 21, 2018.*

In the past few years, the US public has been polarized by declining trust in political institutions, credentialed experts, and social elites. Many commentators speak of a deep crisis of authority in the United States (Knag 1997; Hetherington 2005; Hayes 2012; Taranto 2013; Fraser 2017). Analysts point to a cluster of structural causes, including rising inequality levels, increasing socio-cultural and spatio-economic segregation, and diminishing civic and state infrastructures, all of which might be seen as effects of an institutional "unwinding" of America (Packer, 2013) in the wake of neoliberal governance, postindustrial globalization, and the financialization of party politics (see also Bartels 2008; Stiglitz 2012; Noah 2012; Reeves 2017; Fraser 2017). The domestic crisis also seems to affect the nation's authority in the world, as the international community becomes increasingly skeptical about the United States' capability to fulfill its traditional global leadership role (Krastev 2019; Butler 2020; Betts 2012; Haass 2013; Ikenberry 2011, 2018). Of course, diagnosing "crises" is a genre in its own right, prone to what Raymond Williams (1973, 9–10) called the "escalator" effect, when each generation glimpses the golden age just disappearing "over the last hill" of their own remembered past. What seems an overall decline of trust and authority might be better described in terms of shifting centers of power or sources of legitimacy. This collection of essays looks at how the present "crisis" indicates significant transformations of authority in the US.

Let us begin with a working definition: To wield authority is to dominate a social relationship in a manner that those who are dominated consider legitimate. Whereas crude "power," according to Max Weber, can make us follow someone else's "will" against our own "resistance," authority is a power to which we submit willingly because we feel it embodies a higher good (1972, 122; 1947, 324).[1] Unlike tyranny (Snyder 2017), legitimate domination elicits "deference" (Shils 1982; Friedman 1990; Soper 2002), and therefore requires neither authoritarian coercion nor argumentative persuasion (Hannah Arendt quipped that parents can "lose" their "authority" either by beating their kids, i.e., behaving like "tyrant[s]," or by starting to argue with them, i.e. treating them as "equal[s]" [1972, 144]).[2] Deference is a complex structure of feeling (Flatley 2008, 26–7), a sense of the upward pull of legitimacy that centrally involves the experience of trust. The defining premise of this collection is that we can better understand authority as a social phenomenon if we study it in relation to the lived experience of social trust relations.

Trusting authority requires not only specific truth-claims or beliefs (Weber's "Legitimitätsglaube" [1972, 122; 1947, 325]) but also a practical sense of "vertical resonance" (Rosa 2019, 284), the feeling that specific truth-claims or beliefs connect to a higher order (moral, civil-sacred, cultural, religious, etc.). Thus whereas the study of *power differentials* can rely on empirical data about objective statistical dominance (so many tanks, so much economic weight, so many political "assets"), tracing authority requires the hermeneutic and

---

1   See Szelenyi (2016) on Weber's terms "Herrschaft" and "Autorität" and their various translations as "authority," "domination" or "rule."

2   As Arendt explains in "What is Authority?" in 1956: "Since authority always demands obedience, it is commonly mistaken for some form of power or violence. Yet authority precludes the use of external means of coercion; where force is used, authority itself has failed. Authority, on the other hand, is incompatible with persuasion, which presupposes equality and works through a process of argumentation. Where arguments are used, authority is left in abeyance. Against the egalitarian order of persuasion stands the authoritarian order, which is always hierarchical. If authority is to be defined at all, then, it must be in contradistinction to both coercion by force and persuasion through arguments. (The authoritarian relation between the one who commands and the one who obeys rests neither on common reason nor on the power of the one who commands; what they have in common is the hierarchy itself, whose rightness and legitimacy both recognize and where both have their predetermined stable place)" (1961, 92-3).

ethnographic work of reconstructing site-specific and culturally embedded *atmospheres* of trust. The interplay of authority and trust does not only concern questions of political governance, but also extends to various kinds of symbolic action. *Cultural* authority shapes the spatial hierarchies in urban environments, affects the curation of authorized heritage systems (ranging from consecrated sites of memory to literary-artistic canons), and the public relevance of moral value systems that connect religious or civil-sacred hierarchies with the field of cultural production. The study of these phenomena requires an interdisciplinary and historicizing approach. This collection gathers writing on authority and trust in the US from a range of disciplines across the humanities and social sciences, from the nineteenth century to the present. The assembled essays explore the recent turn to political populism (Manfred Berg), the shifting legitimacy of expert systems since World War II (Martin Thunert), the impact of domestic politics on the US' international relations (Florian Böller/Sebastian Harnisch), the urban-geographic dimensions of city planning and governance (Ulrike Gerhard/Judith Keller/Cosima Werner), the urban imaginary of the nineteenth-century city novel (Margit Peterfy), charismatic authority claims in antebellum religion and transcendentalism (Claudia Jetter/Jan Stievermann), nineteenth-century representations of Anglo-American power relations (Tim Sommer), conceptualizations of trust by American Renaissance writers (Dietmar Schloss), and the relevance of authority and trust for the hermeneutics of reading (Günter Leypoldt).

Legitimacy and the Civil Sacred

US cultural history has been shaped by a deep-rooted skepticism toward authorities of all kinds. Distrusting state power and embracing anti-elitist and libertarian individualism has been part of an "American Creed" that defines itself against the vaunted scenes of state-interventionist Europe (Lipset 1996; Wills 1999). But the problem of legitimate dominance did not simply disappear with King George III. As John Stuart Mill put it in 1840 (paraphrasing Alexis de Tocqueville's *Democracy in America*), "authority" as a basis of political or social agency "may be rejected in theory, but it always exists in fact" (1840, 25).

Mill and Tocqueville grappled with the question of how authority fits into modern democracy, an issue that has remained important to twentieth- and twenty-first-century debates about legitimate governance. Weber's influential distinction between "traditional," "rational-legal," and "charismatic" types of authority can be viewed as an elaboration on Tocqueville's analysis of democratic change (Furedi 2013). In Weber's view, modernity's relentless process of "rationalization" undermines traditional sources of legitimacy (the felt "sanctity [Heiligkeit] of immemorial traditions"). This poses the question of whether abstract rational-legal systems can make up for the delegitimized tradition and provide similarly solid trust foundations. In his famous thoughts on "charismatic authority,"[3] Weber reflects upon the relevance of the sacred in modern secular societies, where traditional religion (as Weber thought) was going to become residual. How do societies shaped by purpose-rational "objectification [Versachlichung]" grapple with the moral economies of inalienable ideals? (See Jetter/Stievermann in this volume on how charismatic notions of poetic and religious experience negotiate the religious crisis of authority in the antebellum period).

While Weber seems to have regarded charismatic rule as a throwback to the premodern that would ultimately disappear with bureaucratic reason (Alexander 2011, 2), the American Weberian Edward Shils suggested that all modern societies require a "charismatic center" (1982) that stabilizes their core values (see Schlette 2013). And where Weber framed charisma as an exceptional force that rarely survives "routinization [Veralltäglichung]" or "institutionalization" (1972, 142; 1947, 363), Shils theorized the charismatic as a more lasting, often low-grade intensity at the level of "the routine functioning of society" that "not only disrupts social order" but "also maintains or conserves it" (1982, 120). In contrast to Weber's focus on charisma as personal authority, moreover (which inspired today's vernacular meaning of charisma as powerful individual magnetism), Shils emphasized the structure of social relations: charismatic legitimacy happens to individuals or things, spaces, and institutions that performatively embody a society's charismatic center.

Shils' interpretation remained a minority view as long as the humanities and social sciences tended towards various "subtraction stories" (Taylor 2007, 22) that defined modernization and democratization in terms of an erosion of authority—a decline of the sacred, devaluation of moral norms, loosening

---

3   Defined by people's extraordinary "devotion [außeralltäglichen Hingabe]" to the "specific and exceptional sanctity, heroism or exemplary character [Heiligkeit, Heldenkraft, Vorbildlichkeit]" of "an individual person" and the "normative patterns" created or "revealed" by this person (Weber 1972, 124; 1947, 328).

of social status hierarchies and pluralization of lifestyles. The subtraction narrative often posits a zero-sum conflict between hierarchical power on the one hand and individual self-fulfillment on the other—John Stuart Mill's *On Liberty* (1859) invokes a historical "struggle between Liberty and Authority" (1997, 41) and hopes for a future liberated from centrally authorized hierarchies. The "countercultural" climate of the 1960s often drew its sense of weakening hierarchies from interpreting the increasing individualization of lifestyles as a radical pluralization of values. "[T]he notion of moral authority is no longer a viable notion," Alasdair MacIntyre wrote in 1964, for authority only makes sense "in a community and in areas of life in which there is an agreed way of doing things according to accepted rules" (1967, 53). The impression that moral authority was a thing of the past inspired a wealth of countercultural liberation narratives (Binkley 2007, Frank 1997), but it also cohered well with the ideal of a liberal "procedural republic" (Sandel 1998) in which all values are to be treated as equally valid (Rawls 1971, 1993). Proceduralist thinking suggests that radical pluralism can be managed with content-blind mechanisms of elimination that exclude from the "public square" all that is merely private (religion) or lacks reasonable common sense. The assumption is that open societies can practice radical tolerance, yet defend themselves against illiberal threats by rejecting "populists" or "racists" on the grounds of their flawed or irrational "logic."[4]

As more recent social and cultural theory has pointed out, however, the most liberal democratic value systems are shaped by moral economies that command considerable public authority. According to Hans Joas, even such apparently self-evident moral-ethical values as human rights owe their legitimacy to processes of consecration similar to Weber's charismatic authority: Certain values strike us with a sense of "subjective self-evidence and affective intensity" (Joas 2013, 5) that immunizes us against the skeptical questions of rational or scientific argument. Jeffrey Alexander makes a similar point when he argues that modern democracies are shaped by a "civil sacred" whose institutional basis rests in the civil sphere (at the interstices of political, economic, religious, and literary-artistic fields). The civil sacred produces moral binaries

---

4   See, for example, Jan-Werner Müller's claim that populism has an "inner logic" based on a deceptive "illusion" (2016, 10–11), in contrast to Mudde/Kaltwasser (2017), who argue that a populist logic can have good or bad political effects, and Mouffe (2018), who in the spirit of Laclau (2005) interprets populism as a specific form of democratic dissent and calls for a new left-wing populism.

by which the public distinguishes "civil" from "uncivil" ways of life along the lines of higher or lower human decency, moral integrity, social justice, solidarity, and so on (2006, 57–9). While the civil sacred revolves around an ideal of democratic equality, in social performance it withholds equal recognition from those who are considered to "profane" or to "pollute" society's moral core. Alexander's account shows the eminently public nature of moral authority: Disagreements about what counts as human decency or social justice tend to spill over onto the public square, especially when they happen to resonate with the sort of "hot-button issues" that drive the US culture wars (Hartman 2015).

The pitched battles between today's culture-warriors over public moral authority can seem to inhabit an alternative universe to the proverbially relaxed sensibilities of the countercultural 1960s (Binkley 2007). Subtraction models like to explain this by invoking the "return of authority" as a large-scale conservative reaction. In Fredric Jameson's account, for example, the 1960s were a "moment of universal liberation" followed, in the 1970s, by "powerful restorations of the social order and the renewal of the repressive power of the various state apparatuses" (1988, 207–8). Pippa Norris and Ronald Inglehart's "cultural-backlash" theory provides a more complex picture. They suggest that a "silent revolution" in the prosperous 1950s and 1960s brought on an "intergenerational value shift among the Western publics" that prioritized "post-materialist" values revolving around "individual free choice and self-expression" (2019, 32–3). The gradual mainstreaming of these values (which in the 1970s and 1980s had been called "countercultural" but in the 1990s became common enough in high-income societies to make this term somewhat outmoded) provoked a defiant counter-reaction by older cohorts of social conservatives that dominated the "heartland" or "Middle America" (Taggart 2000, 93). These became "resentful at finding themselves becoming minorities, stranded on the losing side of history" (Norris/Inglehart 2019, 47–8)—"strangers in their own land" (Hochschild 2016). While this resentment was palpable in many Western publics, the cultural backlash in the US required a distinct political figuration. In the Republic of Ireland, for instance, misgivings about post-materialist change among older age cohorts were comparable to those among social conservatives in the US, but as we can gather from the Irish campaigns for the legalization of gay marriage (2015) and abortion (2018), the conservative position did not create powerful political alignments outside the Catholic Church, with the result that the public referenda about these issues showed little signs of divisive culture war (see Murphy 2016; Earner-Byrne/Urquhart

2019). In the US, by contrast, a series of political cleavages and voter realignments since 1968 helped to empower the conservative position with new political coalitions.[5] As Manfred Berg points out in his essay below, by 2016 this political coalition had grown into the formidable platform of authoritarian populism.

If political platforms make up one foundation of authority claims, another has to do with civil society's shifting sense of what counts as its moral core. It is helpful to recall that the silent revolution's pluralization of value (Inglehart 1977) mostly (and most lastingly) transformed the domain of lifestyle and consumption practices (Frank 1997), a domain that tends to be shaped by what Charles Taylor describes as "weak evaluation" (Taylor 1985, 16, see Leypoldt below). Weak evaluation typically concerns everyday choices that people may be passionate about without considering them as central to their moral core, which makes it relatively easy to practice a near relativist tolerance of difference. In the domains of "strong evaluation," which concern identity-defining "hypergoods" (in Taylor's parlance), it becomes a lot harder to tolerate difference. Subtraction narratives tend to mistake the pluralization of weak values for a large-scale indifference to authority that can be framed either as a heroic breakthrough (Woodstock's defeat of the "authoritarian personality") or a deplorable declension (the "closing of the American mind" at the hands of a relativistic left [Bloom 1987]). What encourages such category mistakes is that the borders between weaker and stronger value domains are constantly shifting.

The transformation of religious authority that has been associated with the decline of church memberships and the rise of individualized religiosities or spiritualities since the 1960s offers pertinent examples of this. Consider the hyper-individualist religious ethos Robert Bellah called "Sheilaism,"

---

5   The most decisive political realignment concerned the breakup of the New Deal coalition that shifted large parts of the working class vote to the Republican Party, which in the late 1960s came to unite the interests of those who wanted to see greater states' rights, more authoritarian policing, a more thorough move towards laissez faire economics, and a more central place for Christianity on the public square. This shift first emerged in the campaign of George Wallace that, in Joseph Lowndes' formulation, invoked, as the most representative figure of the "signifier America," the "white middle-class male from every region who is pushed around by an invasive federal government, threatened by crime and social disorder, discriminated against by affirmative action and surrounded by increasing moral degradation" (2005, 148).

after an interviewee ("Sheila Larson") who said she was religious but only according to a "faith" based on "[j]ust my own little voice." Bellah was troubled by Sheilaism because he thought it suggested "the logical possibility of over 220 million American religions, one for each of us" (2007, 221). He pointed out that a religious framework based on the beliefs of a single person can no longer supply identity-defining moral authority. Indeed, the presence of 220 million religions in the US would surely downgrade their differences to the level of weak-value consumption choices. At first glance, the rise of Sheilaism therefore seemed to support the "de-intensificiation" theory of secularization (Partridge 2006, 8), the claim that commerce and individualism replaced religious authority with "low-intensity" spiritualities and consumerist "life style" religions (Turner 2011, 279; see Wilson 1979). On a closer look, however, Larson's seeker-spirituality (Wuthnow 1998) combines an individualist theology with widely shared non-theistic forms of moral virtue: Her sense of "something beyond" her mundane self (Ammerman 2013, 269) might have little to do with traditional clerical-religious authorities, but remains nonetheless beholden to the civil sacred in Alexander's sense ("I think [God] would want us to take care of each other," Larson says, invoking strong-valued notions of democratic solidarity [Bellah et al. 2007, 221]).

Seeker spiritualities have more dispersed sources of moral authority (Woodhead/Heelas 2000, 354), but they do not necessarily retreat to a realm of private indifference. This is perhaps most obvious in the recent debates about "#MeToo," "#OccupyWallStreet," "#BlackLivesMatter," "#RhodesMustFall," or the "Confederate Monument" affair, when younger and more liberal age cohorts (which tend to have a lower voter turnout) felt compelled to take a public stand against what they experienced as "uncivil" or "toxic." Toxicity might be viewed as the negative slope of moral authority: People or things become toxic when they enjoy a high degree of cultural presence (i.e., as cultural icons) while facing increasing doubts about their moral legitimacy. While the delegitimization of unconsecrated people and things tends merely to inspire contempt (we only notice them long enough to dismiss them as not worth our attention), toxic cultural icons produce a stigmatized presence that inspires disgust. As a strong affect, disgust upsets the public sphere, triggering a sense that one's self needs to be purged of an identity-polluting influence, one that seems wrongfully consecrated by "the authorities" and cannot just be ignored. Disgust with a toxic cultural icon is thus an eminently public, community-building emotion that encourages the agonistic conviviality of "cancel culture" (Asmelash 2019, see Leypoldt below).

The production of authority relies on a layered "public sphere" that sits at the periphery of political and economic power and connects the "problem brokers" of the civil sphere (Knaggård 2015) with a variety of media systems (Chadwick 2017), differing in their degrees of functional autonomy, participatory openness, and cultural relevance. At the one end of the spectrum, there is a large-scale cultural marketplace whose commercially regulated media ecologies show high levels of democratic inclusiveness. At the other end we find a hierarchically organized "restricted" cultural market (Bourdieu 1995) that thrives on *symbolic* economies because it is shaped by authorized expert systems, including curation cultures, taste-making networks, and peer-oriented consecrating institutions (English 2005; McGurl 2009; Balzer 2014; Leypoldt 2015; Bhaskar 2016). While the large-scale cultural marketplace does most of the economic heavy lifting—as a space of blockbuster entertainment, multi-million dollar book deals, a culture of infotainment and commercial ratings systems—the restricted market has an inordinate impact on the public sense of what can count as "legitimate" cultural production and identity-defining ("canonical") cultural heritage (see Tim Sommer's essay below on the nineteenth-century legitimation of Anglo-American heritage). Indeed the challenge in understanding how today's media systems differ in their impact on the production of authority, is to recognize the complex relation between numbers (i.e., sales figures, Nielsen ratings, and the like) and public prestige (i.e., the ability to shape the aesthetic and moral hierarchies of public space). This is all the more important when dealing with the cultural authority of "literary culture," a term that is generally used to include both the "laureate position" in the literary field—the peer-oriented system of literary prizes in which authorized networks consecrate works of high intellectual ambition—and a market-regulated space of popular entertainment that is often less relevant to the production of cultural authority (think of the gulf between Toni Morrison's difficult but Nobel-consecrated and hence highly iconic works and the more accessible but virtually invisible writings of Danielle Steel, who sold more than 600 million copies of her 61 novels between 1973 and 2004 [Maryles 2004]). If the literary prize system resembles a kind of "media bubble"—catering as it does to a small and predominantly affluent and well-educated audience (Griswold 2008, 65)—unlike more recent "social media echo chambers" (Nguyen 2020), it remains shaped by the more traditional expert systems linked to the liberal professions (Leypoldt 2020). Yet all media professionalisms—in literature or journalism—can clash with the democratic ethos of the civil sphere if gatekeeping practices come across as repressive acts of exclusion. The professionalization of knowledge production is not a recent development (Shapin 1994; Kitcher 2011; Millgram 2015), and, as Martin Thunert points out in his essay below, people habitually defer to credentialed experts in matters of "hard" science. Once knowledge production touches upon moral values, cultural tastes, or the ethics of a good life, however, professional expertise can be perceived as cultural imperialism or elite snobbism. The ominous charge of "fake news" that populists have levelled at traditional news outlets reflects an increasing mistrust in credentialed curation cultures. The sociocultural causes of such mistrust have not yet been adequately understood.

Authority and Trust

People's sense of legitimate power hinges on the experience of trust. Over the past thirty years, the concept of trust has become a more prominent topic in the humanities and social sciences. Here, the sociological insight that modern societies require a high degree of social and political trust (Giddens 1990; Luhmann 2009; see Dietmar Schloss' essay below) has encouraged inquiries into whether we are presently witnessing an impending erosion of trust that might undermine "social cooperation, solidarity and consensus" (Misztal 1996). One salient source of low-trust atmospheres in the US is of course the rise of "hyperpartisan publics" (Waisbord et al. 2018, 32). The increasing value gap between Democratic and Republican voting cultures since the 1970s seems to have led to an "affective polarization" (Iyengar et al. 2019) that shapes people's trust in experts and defines their sense of what counts as "fake news" (Rini 2017)—a recent study of the COVID pandemic showed that compliance with social distancing regulations aligned mostly with partisan lines, even in communities with high infection rates (Clinton et al. 2020). Whereas modernity, according to Anthony Giddens, produces "disembedding mechanisms" that "lift out" social trust relationships from "localised contexts" and attach them to more abstract expert systems (1990, 53), political polarization might be said to produce "reembedded contexts of action" (1990, 80) that tie the perception of trust to partisan networks (Svolik 2020, McCoy/Somer 2019). These re-embedding effects are most obvious in the polarized climate of "culture war," when having a moral stance on abortion, wearing a Corona face mask in a supermarket, or debating the legitimacy of specific monuments, are overdetermined by a political cleavage that resonates with specific sociocultural positions (i.e., affiliation to specific life worlds, regions, class locations, or racial or ethnic identity). This tribalization of trust has significant effects on the public perception of authority. To be considered a legitimate form of power, authority requires people's trust that the ruling government represents something they recognize as a higher good. If affective polarization undermines such trust, it can lead to a vicious circle of popular distrust and coercive governance. The recent conflicts over police violence against African Americans exemplify this dynamic all too well: A police force that loses the citizenry's trust will face angry and uncompliant protesters; angry and uncompliant protesters provoke coercive backlash, in turn increasing the citizenry's distrust, and so on (see Manfred Berg below). The hyperpartisan cleavage in the US tends to escalate this downward spiral such that the polarized camps mistrust each other's truth-claims: one party's "excessive police brutality" then becomes another's "law and order."[6]

Trust research hopes to understand such crises by inquiring into the civic foundations of trust. Since Tocqueville, trust has been associated with a vivid democratic civil sphere ("Americans of all ages, all conditions, all minds constantly unite" in "thousand" kinds of "associations," he wrote in 1840 [2000, 489]). Neo-Tocquevillians like Robert Putnam (1993; 2000) or Francis Fukuyama (1995) argue that there is a significant link between people's trust in government institutions and their involvement in "civic community," that is, their participation in networks based on spontaneous sociability rather than kinship. In his influential *Making Democracy Work* (1993), Putnam drew this argument from the study of Italian political institutions: Whereas northern Italy was shaped by "vibrant networks and norms of civic engagement" that led to a culture of "trust and cooperation," southern Italy was hampered by "vertically structured politics, a social life of fragmentation and isolation, and a culture of distrust" (1993, 15). The difference between these regions, Putnam argued, was their unequal production of "social capital," that is, the amount of "weak ties" that sustained the moral contract of civic collaboration.[7] Low social capital undermined what Putnam called "generalized reciprocity" (the

---

6   On the relevance of the "law and order" discourse for Nixon in 1968 and Trump in 2020, see Taylor/Morris 2018 and Shapiro 2020.

7   Putnam distinguishes social capital into "bonding capital" that defines close association between friends, and "bridging capital" that links more distant acquaintances. Following Granovetter's thesis that "weak ties" linking people to less familiar circles can be more important for getting ahead than the strong ties linking people to intimate friends, Putnam ascribes to bridging capital a stronger civic and democratic function (2000, 22-3).

willingness to do something for someone not because they are more powerful or because they will return the favor but because I trust that "someone else will do something for me down the road" [2000, 21]).[8] "Building social capital will not be easy," Putnam concluded, "but it is the key to making democracy work" (1993, 185). In the mid-1990s, he applied his model to the US and found that its civic networks had become thinner since the 1960s—his image of a person "bowling alone" rather than in groups (literally a reference to a 40 percent decline in league bowling concomitantly to a 10 percent rise of individual bowlers from 1980 to 1993 [Putnam 1995]) became an iconic metaphor for how modern individualism undermines the ties that bind democratic communities.

Putnam's work has drawn substantial critiques (Kaufman 2002; Tilly 2007, 85–6), but his thesis that declining trust in authority in the US might be causally linked to the nation's sense of social cohesiveness as a whole is a familiar theme of empirical trust research (see Martin Thunert below). A recent Pew survey (see Rainie et al. 2019) indicates that Americans who express distrust in governmental and institutional authorities are more likely to express lower "interpersonal trust" in the efficiency and fairness of the community. Unsurprisingly, the poll also shows that the major predictors for low interpersonal trust are lower household income, lower levels of education, and non-white race or ethnicity.

The relevance of identitarian boundaries is confirmed by research on how trust emerges in residential neighborhoods (see the essay by Ulrike Gerhard/Judith Keller/Cosima Werner below). Black and Hispanic residents in general report lower levels of trust than "native-born whites," and while the latter express higher trust in "in-group" communities, their trust levels are more likely to decrease in proportion to increasing neighborhood diversity, especially related to "blacks and, to a lesser extent, Hispanics—not Asians or others" (Abascal/Baldassarri 2015, 748, 754). Some studies conclude from this that neighborhood diversity is detrimental to social trust in general. Robert Putnam thinks that "people in ethnically diverse settings appear to 'hunker

---

8   Putnam leans towards rational-choice theoretical concepts that explain trust relationships in terms of interest-based reciprocity (see Hardin 2002). Many other theorists suggest that genuine trust requires a "leap of faith" (Möllering 2006, 7; Frevert 2013, 220) grounded by affective-emotional and moral-cultural investments. Georg Simmel speaks with reference to the banking industry of a "social-psychological" form of "belief" related to "religion" (1900, 151-196; Möllering 2001); Giddens describes trust as "a commitment to something rather than just a cognitive understanding" (1990, 27).

down'—that is, to pull in like a turtle" (2007, 149). Other scholars suggest that the problem with diversity concerns a gap between discourse and practice. In her research on a racially diverse neighborhood of Chicago, Meghan Burke finds that whites will engage in "pro-diversity happy talk" (2012, 98) while their "social action" in the community or the real estate market tends to support a "white center in its sensibilities, safety, and security (economic and otherwise)" (2012, 98, 118; see Bell/Hartmann 2007). Social psychologists get a great deal of media attention (Friedersdorf 2019; Edsall 2018, 2020) by attributing mistrust in diversity to a "heritable" psychological disposition: some people, the argument goes, have an "authoritarian" mindset that comes with a "lack of openness" and other "cognitive limitations" that "reduce" their "willingness and capacity (respectively) to tolerate complexity, diversity, and difference" (Stenner/Haidt 2018, 183). More convincingly, scholarship that pays attention to social interdependencies (Wilson 2007; Wacquant 2007) re-places blanket references to diversity with a more nuanced study of how trust relates to structural inequalities (Uslaner 2002, 2008, 2012; Rothwell 2012). According to Maria Abascal and Delia Baldassarri, "it is not the diversity of a community that undermines trust, but rather the disadvantages that people in diverse communities face" (2016 np).[9]

Trust relations are hard to establish, since empirical surveys can capture only "attitudinal"—self-reported—trust in response to generic survey questions. The world value survey, for example, asks: "Generally speaking, would you say that most people can be trusted or that you cannot be too careful in dealing with people?" Scholars have noted that "it is not entirely clear what this question exactly measures," and how the interviewees' answers relate to their lived practice (Sapienza et al. 2013, 1313). Some think that attitudinal

---

9   Poor neighborhoods tend to have "smaller social networks" than more affluent com-munities, which makes it harder for them "to mobilize their ties to secure resources." Another predictor is residential stability: "homeownership strongly and positively pre-dicts trust in neighbors and neighborhood cooperation." Finally: "Indicators of eco-nomic conditions, especially education and economic satisfaction, positively predict several measures of trust. In addition, household income is strongly, positively asso-ciated with neighborhood cooperation, while unemployment is strongly, negatively associated with trust in neighbors. In short, we find that individual and contextual in-dicators of racial/ethnic differences, residential stability, and economic well-being are the strongest predictors of trust and cooperation, thus swinging the pendulum of the determinants of trust away from ethnic diversity and towards well studied economic and social indicators" (Abascal/Baldassarri 2015, 734, 748–50).

measures are particularly misleading across identitarian boundaries. For example, Abascal and Baldassarri find that blacks constantly report lower attitudinal trust than whites but "in trust games that require individuals to make consequential economic decisions," the gap between blacks and whites disappears (2015, 729). Writing as a historian, Geoffrey Hosking stresses that trust "has to be teased out 'between the lines'" of people's utterances (2014, 24). The social historian Charles Tilly, similarly, argues that while attitudinal markers provide a "first indication" of trust relationships, it is key to look at their participants' moves and practices: "if you trust me," Tilly says, "don't just tell me so; let me take charge of your children's education, lend me your life's savings for investment, take medicines I give you, or help me paint my house on the assumption that I will help you paint yours. If you don't trust me, prove it by doing none of these things, and nothing like them" (2005, 12). This seems good advice not only for the survey culture of the empirical social sciences but also for textualist scholarship in the humanities that would take Hosking's warning about trust having to be teased out from "between the lines" as a call to more intense but nonetheless object-centered "close reading" (see Margit Peterfy's essay on the literary ethnography of trust).

Tilly's work suggests that democracies do not just require disembedded forms of trust (Giddens) or the social capital of weak ties (Putnam), they also need to find ways to incorporate tightly-knit "trust networks" that have existed outside or inside state rule structures for thousands of years—his examples range from kinship ties to religious sects, trade diasporas, migration networks, artisanal groups, patron-client chains, credit networks, societies of mutual aid, and many others (2005, 6). Trust networks, according to Tilly, involve "ramified interpersonal connections" that consist "mainly of strong ties" and place "valued" and "long-term resources and enterprises" at risk to the "malfeasance, mistakes, and failures of individual members" (2007, 81–2). In the twentieth and twenty-first centuries, people continue to rely on trust networks "for such practical activities as getting jobs, migrating long distances, making major purchases, borrowing money, engaging in high-risk political activity, and finding marriage partners" etc. (2005, 13–14). Tilly's claim is that democratization requires trust networks to be integrated into public politics, to allow the state to profit from these networks' resources and shift from coercive to commitment-based forms of rule. By the same logic, "extensive withdrawal of trust networks from public politics" can be damaging to democracy (2005, 11). Even in affluent and powerful modern societies, Tilly argues with a view to the United States, "democracy remains vulnerable" if the withdrawal of trust networks divides privileged groups from the larger social whole: "Privatization of social security or health care, withdrawal of elites or minorities from public schools," retrenchment into "exclusive clubs and religious sects, gated communities, and capture of governmental agencies or offices for private profit," all of these produce de-democratizing effects by allowing economic and political elites "to secure their own advantages without subjecting themselves to the costs and constraints of public politics" (2005, 150, 11).

Tilly's study of trust networks coheres well with recent research on the network-related making and unmaking of group identity. Since democratic politics involves "pressures to associate for collective action," it creates "us-them boundaries" that "threaten naturally accumulated trust" (Tilly 2007, 93). Andreas Wimmer (2013; 2018) has shown that boundaries between groups harden into quasi-ethnic boundaries in proportion to their social closure (when members of one network have fewer ties to members of others), and also in proportion to the power inequalities between the separated groups (when one socially closed network has more politico-economic or status-related assets than others). The takeaway point is that identitarian boundaries do not express intrinsic group differences, but rather emerge when socio-institutional figurations happen to give certain (often arbitrary) group differences identity-defining social and moral resonance. This separation of groups may evolve gradually over time, as in the division between Protestant and Catholic Northern Ireland (where longstanding power inequalities between socially closed networks turned a religious difference that most modern Europeans find uninteresting into a veritable "ethnoreligious divide" that organizes central dimensions of Northern Irish social life). Boundaries can also erupt more suddenly, as when in 1990s Yugoslavia the collapse of Communism's political networks unleashed ethnonational and ethnoreligious loyalties that during the communist regime had little social importance.

Wimmer's work demonstrates the fluidity of the groups that are commonly treated as the hard-wired ethno-racial segments of American "diversity." Network effects can render such seemingly binary differences as the black/white distinction so fuzzy as to confuse insiders to which group they belong. The significant variations of the "color-line" across the world (a one-drop rule in the US and South Africa vs. a somatic continuum in Brazil, Cuba, Puerto Rico or Colombia) correlates, according to Wimmer, with patterns of economic and political interdependencies.[10] Trusting the cultural "other" is thus not just a question of tolerance or "empathy" (as public debates about "racism" often imply), but depends on structural interdependencies that are shaped by political and economic policy (Wacquant 2007; Wilkerson 2020). Building trust therefore also means to reverse the segregating effects of neoliberal programs.[11] If today's political cleavages can divide groups that would not normally describe their difference in identitarian terms, such as the affectively polarized and mutually mistrusting blocks of Republican and Democrat voters in the US, building networks that transcend identitarian and class boundaries might soften the most rigid socio-cultural divides.

---

10   Wimmer's comparison with Brazil seems helpful here: "When slavery was abolished and restricted forms of democracy introduced, Brazil's elite relied on an extensive network of clientelist ties stretching far into the intermediate class of mixed racial origin that had emerged in previous centuries. In the United States, however, this intermediate class was composed of Anglo-American peasants and tradesmen [...], and no transracial political ties had previously developed. Accordingly, Brazil's new political elites aimed at integrating and mixing peoples of different racial origin, while in the United States the nation was imagined as white and mixing conceived and treated as a horribilum to be avoided at all costs [...]. The lack of well-established transracial political networks helps explain why nation building in America was set off against the 'black' population as its inner other rather than against the nation of competing neighboring states as in much of Europe" (2008, 996). A further hardening of boundaries occurred with an increasing "overlap of interests" (2013, 98) between the dominant and dominated groups in the US. Interest overlaps occur to the degree that owning an ethnic ascription yields rewards (for example, group honor and moral dignity, or access to professions, public goods, and political power). On how the black ghetto in the Northern rust belt between 1930 and 1960 produced such overlapping interests, see Wacquant 2011.

11   As Nancy Fraser (2017) points out, since the Clinton administration the neoliberal program has been a bipartisan affair. Alongside the "reactionary neoliberalism" housed in the Republican Party (which combines laisser-faire capitalism with social conservatism), Clinton's "progressive neoliberalism" helped to disarticulate the remnants of the new deal alliance by "forging a new alliance of entrepreneurs, bankers, suburbanites, 'symbolic workers,' new social movements, Latinos, and youth, while retaining the support of African Americans, who felt they had nowhere else to go." The Clintonite wing of the democratic party, according to Frasier, "won the day by talking the talk of diversity, multiculturalism, and women's rights, even while preparing to walk the walk of Goldman Sachs."

The Essays in this Collection

Our contributors look at the nexus of authority and trust in the US from a number of disciplines and thematic angles from the nineteenth century to the immediate present. Manfred Berg's "The Decline of Political Trust and the Rise of Populism in the United States" takes a historian's look at how the dramatic upsurge of right-wing populism has led to a general crisis of liberal representative democracy. Exploring how the declining political trust relates to the recent shift towards the political right, Berg probes the historical and structural roots of American populism. There is a long-standing tradition of distrust in American political culture, he argues, which has driven populist movements throughout American history. Berg's essay shows how Donald Trump's presidential campaign built on this tradition, and profited from a radically altered media environment that undermined not only political trust but trust in authority generally.

Martin Thunert's "Waning Trust in (Scientific) Experts and Expertise?" examines the authority of expert systems from a political science perspective. Looking at a wide range of empirical data on the United States and Great Britain, Thunert complicates the widely noted "crisis of expertise." His essay shows that while trust in medical experts has actually increased in the past few years, other forms of expertise have a more checkered trust record. The greatest factor in the mistrust of expertise, Thunert shows, are partisan divides that lead to the politicization of professional knowledge, especially in such fields as journalism and politics and in the context of partisan-oriented spaces of intellectual inquiry such as corporate-funded think tanks.

Florian Böller and Sebastian Harnisch's "Shifting Meridians of Global Authority" applies the methodology of International Relations to America's recent (and not so recent) foreign and security policies, and how they affected its authority in the world. Proposing a relational and role-theoretical concept of international authority, the authors suggest that in order to understand how global authority relations can shift along with foreign policy choices, we need to have a closer look at how international policy is shaped at the domestic level. Böller and Harnisch's focus lies on the effects of state-society relations (politicization and populism), inter-institutional relations (domestication), and state-corporate relations (economization). On the international level, they argue, states can only claim authority within regimes and institutions if their policies are perceived as legitimate. In turn, how states choose to react to the transformation of authority will have a significant effect on the persistence of that order and the direction of its transformation. Their essay concludes that current (as well as previous) foreign policy choices have (unintended) consequences that may negatively affect the international perception of U.S. authority and the liberal international order.

Ulrike Gerhard, Judith Keller, and Cosima Werner's "Trust and the City" takes a geographic perspective to consider how transformations of authority and trust manifest themselves in urban space. Using trust as a sociospatial concept, the authors highlight two central urban-geographic dimensions—the relational and the mobile—that shape the relevance of urban trust relations for urban development and governance. These are exemplified with regard to four related themes: (1) the cultural representations of the city as an imaginative space, (2) the residents' neighborhood-level urban practices that turn the city into a social space, (3) the temporal dimension of urban development as described by urban planning measures, and (4) the meaning of "home" and "housing." These themes, the authors argue, touch upon important challenges that cities have faced over the last decades. A socio-spatial concept of trust can help to a better understanding of these issues within urban geography.

Margit Peterfy's "William Dean Howells's Urban Theory of Trust and Trustworthiness in *A Hazard of New Fortunes*" combines urban with literary studies to discuss how the late-nineteenth-century novel imagines new kinds of trust relationships in the urban environment of metropolitan modernity in the US. These new relationships concern transport, work, economic and labor relations, and changes in the perception of women in the public space. Peterfy looks at how Howells tries to make sense of trust and trustworthiness in a "realist" or "documentary" register. Her thesis is that—as the issue of trust does not lend itself well to representational objectivity claims—Howells chooses highly symbolic modes of description that revolve around the urban scenes of New York.

Claudia Jetter and Jan Stievermann's "Joseph Smith, Ralph Waldo Emerson and the Transformation of Religious Authority in the Antebellum Period" combines literary and religious studies to read Smith and Emerson in the context of the profound crisis of religious authority in the nineteenth-century US. Drawing from Weber and current research on trust, they argue that Smith and Emerson attempt to come to grips with a rising distrust in the authority of existing clerical institutions and traditional biblical exegesis. The work of both men can be seen as related attempts at restituting a charismatic authority grounded in immediate experience of presence. Whereas Smith stuck to a

Protestant notion of supernatural revelation (claiming for himself the role of the chosen prophet), Emerson's performance of charismatic authority, Jetter and Stievermann argue, was rooted in a naturalized understanding of revelation and a radically-individualized seeker spirituality.

Dietmar Schloss's "The Trust Debate in the Literature of the American Renaissance" analyzes mid-nineteenth century American literature in relation to contemporary sociological theories of trust. The writers of the American Renaissance, Schloss argues, addressed issues of trust and self-trust out of a deep concern about human agency under modern conditions. Using Anthony Giddens' sociology as a conceptual framework, Schloss compares the different positions of Nathaniel Hawthorne, Herman Melville and Ralph Waldo Emerson, concluding that all three considered "self-consciousness"—or what Giddens called the "self-reflexivity of modernity"—as a central problem of trust in modernity. While Hawthorne and Melville considered this problem as almost unsurmountable, Schloss argues, Emerson developed a trust theory that anticipated Giddens' modern way of "doing" trust. Thus Emerson's apparently individualistic, anti-social ethos of self-reliance was designed to act as a stabilizing force in the new risk environment of modern democratic society.

Tim Sommer's "Authority, Genealogy, Infrastructure: Nineteenth-Century Discourses of Transatlantic Relationality" examines how important nineteenth-century intellectuals (Thomas Paine, Washington Irving, Thomas Carlyle, Ralph Waldo Emerson, Frederick Douglass, Walt Whitman) negotiate questions of transatlantic authority. Sommer argues that nineteenth-century Anglo-American relations were expressed in two kinds of images, (1) the language of race and ancestry (revolving around notions of a shared "Anglo-Saxon" pedigree and metaphors of family relationships), and (2) debates about transatlantic infrastructure that highlighted technological developments (national railway systems, transatlantic steam travel, networks of communication, and the like). Both discourses, Sommer suggests, provided the conceptual language through which nineteenth-century writers could imagine relations between the US and British culture as marked by shifting authorities that continuously redefined the character of transatlantic contact.

Günter Leypoldt's "Shoppers, Worshippers, Culture Warriors" explores how the hermeneutics of reading is shaped by different kinds of trust relations. Setting out from George Steiner's account of the "hermeneutic motion" (as a four-fold process involving trust, prejudgment, incorporation, and restoration), Leypoldt reworks received notions of the hermeneutic process using Charles Taylor's theory of moral "frameworks." Whereas traditional hermeneutics focusses on notions of hermeneutic equilibrium and "critical openness," Leypoldt points to three common (if ideal-typical) hermeneutic biases: readers as purpose-oriented consumers, as worshippers trusting a higher good, and as culture warriors revolted by a "toxic" kind of sacred. With a look at the reception history of Henry Wadsworth Longfellow's *Evangeline* (1847), Leypoldt discusses the difficult ontological status of hermeneutic trust—or trust "atmospheres"—and the conflicting moral frames involved in the making of authorized canons.

Works Cited

Abascal, Maria, and Delia Baldassarri (2015). "Love Thy Neighbor? Ethnoracial Diversity and Trust Reexamined." *American Journal of Sociology* 121.3 (November): 722–82.

Abascal, Maria, and Delia Baldassarri (2016). "Don't Blame Diversity for Distrust." *New York Times*, May 20. https://www.nytimes.com/2016/05/22/opinion/sunday/dont-blame-diversity-for-distrust.html. Accessed May 7, 2020.

Alexander, Jeffrey C. (2006). *The Civil Sphere* (Oxford UP).

Alexander, Jeffrey C. (2011). *Performance and Power* (Cambridge: Polity).

Ammerman, Nancy T. (2013). "'Spiritual But Not Religious': Beyond Binary Choices in the Study of Religion." *Journal for the Scientific Study of Religion* 52.2: 258–78.

Arendt, Hannah (1961). *Between Past and Future: Six Exercises in Political Thought* (NY: Viking).

Arendt, Hannah (1972). *Crises of the Republic: Lying in Politics. Civil Disobedience. On Violence. Thoughts on Politics and Revolution* (NY: Mariner).

Asmelash, Leah (2019). "Why 'Cancel Culture' Doesn't Always Work." *CNN*, September 21. https://edition.cnn.com/2019/09/21/entertainment/cancel-culture-explainer-trnd/index.html. Last accessed June 17, 2020.

Balzer, David (2014). *Curationism: How Curating Took Over the Art World and Everything Else* (Toronto: Coach House Books).

Bartels, Larry M. (2008). *Unequal Democracy: The Political Economy of the New Gilded Age* (NY: Sage).

Bell, Joyce M., and Douglas Hartmann (2007). "Diversity in Everyday Discourse: The Cultural Ambiguities and Consequences of 'Happy Talk.'" *American Sociological Review* 72 (December): 895–914.

Bellah, Robert N., et al. (2007). *Habits of the Heart: Individualism and Commitment in American Life* (Berkeley: U of California P).

Betts, Richard K. (2012). *American Force: Dangers, Delusions, and Dilemmas in National Security* (NY: Columbia UP).

Bhaskar, Michael (2016). *Curation: The Power of Selection in a World of Excess* (London: Piatkus).

Binkley, Sam (2007). *Getting Loose: Lifestyle Consumption in the 1970s* (Durham, NC: Duke UP).

Bloom, Allan (1987). *The Closing of the American Mind: How Higher Education Has Failed Democracy and Impoverished the Souls of Today's Students* (NY: Simon and Schuster).

Bourdieu, Pierre (1995). *The Rules of Art: Genesis and Structure of the Literary Field* (Stanford: Stanford UP).

Burke, Meghan A. (2012). *Racial Ambivalence in Diverse Communities: Whiteness and the Power of Color-Blind Ideologies* (Lanham, MD: Lexington Books).

Butler, Katharine (2020). "Europeans' Trust in US as World Leader Collapses During Pandemic." *The Guardian* June 29. https://www.theguardian.com/world/2020/jun/29/europeans-trust-in-us-as-world-leader-collapses-during-pandemic? Accessed, July 5, 2020.

Chadwick, Andrew (2017). *The Hybrid Media System: Politics and Power* (Oxford: Oxford UP).

Clinton, Joshua, et al. (2020). "Partisan Pandemic: How Partisanship and Public Health Concerns Affect Individuals' Social Distancing During COVID-19" (July 9, 2020). Available at SSRN: https://ssrn.com/abstract=3633934 or http://dx.doi.org/10.2139/ssrn.3633934. Accessed July 27, 2020.

Earner-Byrne, Lindsey, and Diane Urquhart (2019). *The Irish Abortion Journey, 1920–2018* (London: Palgrave).

Edsall, Thomas B. (2018). "The Contract With Authoritarianism." *New York Times*, April 5. https://www.nytimes.com/2018/04/05/opinion/trump-authoritarianism-republicans-contract.html?referringSource=articleShare. Accessed July 23, 2020.

Edsall, Thomas B. (2020). "Why Trump Persists." *New York Times*, Jan. 20. https://www.nytimes.com/2020/01/22/opinion/trump-voters.html?referringSource=articleShare. Accessed July 23, 2020.

English, James (2005). *The Economy of Prestige: Prizes, Awards, and the Circulation of Cultural Value* (Cambridge: Harvard UP).

Flatley, Jonathan (2008). *Affective Mapping: Melancholia and the Politics of Modernism* (Cambridge, MA: Harvard UP).

Frank, Thomas (1997). *The Conquest of Cool: Business Culture, Counterculture, and the Rise of Hip Consumerism* (Chicago: U of Chicago P).

Fraser, Nancy (2017). "From Progressive Neoliberalism to Trump and Beyond." *American Affairs* 1.4 (Winter). https://americanaffairsjournal.org/2017/11/p rogressive-neoliberalism-trump-beyond/. Accessed July 30, 2020.

Frevert, Ute (2013). *Vertrauensfragen: Eine Obsession der Moderne* (München: Beck).

Friedersdorf, Connor (2019). "What Ails the Right Isn't (Just) Racism." *Atlantic Monthly*, August 9. https://www.theatlantic.com/ideas/archive/2019/08/w hat-if-left-was-right-race/595777/. Accessed July 23, 2020.

Friedman, R.B. (1990). "On the Concept of Authority in Political Philosophy." *Authority*. Ed. Joseph Raz (NY: New York University P) 56–91.

Fukuyama, Francis (1995). *Trust: The Social Virtues and the Creation of Prosperity* (NY: Free Press).

Furedi, Frank (2013). *Authority: A Sociological History*. (Cambridge: Cambridge UP).

Giddens, Anthony (1990). *The Consequences of Modernity* (Cambridge: Polity).

Griswold, Wendy (2008). *Regionalism and the Reading Class* (Chicago: U of Chicago P).

Haass, Richard (2013). *Foreign Policy Begins at Home: The Case for Putting America's House in Order* (NY: Basic Books).

Hardin, Russell (2002). *Trust and Trustworthiness* (NY: Russell Sage Foundation).

Hartman, Andrew (2015). *A War for the Soul of America: A History of the Culture Wars* (Chicago: University of Chicago P).

Hayes, Christopher (2012). *Twilight of the Elites: America after Meritocracy* (NY: Crown).

Hetherington, Marc (2005). *Why Trust Matters: Declining Political Trust and the Demise of American Liberalism*. (Princeton: Princeton UP).

Hochschild, Arlie Russell (2016). *Strangers in Their Own Land: Anger and Mourning on the American Right* (NY: The New Press).

Hosking, Geoffrey A. (2014). *Trust: A History* (Oxford: OUP).

Ikenberry, G. John (2011). *Liberal Leviathan: The Origins, Crisis, and Transformation of the American World Order* (Princeton: Princeton UP).

Ikenberry, G. John (2018). "The End of Liberal International Order?" *International Affairs* 94.1: 7–23.

Inglehart, Ronald (1977). *The Silent Revolution: Changing Values and Political Styles among Western Publics* (Princeton: Princeton UP).

Iyengar, Shanto et al. (2019). "The Origins and Consequences of Affective Polarization in the United States." *Annual Review of Political Science* 22.1. 129–146.

Jameson, Fredric (1988). *The Ideologies of Theory: Essays, 1971–1986. Vol. 2: The Syntax of History* (Minneapolis: U of Minnesota P).

Joas, Hans (2013). *The Sacredness of the Person: A New Geneaology of Human Rights* (Washington, D.C.: Georgetown UP):

Kaufman, Jason (2002). *For the Common Good? American Civic Life and the Golden Age of Fraternity* (Oxford: Oxford UP).

Knag, Sigmund (1997) "The Almighty,Impotent State, Or, the Crisis of Authority." *The Independent Review* I.3 (Winter): 397–412.

Knaggård, Åsa (2015). "The Multiple Streams Framework and the Problem Broker." *European Journal of Political Research* 54.3. 450–465.

Kitcher, Philip (2011). *Science in a Democratic Society* (NY: Prometheus).

Krastev, Ivan (2019). "Will Europe Ever Trust America Again?" *New York Times* Dec. 3. https://www.nytimes.com/2019/12/03/opinion/trump-nato-europe.html. Accessed, July 7, 2020.

Laclau, Ernesto (2005). *On Populist Reason* (London: Verso).

Leypoldt, Günter (2015). "Shifting Meridians: US Authorship in World-Literary Space." *American Literary History* 27.4 (Winter): 768–787.

Leypoldt, Günter (2020). "Spatial Reading: Evaluative Frameworks and the Making of Literary Authority." *American Journal of Cultural Sociology* 9. Special Issue on Reading, ed. Angelica Thumala. https://doi.org/10.1057/s41290-020-00107-w.

Lipset, Seymour Martin (1996). *American Exceptionalism. A Double-Edged Sword* (NY: Norton).

Lowndes, Joseph (2005). "From Founding Violence to Political Hegemony: The Conservative Populism of George Wallace." *Populism and the Mirror of Democracy.* Ed. Francisco Panizza (London: Verso): 144–171.

Luhmann, Niklas (2009). *Vertrauen: Ein Mechanismus der Reduktion sozialer Komplexität* (Stuttgart: UTB).

Maryles, Daisy (2004). "Steel at 61." *Publisher's Weekly* July 14. http://publishersweekly.com/pw/print/20040712/29130-steel-at-61.html. Accessed August 14, 2020.

McGurl, Mark (2009). *The Program Era: Postwar Fiction and the Rise of Creative Writing* (Cambridge: Harvard UP).

MacIntyre, Alasdair (1967). *Secularization and Moral Change* (Oxford: OUP).

McCoy, Jennifer, and Murat Somer (2019). "Toward a Theory of Pernicious Polarization and How It Harms Democracies: Comparative Evidence and Possible Remedies." *The Annals of the American Academy of Political and Social Science* 681.1. 234–271.

Millgram, Elija (2015). *The Great Endarkenment: Philosophy for an Age of Hyperspecialization* (NY: Oxford UP).

Mill, John Stuart (1840). "[Review of Tocqueville, *Democracy in America*]." *Edinburgh Review* CXLV (October): 1–47.

Mill, John Stuart (1997). *The Spirit of the Age, On Liberty, The Subjection of Women.* Ed. Alan Ryan (NY: Norton).

Misztal, Barbara (1996). *Trust in Modern Societies: The Search for the Bases of Social Order* (Cambridge: Polity Press).

Möllering, Guido (2001). "The Nature of Trust: From Georg Simmel to a Theory of Expectation, Interpretation and Suspension." *Sociology* 35.2 (2001): 403–20.

Möllering, Guido (2006). *Trust: Reason, Routine, Reflexivity* (Amsterdam: Elsevier).

Mouffe, Chantal (2018). *For a Left Populism* (London: Verso).

Mudde, Cas, and Cristóbal Rovira Kaltwasser (2017). *Populism: A Very Short Introduction* (Oxford: Oxford UP).

Müller, Jan-Werner (2016). *What is Populism?* (London: Penguin).

Murphy, Yvonne (2016). "The Marriage Equality Referendum 2015." *Irish Political Studies* 31.2. 315–30.

Nguyen, C. Thi (2020). "Echo Chambers and Epistemic Bubbles." *Episteme* 17.2 (June): 141–61.

Noah, Timothy (2012). *The Great Divergence: America's Growing Inequality Crisis and What We Can Do About It* (NY: Bloomsbury P).

Norris, Pippa, and Ronald Inglehart (2019). *Cultural Backlash: Trump, Brexit, and Authoritarian Populism* (Cambridge: Cambridge UP).

Packer, George (2013). *The Unwinding: An Inner History of the New America* (NY: Farrar, Straus and Giroux).

Partridge, Christopher (2006). *The Re-Enchantment of the West: Alternative Spiritualities, Sacralization, Popular Culture and Occulture. Vol I* (London: T. & T. Clark International).

Putnam, Robert D. (1993). *Making Democracy Work: Civic Traditions in Modern Italy* (Princeton: Princeton UP).

Putnam, Robert D. (1995). "Bowling Alone: America's Declining Social Capital." *Journal of Democracy* 6.1. 65–78.

Putnam, Robert D. (2000). *Bowling Alone: The Collapse and Revival of American Community* (NY: Simon & Schuster).

Putnam, Robert D. (2007). "E Pluribus Unum: Diversity and Community in the Twenty-first Century." *Scandinavian Political Studies* 30.2 (June): 137–174.

Rainie, Lee, Scott Keeter, and Andrew Perrin (2019). "Trust and Distrust in America." Pew Research Center, July 22. https://www.pewresearch.org/politics/2019/07/22/trust-and-distrust-in-america/. Last accessed, July 4, 2020.

Rawls, John (1971). *A Theory of Justice* (Cambridge: Belknap).

Rawls, John (1993). *Political Liberalism* (NY: Columbia UP).

Reeves, Richard V. (2017). *Dream Hoarders: How the American Upper Middle Class Is Leaving Everyone Else in the Dust, Why That Is a Problem, and What to Do About It* (NY: Brookings).

Rini, Regina (2017). "Fake News and Partisan Epistemology." *Kennedy Institute of Ethics Journal* 27.2 Supplement (June): E-43–E-64.

Rosa, Hartmut (2019). *Resonance: A Sociology of Our Relationship to the World* (Cambridge: Polity).

Rothwell, Jonathan (2012). "The Effects of Racial Segregation on Trust and Volunteering in US Cities." Urban Studies 48, vol. 10: 2109–2136.

Sandel, Michael (1998). *Democracy's Discontent: America in Search of a Public Philosophy* (Cambridge, MA: Harvard UP).

Sapienza, Paola, et al. (2013). "Understanding Trust." *Economic Journal*. 123 (573): 1313–32.

Schlette, Magnus (2013): "'… das Charisma auf seinem schicksalsreichen Wege …' Max Webers und Edward Shils' Beiträge zu einer Soziologie des Heiligen." *Das Heilige (in) der Moderne. Denkfiguren des Sakralen in Philosophie und Literatur des 20. Jahrhunderts.* Ed. Héctor Canal et al. (Bielefeld: transcript) 141–160.

Shapin, Steven (1994). *A Social History of Truth: Civility and Science in Seventeenth-Century England* (Chicago: U of Chicago P).

Shapiro, Walter (2020). "The Flawed Politics of a Law-and-Order Campaign." *New Republic*, May 31. https://newrepublic.com/article/157939/flawed-politics-law-and-order-campaign. Accessed August 5, 2020.

Shils, Edward (1982). *The Constitution of Society* (Chicago: U of Chicago P).

Simmel, Georg (1900). *Philosophie des Geldes* (Berlin: Duncker & Humblot).

Snyder, Timothy (2017). *On Tyranny: Twenty Lessons from the Twentieth Century* (London: Bodley Head).

Soper, Philip (2002). *The Ethics of Deference: Learning from Law's Morals* (Cambridge: Cambridge UP).

Stenner, Karen, and Jonathan Haidt (2018). "Authoritarianism Is Not a Momentary Madness, But an Eternal Dynamic Within Liberal Democracies." *Can it Happen Here? Authoritarianism in America*. Ed. Cass R. Sunstein (NY: HarperCollins) 175–219.

Stiglitz, Joseph E. (2012). *The Price of Inequality: How Today's Divided Society Endangers Our Future* (NY: Norton).

Svolik, Milan W. (2020). "When Polarization Trumps Civic Virtue: Partisan Conflict and the Subversion of Democracy by Incumbents." *Quarterly Journal of Political Science* 15.1: 3–31.

Szelenyi, Iván (2016). "Weber's Theory of Domination and Post-Communist Capitalisms." *Theory and Society* 45 (2016):1–24.

Taggart, Paul (2000). *Populism* (Buckingham: Open UP).

Taranto, James (2013). "A Crisis of Authority: The Deeper Meaning of the Obama Scandals." *Wall Street Journal* May 20. https://www.wsj.com/articles/SB10001424127887324787004578494961837484232. Accessed July 10, 2020.

Taylor, Charles (1985). "What is Human Agency?" *Human Agency and Language: Philosophical Papers, Vol. 1* (Cambridge: Cambridge UP) 15–44.

Taylor, Charles (2007). *A Secular Age* (Cambridge: Harvard UP).

Taylor, David, and Sam Morris (2018). "The Whole World is Watching: How the 1968 Chicago 'Police Riot' Shocked America and Divided the Nation." *Guardian*, August 9. https://www.theguardian.com/us-news/ng-interactive/2018/aug/19/the-whole-world-is-watching-chicago-police-riot-vietnam-war-regan/. Accessed August 20, 2020.

Tilly, Charles (2005). *Trust and Rule* (Cambridge: Cambridge UP).

Tilly, Charles (2007). *Democracy* (Cambridge: Cambridge UP).

Tocqueville, Alexis de (2000). *Democracy in America*. Ed. Harvey Mansfield and Delba Winthrop (Chicago: U of Chicago P).

Turner, Bryan S. (2011). *Religion and Modern Society: Citizenship, Secularization and the State* (Cambridge UP).

Uslaner, Eric M. (2002). *The Moral Foundations of Trust* (Cambridge: Cambridge UP).

Uslaner, Eric M. (2008). *Corruption, Inequality, and the Rule of Law: The Bulging Pocket Makes the Easy Life* (Cambridge: Cambridge UP).

Uslaner, Eric M. (2012). *Segregation and Mistrust: Diversity, Isolation, and Social Cohesion* (Cambridge: Cambridge UP).

Wacquant, Loïc (2007). *Urban Outcasts: A Comparative Sociology of Advanced Marginality* (Cambridge: Polity).

Wacquant, Loïc (2011). "A Janus-Faced Institution of Ethnoracial Closure: A Sociological Specification of the Ghetto." *The Ghetto: Contemporary Global Issues and Controversies*. Ed. Ray Hutchison and Bruce D. Haynes (Boulder: Westview, 2011) 1–31.

Waisbord, Silvio, et al. (2018). "Trump and the Great Disruption in Public Communication." *Trump and the Media*. Ed. P. J. Boczkowski, and Z. Papacharissi (Boston: MIT) 25–32.

Weber, Max (1972). *Wirtschaft und Gesellschaft* (Tübingen: Mohr-Siebeck).

Weber, Max (1947). *The Theory of Social and Economic Organization*. Ed. Talcott Parsons (NY: Oxford UP).

Wilkerson, Isabel (2020). *Caste: The Lies that Divide Us* (London: Allen Lane).

Williams, Raymond (1973). *The Country and the City* (NY: Oxford UP).

Wills, Garry (1999). *A Necessary Evil: A History of American Distrust of Government* (NY: Touchstone).

Wilson, Bryan (1979). *Contemporary Transformations of Religion* (Oxford: Clarendon).

Wilson, David (2007). *Cities and Race. America's New Black Ghetto* (London: Routledge). .

Wimmer, Andreas (2008). "The Making and Unmaking of Ethnic Boundaries: A Multilevel Process Theory." *American Journal of Sociology* 113.4 (January): 970–1022.

Wimmer, Andreas (2013). *Ethnic Boundary Making: Institutions, Power, Networks* (Oxford: Oxford UP).

Wimmer, Andreas (2018). *Nation Buildung: Why Some Countries Come Together While Others Fall Apart* (Princeton: Princeton UP).

Woodhead, Linda, and Paul Heelas, eds. (2000). *Religion in Modern Times: An Interpretive Anthology* (London: Blackwell).

Wuthnow, Robert (1998). *After Heaven: Spirituality in America since the 1950s* (Berkeley: U of California P)

The Decline of Political Trust and the Rise of Populism in the United States

Manfred Berg

In his state-of-the-union address of January 12, 2016, U.S. President Barack Obama (Obama-white-house 2016) reminded the American people that

> democracy does require basic bonds of trust between its citizens. It doesn't work if we think the people who disagree with us are all motivated by malice. It doesn't work if we think that our political opponents are unpatriotic or trying to weaken America. Democracy grinds to a halt without a willingness to compromise, or when even basic facts are contested, or when we listen only to those who agree with us. Our public life withers when only the most extreme voices get all the attention. And most of all, democracy breaks down when the average person feels their voice doesn't matter; that the system is rigged in favor of the rich or the powerful or some special interest.

Ten months later, nearly sixty-three million American voters cast their ballots for a presidential candidate who, it seems fair to say, had run his campaign on messages that represent what Obama had warned against. Donald Trump denounced his opponent, former Secretary of State Hillary Clinton, as "the ringleader of a criminal enterprise that has corrupted our government at the highest levels" (Trump Pueblo Rally 2016). Presenting himself as the avenger of a wronged people, the Republican contender promised that he would "drain the swamp" and warned that the Democrats were plotting massive electoral fraud to stop him (Trump Grand Junction Rally 2016). When the vote count showed that he had won a majority in the Electoral College but trailed Clinton in the popular vote, the president-elect kept insisting that her three-million vote lead resulted from "the millions of people who voted illegally" (@realDonaldTrump, November 27, 2016).

Since November 9, 2016, pundits and scholars debate why nearly half of the electorate was willing to entrust America's—and arguably the world's—most powerful political office to a businessman of dubious reputation who had no experience of public service—a man whose vulgarity, vanity, and mendacity made his candidacy appear so outlandish that observers claimed it was the publicity stunt of a brazen self-promoter (Wolff 2018). Analysts disagree whether racial resentment, sexism, or socio-economic grievances played the largest role in Trump's startling victory. But nobody contests that the basic motivation of Trump voters was a deep-seated distrust of America's political elites and institutions. According to political scientist Thomas E. Patterson, Trump "rode the wave of distrust all the way to the Oval Office" (2019: 68).

Clearly Trump thrived on spreading distrust, but he did not create it. Indeed, trust in government has been declining since the mid-1960s when 75 percent of Americans declared that they trusted government to do what is right just about always or most of time; by comparison, in 2016 fewer than 20 percent agreed with that statement (Pew Research Center 2017: 1). To be sure, trust in government has fallen significantly in all Western democracies (Dalton 2017: 376). Many political scientists have interpreted this trend as evidence of rising expectations among the "critical citizens" of mature democracies (Norris 1999 and 2011). However, with the dramatic upsurge of right-wing populism, including the "Trump Movement," distrust of government appears to have transmuted into a general crisis of liberal representative democracy (Mudde/Kaltwasser 2017; Müller 2017; Mounk 2017).

In this essay, I explore the relationship between the decline of political trust and the rise of right-wing populism in contemporary America. I will begin by introducing the concept of political trust and review some relevant academic debates. I will then probe the historical and structural roots of American populism. Finally, I will look at the role political distrust has played in Donald Trump's ascendency to the presidency of the United States. Political distrust, I argue, is the key to understand both the history of American populism and the "Trump phenomenon."

Political Trust

Although there is no universally accepted definition of political trust, most scholars agree that the term refers to generalized trust in political institutions and elites. It is thus distinct from trust between individuals in face-to-face relationships, as well as from generalized social trust, defined as trust in local communities and society at large (Uslaner 2018). The delegation of political authority requires that the governed trust that the governing elites will not abuse their power, but rather act in the best interest of the polity. Levels of political trust range from affective belief in the principal benevolence of authorities, to skepticism, deep cynicism, and alienation. Moreover, people may identify with the core principles of a political system but distrust individual officeholders, or be dissatisfied with the performance of particular institutions (Norris 2017).

Political scientists are mostly interested in trust at the systemic level. When they ask American citizens the standard question, "How much of the time do you think you can trust the government in Washington to do what is right—just about always, most of the time, only some of the time, or never?" they seek to measure levels of trust in the system of government and not in the current administration (Hetherington 2005: 11). To be sure, incumbents do affect the levels of trust among their supporters and opponents, although historically the correlation was never strong. This has changed in recent years. During the presidency of Barack Obama (2009–2017), trust in government reached an all-time low among Republicans. After Donald Trump's election, Democrats, who usually express higher levels of political trust compared to Republicans, have professed the lowest trust in government in nearly six decades, whereas trust among Republicans increased significantly (Pew 2015: 9; Pew 2017: 1–2; 7–8; 10). Some researchers see the growing salience of negative partisanship, i.e. voters' dislike for the opposite party exceeds approval for their ideological preference, as an indicator that polarization is undermining trust in institutions (Hetherington/Rudolph 2015; Abramowitz 2018).

Clearly government performance, especially in the area of economic and welfare policies, affects trust (Kumlin/Haugsgjerd 2017). Political scientist Marc Hetherington defines political trust as "the degree to which people perceive that government is producing outcomes consistent with their expectations." As Hetherington points out, however, perceptions and expectations are subjective categories that often lead to distortions and inconsistencies. For example, most Americans grossly overrate the extent of government waste and corruption, which then negatively affects their political trust (Hetherington 2005: 9–10). Moreover, government performance is not confined to the delivery of material benefits. Citizens expect institutions to be fair and accessible, and elites to perform their duties in a competent, impartial, and unselfish way. With respect to these standards, surveys show that Americans are deeply distrustful of their elected officials. According to a 2015 study by the Pew Research Center (12–13), 74 percent suspect elected officials to put their personal interests ahead of the country's, while 55 percent believe that ordinary Americans would do a better job at solving the country's problems. Nearly 70 percent of Americans hold an unfavorable view of Congress, which is the least trusted government institution in America, although it represents the elected branch of government (58; see also Pew 2019b: 1–10). Virtually all surveys on trust indicate that large parts of the American citizenry have developed a cynical perception of their country's political process and of elites as being inherently corrupt and incompetent. Fifty-seven percent of respondents declared they were "frustrated," and 22 percent expressed outright anger with government; among Republicans the angry group amounted to 32 percent. Nearly 90 percent of GOP voters showed a high level of general distrust of government (Pew 2015: 9). At the same time, most Americans appear to be deeply worried about the decline of both political trust and social trust. A recent study on *Trust and Distrust in America* by the Pew Research Center found that up to 70 percent of respondents wished that trust in government and interpersonal trust could be improved because low trust made it more difficult to solve vital problems. America's political culture, the study notes, is widely perceived as broken (Pew Research Center 2019a: 3–4, 16–29).

This bleak assessment stands in stark contrast to the halcyon picture which Gabriel Almond and Sidney Verba, the pioneers of political culture research, painted of political trust in America in their pathbreaking work *The Civic Culture*, first published in 1963 (1995). Probing the cognitive and emotional orientations of citizens toward the political system, the authors identified trust as a key pillar of a democratic civic culture that combines active participation with traditional loyalty to authorities: "General social trust is translated into politically relevant trust" (214). In contrast to the citizens of Italy, Mexico, Germany, and Great Britain—the study's comparative frame of reference—postwar Americans showed high levels of social trust, which induced them to join voluntary associations and participate in politics. Social trust supposedly led to an "open pattern of partisanship in the United States." Voters cared about the outcome of elections, but this did not mean "complete rejection of one's political opponent." Hence, U.S. citizens combined "generalized system affect" and a "satisfaction with specific governmental performance" (313–315).

Although *The Civic Culture* subsequently came under criticism for methodological flaws and a white, middle-class bias, its conceptual linkage between trust and democratic stability has remained influential among both scholars and the general public. As the editors of the 2017 *Handbook of Political Trust* summarize the conventional wisdom: "Political trust thus functions as the glue that keeps the system together and as the oil that lubricates the political machine." Once trust gives way to distrust and cynicism, the "very survival of representative democracy and its institutions may be at stake" (Zmerli/van der Meer 2017: 1).

The premise that democracy depends on trust appears plausible. People need to have confidence in the integrity of political leaders, while elected leaders need the trust of their constituents to make necessary, albeit unpopular decisions (Patterson 2019: 50). And, yet, as political scientist Mark E. Warren points out, "trust and democracy have an essential but paradoxical relationship to one another" because the institutions of democracy, and especially the American constitutional system of checks and balances, "were founded on *distrust*" (2017: 33; emphasis in the original). The paradox can be solved, Warren argues, if citizens learn to distrust officeholders without losing confidence in political institutions (35–36). Other scholars insist, however, that Americans must cherish the Madisonian tradition that sees government as a necessary evil (Rossiter 1961: 322; see also Wills 1999). In an essay entitled "Government without Trust," the late Russell Hardin, a leading scholar of trust and a proponent of rational choice and libertarian economic theory, disputed that citizens could or should trust institutions or elites (2013). According to Hardin, distrust is the only rational attitude because government will always be much more powerful than individual citizens and thus be a threat to their liberty: "Liberal distrust of government is historically distrust of its use of power," he stated (38). Therefore, in Hardin's view, the decline of trust in recent decades, far from giving us occasion for concern, simply indicates the transition to a new political era when "big government" is no longer needed because markets will function smoothly by themselves (49).

If distrust of government is indeed a wholesome civic virtue, the citizens of Western democracies have learned their lesson according to those social scientists who have studied value change in the "postmaterialist societies" of North America and Western Europe. As Western societies have become more affluent, better educated, and more individualistic over the past half century, their political cultures have undergone a silent, but fundamental revolution. Hence, for Ronald Inglehart, Pippa Norris, Russell Dalton, and others, the decline of political trust does not signal a crisis of democracy but, on the contrary, mirrors increased expectations about how democratic government should perform. The "critical citizens" of democracies, Dalton argues, are "dissatisfied democrats," who "distrust government and political institutions but are supportive of democratic principles" (2017: 282; Norris 1999 and 2011). The age of deferential citizenship, when trust of elites could be more or less taken for granted, has given way to a "new civic culture." "We have entered a new period when governments must confront a public skeptical of their motivations, doubtful about the institutions of representative democracy, and willing to challenge political elites," writes Russell Dalton (391).

But how long does it take until dissatisfied democrats will lose patience with democratic rule—or at least with representative democracy? Yascha Mounk contends that persistent dissatisfaction with government performance will sooner or later undermine loyalty to democracy itself. Mounk points to surveys that indicate growing support for authoritarian rule across North America and Western Europe, especially among younger age cohorts. According to findings of the World Values Survey, roughly one in three Americans today endorses government by a strong leader who does not have to bother with Congress or elections (Mounk 2017: 103–112). Ten years ago, we might not have seen such numbers as alarming. With Donald Trump in the White House, we can no longer be so sure.

The Historical and Structural Roots of American Populism

The "critical citizens" approach has much plausibility in explaining what we could call the "left wing of political distrust," represented by the new social movements and an activist civil society. But how do we account for the rise of right-wing populism, illiberalism, and authoritarianism in Western societies? After all, the leaders and followers of right-wing populism also claim to be "critical citizens" who challenge the "undemocratic" rule of a self-serving "establishment." Populists, scholars agree, define politics as a moral conflict between the "pure people" and "corrupt elites," and they reduce democracy to executing the alleged "will of the people" (Mudde/Kaltwasser 2017: 5–6; see also Eichengreen 2018; Müller 2017; Judis 2016). Left-wing and right-wing populists agree in their distrust of representative democracy, but differ in their conception of who is included in the "people." Right-wing populism defines the people as an ethnocultural community, whereas left-wing populists emphasize the common socio-economic interests of the "Ninety-Nine Percent," as the catchy, but misleading slogan of the so-called Occupy Wall Street Movement during the Great Recession had it.

Unlike fascism or communism, populism is not a fixed ideology but a political idiom. Historian Michael Kazin defines it as "a language whose speakers conceive of ordinary people as a noble assemblage not bounded narrowly by class, view their elite opponents as self-serving and undemocratic, and seek to mobilize the former against the latter" (1995: 1). Distrust of government has always formed the core of populist thought and rhetoric. In American popular memory, this tradition goes back to the Revolutionary Era when virtuous Patriots rebelled against the corrupt British monarchy. Subsequently, it shaped Anti-Federalist opposition to a powerful federal government. During the Jacksonian Era, which Alexis de Tocqueville famously described in his treatise on *Democracy in America* (1990), the populist mood became dominant as the United States developed into a mass democracy. The "people," conceived as the egalitarian community of white men who earned their livelihoods as independent farmers and mechanics, needed to be constantly on guard against greedy capitalists and crooked politicians (Kazin 1995: 19–22; Formisano 2008; Wills 1999). Indeed, the populist idiom and style have shaped American political history to an extent that makes it difficult to distinguish between populist insurgents and folksy mainstream politicians.

According to historian Ronald Formisano, American populist movements have been driven by "fear of centralized power" and by resistance of local communities against "external forces that are perceived to threaten their autonomy, political rights, or economic security" (2008: 10). Formisano distinguishes between a progressive variety of American populism, which fights for social reforms and equal opportunity for ordinary people, and a reactionary branch, which touts illiberal messages and scapegoats vulnerable minorities instead of confronting the privileged and powerful (2008: 10–14). From the agrarian protest movement of the late 19th century (Postel 2007) to Huey Long's "Share Our Wealth" campaign during the Great Depression (Brinkley 1983), American populists primarily focused on defending the interests of small producers and workers against plutocratic capitalists. With the onset of the Cold War and postwar affluence, however, populism began to take a conservative turn. Americans no longer distrusted business leaders but began to focus on liberal intellectual elites, whom they suspected of secretly sympathizing with communism and the Soviet Union. Senator Joseph McCarthy (R–WI), the most prominent protagonist of the anticommunist hysteria of the early Cold War, alleged that America's liberal foreign policy establishment was engaged in a "conspiracy on a scale so immense as to dwarf any previous such venture in the history of man" (Kazin 1995: 165–193; Oshinsky 2005: 191). At its core, McCarthyism represented a populist culture war of patriotic, god-fearing Americans against supposedly cosmopolitan and secularist elites.

When the liberal consensus, which Almond and Verba had celebrated in *The Civic Culture*, fell apart during the upheavals of the Vietnam-Watergate Era, the white working and middle classes, which had previously formed the backbone of the Democratic New Deal Coalition, staged what the Republican strategist Kevin Philipps diagnosed as "a populist revolt of the American masses ... against the Mandarin caste of the liberal establishment" (quoted in Boyd 1970: 25). The immediate beneficiary was George Wallace, a former governor of Alabama, who posed as an uncompromising defender of white supremacy and raged against unelected judges and hypocritical liberal elites trying to impose racial integration on ordinary white folks, while sending their own children to expensive private schools (Kazin 1995: 228–242; Carter 1995). In the 1968 presidential election, Wallace ran as an independent and garnered an impressive 13.5 percent of the nationwide popular vote. More important in the long run, however, was the transformation of the Republican Party. The Grand Old Party began to shed its liberal wing and to appeal to the "silent majority" of (white) Americans who saw themselves as the losers of the civil rights reforms and the cultural revolution of the Sixties. Republicans promised they would restore traditional moral and religious values, and protect hard-working Americans against the encroachments of arrogant and inefficient government bureaucrats. In his first inauguration of January 1981, President Ronald Reagan famously summed up the anti-government message: "Government is not the solution to our problem, government is the problem" (Schaller 2002: 83; Lütjen 2016). The conservative turn of populism was followed by a populist turn of conservatism.

The GOP's espousal of "traditional family values" and its alliance with the emerging Religious Right could easily obscure the fact that the party's anti-government rhetoric was at odds with traditional conservatism, which had favored strong institutions (Patterson 2019: 55–56). In fact, the relentless assault on government interference with the economy represented a radical libertarianism, which had made its first, forceful national appearance with Barry Goldwater's capture of the Republican presidential nomination in 1964 (Perlstein 2001). In her controversial book *Democracy in Chains*, historian Nancy MacLean (2016) claims that the political advance of neoliberal economics followed a "stealth plan" connived by a small group of libertarian ideologues and right-wing billionaires to undermine American popular democracy. But neoliberalism was no conspiracy, and libertarians never concealed their conviction that individual economic freedom must enjoy precedence over state intervention. On the contrary, Thomas Patterson credits the success of Republican leaders in undermining trust in government to their ability to tell a simple popular message: "Big government is the problem, cutting taxes and regulation the solution; a rising tide will then lift all the boats and those who work hard will live the American Dream" (2019: 57).

But why did this message resonate so strongly among the working and middle classes, which had supposedly supported the regulatory and welfare regime of the New Deal Era? Why have many ordinary Americans, whose wages and incomes have stagnated for decades, consistently voted for policies, including tax breaks for the rich and deep cuts of the welfare state, which have contributed to a massive redistribution of wealth in favor of the top ten percent and, mostly, the top one percent (Bartels 2008; Stiglitz 2012; Saez/Zucman 2019)? Is it because average voters fail to grasp the redistributive effects of tax cuts and merely focus on their personal tax burden (Bartels 2008: 23–24)? Or is it the "false consciousness," to resurrect a venerable Marxist concept, of people "getting their fundamental interests wrong," as Thomas Frank lamented in his much-debated book *What's the Matter with Kansas?* (2004: 1)? Frank summed up liberal frustration in blunt words. The new conservative populism represented "a working-class movement that has done incalculable, historic harm to working-class people.... Like a French Revolution in reverse—one in which the Sansculottes pour down the streets demanding more power for the aristocracy." Employing the anti-elitist rhetoric of populism, the strategists of plutocracy had hoodwinked Middle Americans into culture wars over abortion, gay rights, school prayer, etc. "Cultural anger is marshaled to achieve economic ends," Frank complains. "The trick never ages; the illusion never wears off. Vote to stop abortion; receive a rollback in capital gains taxes. Vote to make our country strong again; receive deindustrialization. Vote to screw those politically correct college professors; receive electricity deregulation" (5–9). Like other liberals of the New Deal tradition, Frank scolds the Democratic Party for abandoning its traditional blue-collar constituencies and for embracing neoliberalism, cultural elitism, and identity politics for racial and sexual minorities (Frank 2016; see also Lilla 2017).

American culture wars epitomize a larger sociocultural conflict in postindustrial Western societies, which many researchers see as the basic structural cause of the populist insurgency. According to Andreas Reckwitz (2019) and others, the traditional antagonism between capital and labor of the industrial era has been replaced by a new cleavage between the winners and losers of globalization and modernization—a conflict that pits liberal, educated, "cosmopolitan" elites, and the so-called creative classes against the "old" working and middle classes, who have experienced continuous economic decline and feel alienated from and despised by the liberal mainstream culture—"strangers in their own land," as sociologist Arlie Hochschild entitled her acclaimed exploration of the mentalities of poor whites in rural Louisiana (2016). Right-wing populism offers them an outlet to assert their identities and articulate their protest against a federal government they see as unfairly favoring clamorous minorities.

Obviously, no analysis of political distrust and the rise of populism in the United States can ignore race. Even historians who emphasize the emancipatory and egalitarian impetus of American populism acknowledge the destructive impact of racism (Postel 2007: 173–203). Southern populists, such as George Wallace, waged their struggle for white supremacy, first and foremost, against Northern liberal elites and an intrusive federal government trying to force the "social equality" of blacks upon ordinary white people. When, in 1970, Kevin Philipps advised the Republican Party to build a new electoral majority on the support of the "negrophobe whites of the South" (Boyd 1970: 105), he correctly anticipated that combining racial resentment with social conservatism and anti-government rhetoric would be a winning strategy. In subsequent decades, a vast majority of Southern whites shifted their party allegiance from the Democrats to the Republicans, making the GOP the dominant party in the South. By and large, white voters rallied along racial and religious lines, regardless of economic status (Black/Black 2002: esp. 370–373).

The so-called white backlash and the process of partisan realignment were not confined to the South. Nationwide, the Republicans have become the party of conservative whites, while the Democrats depend heavily on the support of African Americans, Hispanics, and Asians. Many political scientists see race as the prime driver of partisan polarization (Abramowitz 2018: XII). African American critics contend that, despite the civil rights reforms of the 1960s, American society has remained structurally racist, and that white Americans resent whatever advancements blacks have made over the past half century (Anderson 2016). Racial prejudice is also often cited as a cause for the decline of political trust. Polls show that many working and middle-class whites view themselves as victims of "reverse discrimination" because of government-mandated affirmative action programs (Patterson 2019: 58).

Moreover, race has played a key role in undermining support for welfare programs. Ironically, the expansion of the welfare state during the Sixties' "War on Poverty" was part of a liberal effort to pacify racial unrest and bring poor blacks into the mainstream of what President Lyndon Johnson dubbed the Great Society (Andrew 1998). Conservatives denounced the War on Poverty as a misguided liberal crusade at taxpayers' expense, which had resulted in discouraging personal responsibility and in creating a permanent underclass of dependents who knew how to exploit the system (Murray 1984). Prominent Republican politicians such as Ronald Reagan touted anecdotes about "welfare queens" who allegedly drove Cadillac cars and bought T-Bone steaks with food stamps. Apart from their racialized content, such stories sent the message that government was inherently wasteful and incapable of solving social problems (Hetherington 2005: 78–79).

In his study on declining political trust, Marc Hetherington found that Americans continue to favor government programs that benefit most citizens, but oppose redistributive policies which smack of preferential treatment for racial minorities. Paradoxically, support for the principle of racial equality has increased strongly since mid-20th century. Hetherington explains this gap by citing lack of political trust, rather than racism, as the key reason: "Many whites simply do not trust the government enough to implement and administer the programs designed to make racial equality a reality" (Hetherington 2005: 99–119, 119). But maybe distrust of government has simply become a proxy for racism in the same vein as "states' rights" was a code for white supremacy in the age of Jim Crow. As Theda Skocpol and Vanessa Williamson have observed with regard to the Tea Party movement, anti-government rhetoric often serves as a cover for defending one's privileges. People like the programs from which they benefit, but refuse to pay for those that benefit others (2012: 203).

Recently, scholars have raised the question of whether social solidarity and political trust have declined as a consequence of mass immigration and the ensuing demographic transformation of Western societies (McLaren 2017). In American history, the argument holds, the New Deal consensus on the welfare state during the mid-twentieth century coincided with a restrictive immigration regime that kept levels of immigration at a historic low in the decades between the 1920s and the 1960s. Since the Immigration Reform Act of 1965, tens of millions of newcomers from Latin America and Asia have profoundly altered the country's demographic landscape. In 1960, close to 90 percent of the U.S. population were classified as white; today their share is down to 60 percent (Bureau of the Census 2019). In a few decades, persons of European descent will no longer constitute a majority of the population. Not surprisingly, mass immigration has triggered economic competition and cultural anxieties as well as a nativist backlash, which many analysts see as the major mobilizing factor for right-wing populism. Critics of the liberal, pro-immigration consensus chide cosmopolitan elites and the multicultural left for ignoring the legitimate fears of ordinary people who have seen their jobs being taken away by immigrants (Eatwell/Goodwin 2018; Kaufmann 2018). Before the 2016 election, Francis Fukuyama credited the populist campaigns of Bernie Sanders and Donald Trump with bringing back economic inequality and social class on the American agenda. In order to restore a social equilibrium and a political consensus, he argued, some retreat from globalization was necessary, including "reasonable restrictions on immigration" (Fukuyama 2016). Arguably, no other of Donald Trump's slogans was more popular among his supporters than his promise to build a wall at the Mexican border.

In Fukuyama's view, the surge of populism mirrors an understandable protest against an increasingly dysfunctional political system that has become unresponsive to the interests and concerns of ordinary people. Roger Eatwell and Matthew Goodwin also dispute the notion "that the people are giving up on democracy" simply because they distrust "highly educated and liberal elites whose backgrounds and outlooks differ fundamentally from those of average citizens" (Eatwell/Goodwin 2018: 85). While the political institutions of Western democracies have become more inclusive for women and minorities, the authors observe, representatives of the working classes and people with less formal education have almost been shut out. Half of U.S. senators and congressmen are millionaires in the top one percent of income distribution (108). The view that the political process in America is dominated by lobbyists and powerful interest groups, while being "utterly unresponsive to the policy preferences of millions of low-income citizens," is no populist conspiracy theory, but has often been confirmed by solid social science research (Bartels 2008: 2; Gilens 2012; Hacker/Pierson 2011).

The widespread dissatisfaction with a political system that favors the interests of corporate America and the rich reached new heights in the wake of the financial crisis of 2008. Although the massive bailout of banks was arguably inevitable and successful, it created tremendous outrage, as Washington seemingly saved Wall Street but let Main Street go to the dogs

(Tooze 2018). However, the protest played out differently on the left and the right. The Occupy Wall Street Movement, which emerged in the summer of 2011, claimed to speak for the "Ninety-Nine Percent." But these anti-capitalist protesters were predominantly young and educated members of the white middle classes. Their strict grass-roots egalitarianism won them praise among liberals and the left, but also contributed to the movement's organizational weakness and its fast decline (Kruse/Zelizer 2019: 308–9).

In contrast, the so-called Tea Party Movement on the right, which formed almost immediately after President Barack Obama's inauguration, proved to be much more consequential. The mostly white, conservative, and relatively affluent Tea Partiers fiercely rejected Obama's Wall Street bailout, his plans for universal health care, and his stimulus package to fight the Great Recession as proof of his alleged design to make America a socialist country. Observers debated if the Tea Party was a bona fide populist grass-roots movement or the creature of right-wing media and reactionary billionaires. But the movement clearly had a strong base of committed activists and resonated widely among the electorate. Most importantly, it pushed the Republican Party further to the right by challenging moderates in the party's primaries and committing the GOP to hardline opposition against taxes, immigration, and "socialist medicine." Although the Tea Party was short-lived as an organizational framework, analysts argue that it paved the way for Donald Trump's takeover of the Republican Party (Skocpol/Williamson 2012; Formisano 2012; Kivisto 2018).

Donald Trump and the Politics of Distrust

In the early 2000s, political scientists were debating if the polarization of American politics was perhaps a myth trumped up by the media and a small crust of partisan activists (Fiorina 2005). Today, few people dispute that polarization is real and extends to the very foundations of society and culture (Abramowitz 2018; Campbell 2016). As terms such as "alternative facts," "fake news," and "post-truth" have entered our vocabulary, Americans have come to live in different realities, often referred to as "echo chambers," where people find their own preconceived views and values amplified. In their deeply pessimistic work, *Dueling Facts in American Democracy*, Morgan Marietta and David Barker argue that the inability to agree on facts is rooted in a polarization of values (2019). Whenever there is a conflict over facts, they found, people invariably believe those facts that match their values, regardless of whether they are exposed to fact-checking and regardless of their educational backgrounds. Polarized values lead to a polarization of perceptions and to a "downward spiral of distrust, cynicism, and further political polarization." This process, according to the authors, is driven by "an extreme moralization of politics, a radically altered information environment, and the demise of trust in authority" (12–13). Trust and truth are inextricably linked. Because most of what we believe to be true and factual is far beyond our personal experience, we must trust in sources we consider authoritative and reliable. If there is no longer any basic consensus on which sources are trustworthy, the consequence is "a world of dueling facts, with two separate camps entrenched in their own positions and backed by their own authorities" (XIV).

Since the 1960s, when CBS anchorman Walter Cronkite was known as "the most trusted man in America," Americans have dramatically lost confidence in the mainstream media. In 2015, 65 percent said that the news media affected the country negatively; the worst rating of all non-governmental institutions. Sixty percent believe that the media intentionally withhold information from the public. Distrust of the media is even higher among Republicans, who have long since suspected that the media hold a liberal bias (Pew 2015: 124; Pew 2019a: 11; Patterson 2019: 59–61). The driver of this development has been the fragmentation of the public sphere brought about by the rise of cable tv, talk radio, the internet, and social media in particular (Sunstein 2917: 59–97). While cyber enthusiasts celebrate the advent of a golden age of participatory democracy facilitated by digital technology, critics see the internet as "a polarization machine, fast, efficient, and cheap, and all but automated" with a boundless potential for spreading distrust and conspiracy theories (Lepore 2018: 648; 729–740).

The world of social media was tailor-made for Donald Trump, who employed his Twitter account as a highly effective medium of direct political communication, boasting 11 million followers in 2016. The former reality tv character also knew how to play the mainstream media. Although he relentlessly pounded them as "enemies of the people," fake media," "lying media," and so on, the liberal media were glad to give him all the attention he sought because he drove up ratings. Les Moonves, the chairman of CBS, wryly observed that Trump may not be good for America, but he was "damn good for CBS." Supposedly he received free media coverage worth three billion dollars during the Republican primaries alone. Prior to the general election, the mainstream media tried to demonstrate their objectivity by primarily focusing on Hillary Clinton's alleged scandals (Sunstein 2017: 83; Patterson 2019: 59; Kruse/Zelizer 2019: 337, 340–42).

Donald Trump excelled at sowing distrust, division, and confusion. Volumes could be filled with his blatant lies, vulgar abuses, and wild conspiracy theories. Starting in 2012, he had prepared his presidential bid by posing as a leading spokesman for the so-called "birther" movement that alleged Barack Obama had not been born in the United States and was therefore ineligible for the presidency. Although Obama had released two authenticated versions of his birth certificate, Trump insinuated the documents were forged by an official who had later died under suspicious circumstances (Kruse/Zelizer 2019: 333; @realDonaldTrump, December 12, 2013). During the 2016 campaign, he promised to lock up his opponent, whipped up fear and hate against Mexicans and Muslims, and openly espoused racist and sexist rhetoric. His message "Make America Great Again!" boiled down to a crude nationalism which blamed all of America's problems on treacherous globalist elites, unfair foreign competitors, and illegal immigrants. Moreover, Trump made little effort to conceal that the slogan should also be understood as a promise to restore white hegemony (Simms/Laderman 2017; Blow 2016). In light of America's globalized economy and demographic make-up, Trump's reactionary brand of populism looked hopelessly anachronistic. In the summer of 2016 strategists of both parties expected him to go down in crushing defeat.

It is now clear that most pollsters and pundits had completely misread Trump's appeal. They judged him by conventional standards of politics and found him all bluster with no substance. Surely, Americans, including most Republicans, wanted workable solutions to real problems and would not vote for a political snake oil salesman. But Trump refused to play by conventional rules. Instead he offered his audiences an alternative reality where their gut feelings reigned supreme (Seeßlen 2017: 52–67). Trump, as Arlie Hochschild (2016: 225) put it succinctly, was an "emotions candidate." After attending a Trump rally, she described the atmosphere as one of "whipped-up anger and nationalism." Trump himself gladly admitted that anger was at the root of his appeal: "I am angry, and a lot of other people are angry too, at how incompetently our country is being run. As far as I am concerned anger is o.k. Anger and energy is what this country needs" (quoted in Duhigg 2019: 65). Thus, the warnings by liberals and conservatives alike that Trump was inexperienced, incompetent, and unstable, that he was "a chaos candidate, and he'd be a chaos president," in the words of establishment Republican Jeb Bush, all missed the point. His supporters wanted chaos, and disruption; they wanted an outsider who, at long last, would blow up politics as usual (Rauch 2016). The icono-clastic, left-wing filmmaker Michael Moore predicted that Trump would win because voting for him offered white working and middle-class Americans the opportunity to play "a good practical joke on a sick political system" (Moore 2016).

In his acceptance speech of July 21, 2016, Donald Trump claimed: "Nobody knows the system better than me, which is why I alone can fix it" (Trump Acceptance Speech 2016). In essence, he promised the American people po-litical salvation if only they trust in his extraordinary abilities as a leader and dealmaker. Political scientists point out that his supporters, and the fol-lowers of right-wing populism in general, display strong authoritarian ten-dencies (Kivisto 2017: 51–67; Norris/Inglehart 2019: 9–12; 362–363; Hethering-ton/Weiler 2009). But authoritarianism is only one side of the coin; arguably it is the one that shows up when it comes to repressing "the other." In pursuit of their own rights and interests, however, American twenty-first-century pop-ulists are fiercely antiauthoritarian. In a lucid analysis of the mentality of the Tea Partiers, Mark Lilla (2010) characterizes them as "petulant individuals," who distrust institutions and expertise but are "convinced they can do every-thing themselves if they are only left alone." According to Lilla, the fusion of the anarchism of the Sixties with the neoliberal selfishness of the Eighties has spawned "a nation of cocksure individualists.... They don't want the rule of the people, though that's what they say. They want to be people without rules." It should come as no surprise then that they came to admire Donald Trump, the man who brags about getting away with breaking every rule.

After November 8, 2016, admirers celebrated Trump's stunning victory as the triumph of the common man in the true spirit of American populism (Rosenfielde 2017). In contrast, liberals warned that the United States had entered the slippery slope to authoritarianism (Levitsky/Ziblatt 2017). Polit-ical scientists of the value change school offer us at least some consolation. Trump's election, they claim, marks the apex of a decade-long authoritar-ian backlash against the inexorable liberalization of Western societies. Right-wing populism has peaked in recent years because the "tipping point" has been reached when the once dominant cultural and social groups were becoming minorities and, thus, facing the loss of their hegemony (Norris/Inglehart 2019: esp. 87–91). In other words, Donald Trump may lead the angry white man in his last stand, but the future belongs to an open, liberal, multiethnic society wrought by generational, demographic, economic, and educational change. In order to alleviate the transitional crisis, liberals demand that government must restore trust by addressing the economic grievances and status fears of the losers (see also Reckwitz 2019: 285–304).

Alas, while optimists hope for a gradual transformation, pessimists point to American history for a much gloomier scenario. The American Civil War, which claimed more than 700,000 lives between 1861 and 1865, was preceded by decades of mounting distrust and polarization until the North and the South viewed each other as irreconcilable foes in an irrepressible conflict. When Abraham Lincoln was elected president of the United States in November 1860, the slaveholding South concluded that its economic foundation, political power, and way of life were at stake and, as a result, decided to secede from the Union. Historian David Blight, an authority on the Civil War Era, observes that a polarized country faces an imminent risk of civil war if the outcome of an election becomes unacceptable for the losing side (Wright 2017). In 2016, Donald Trump told his supporters that the system was rigged and he left open whether he would concede defeat. Will he do so should he lose in 2020? Will the Democrats accept defeat if Trump again fails to win the popular vote? Will Americans trust in the integrity of the election? After nearly four years of Trump in the White House, during which polarization and political distrust have reached new heights, these are frightening questions. At the time of this writing (March to May of 2020), they have taken on a truly dramatic dimension, as the Corona pandemic, rather than eliciting a coordinated and unifying national response, appears to be deepening the crisis of political trust and radicalizing the rifts and cleavages in American politics and society (Brownstein 2020). How the situation will look like when this essay comes to print, I do not dare to predict.

Works Cited

Abramowitz, Alan I. (2018): The Great Alignment: Race, Party Transformation, and the Rise of Donald Trump. New Haven: Yale University Press.

Almond, Gabriel A./Verba, Sidney (1995; original 1963): The Civic Culture: Political Attitudes and Democracy in Five Nations, Newbury Park, Calif.: Sage Publications.

Anderson, Carol (2016): White Rage: The Unspoken Truth of Our Racial Divide, New York: Bloomsbury.

Andrew, John A. (1998): Lyndon Johnson and the Great Society, Chicago: I.R. Dee.

Bartels, Larry M. (2008): Unequal Democracy: The Political Economy of the New Gilded Age, Princeton: Princeton University Press.

Black, Earl/Black, Merle (2002): The Rise of Southern Republicans, Cambridge, Mass.,: The Belknap Press of Harvard University Press.

Blow, Charles (2016): "Trump: Making America White Again." New York Times, November 21, 2016. www.nytimes.com/2016/11/21/trump-making-america-white-again.html.

Boyd, James (1970): "Nixon's Southern Strategy: It's All in the Charts." New York Times, May 17, 1970, 25.

Brinkley, Alan (1983): Voices of Protest: Huey Long, Father Coughlin and the Great Depression, New York: Vintage Books.

Brownstein, Ronald (2020): "Red and Blue America Aren't Experiencing the Same Pandemic. The disconnect is already shaping, even distorting, the nation's response," in: The Atlantic, March 22, 2020, https://www.theatlantic.com/politics/archive/2020/03/how-republicans-and-democrats-think-about-coronavirus/608395/.

Bureau of the Census (2019): https://www.census.gov/quickfacts/fact/table/US/PST045219.

Carter, Dan T. (1995): The Politics of Rage: George Wallace, the Origins of the New Conservatism, and the Transformation of American Politics, New York: Simon & Schuster.

Campbell, James E. (2016): Polarized. Making Sense of a Divided America, Princeton: Princeton University Press.

Dalton, Rusell J. (2017): "Political Trust in North America," in: Sonja Zmerli/Tom W. G. van der Meer (eds.): Handbook on Political Trust, Cheltenham, UK: Edward Elgar Publishing, 375–394.

Duhigg, Charles (2019): "Why Are We So Angry?" in: The Atlantic, January/February 2019, 62–75.

Eatwell, Roger/Goodwin, Matthew (2018): National Populism: The Revolt against Liberal Democracy, London: Penguin Books.

Eichengreen, Barry J. (2018): The Populist Temptation: Economic Grievance and Political Reaction in the Modern Era, New York: Oxford University Press.

Fiorina, Morris P. (2005): Culture War? The Myth of a Polarized America, New York: Longman.

Frank, Thomas (2004): What's the Matter with Kansas? How Conservatives Won the Heart of America, New York: Metropolitan Books.

Frank, Thomas (2016): Listen, Liberal, or, What Ever Happened to the Party of the People? New York: Henry Holt Publishers.

Formisano, Ronald P. (2008): For the People: American Populist Movements from the Revolution to the 1850s, Chapel Hill: University of North Carolina Press.

Formisano, Ronald P. (2012): The Tea Party: A Brief History, Baltimore: Johns Hopkins University Press.

Fukuyama, Francis (2016): "American Political Decay or Renewal? The Meaning of the 2016 Election," in: Foreign Affairs 95.

Gilens, Martin (2012): Affluence and Influence: Economic Inequality and Political Power in America, Princeton: Princeton University Press.

Hacker, Jacob S./Pierson, Paul (2011): Winner-Take-All Politics: How Washington Made the Rich Richer-and Turned Its Back on the Middle Class, New York: Simon & Schuster.

Hardin, Russell (2013): "Government without Trust," in: Journal of Trust Research 3, 32–52.

Hetherington, Marc J. (2005): Why Trust Matters: Declining Political Trust and the Demise of American Liberalism, Princeton: Princeton University Press.

Hetherington, Marc J./Weiler, Jonathan Daniel (2009): Authoritarianism and Polarization in American Politics, New York: Cambridge University Press, 2009.

Hetherington, Marc J./Rudolph, Thomas J. (2015): Why Washington Won't Work: Polarization, Political Trust, and the Governing Crisis, Chicago: University of Chicago Press.

Hochschild, Arlie Russell (2016): Strangers in Their Own Land: Anger and Mourning on the American Right, New York: The New Press.

Judis, John B. (2016): The Populist Explosion: How the Great Recession Transformed American and European Politics, New York: Columbia Global Reports.

Kaufmann, Eric (2018): Whiteshift: Populism, Immigration and the Future of White Majorities, London: Penguin.

Kazin, Michael (1995): The Populist Persuasion: An American History, New York: Basic Books.

Kivisto, Peter (2018): The Trump Phenomenon: How the Politics of Populism Won in 2016, St. Petersburg, FL: Emerald Publishing.

Kruse, Kevin/Zelizer, Julian E. (2019): Fault Lines: A History of the United States since 1974, New York: W.W. Norton.

Kumlin, Staffan/Haugsgjerd, Atle (2017): "The Welfare State and Political Trust: Bringing Performance Back In," in: Sonja Zmerli/Tom W. G. van der Meer (eds.): Handbook on Political Trust, Cheltenham, UK: Edward Elgar Publishing, 285–301.

Lepore, Jill (2018): These Truths: A History of the United States, New York: W.W. Norton.

Levitsky, Steven/Ziblatt, Daniel (2017): How Democracies Die: What History Reveals About Our Future, New York: Penguin Random House.

Lilla, Mark (2010): "The Tea Party Jacobins," in: *New York Review of Books*, May 27, 2010 , http://www.uvm.edu/~dguber/POLS125/articles/lilla.htm.

Lilla, Mark (2017): The Once and Future Liberal. After Identity Politics, New York: Harper.

Lütjen, Torben (2016): Partei der Extreme: Die Republikaner. Über die Implosion des Amerikanischen Konservatismus, Bielefeld: transcript.

MacLean, Nancy (2016): Democracy in Chains: The Deep History of the Radical Right's Stealth Plan for America, New York: Viking.

Marietta, Morgan/Barker, David C. (2019): One Nation, Two Realities. Dueling Facts in American Democracy, New York: Oxford University Press.

McLaren, Lauren (2017): "Immigration, Ethnic Diversity, and Political Trust," in: Sonja Zmerli/Tom W. G. van der Meer (eds.): Handbook on Political Trust, Cheltenham, UK: Edward Elgar Publishing in *Handbook on Political Trust*, edited by Sonja Zmerli and Tom W. G. van der Meer. Cheltenham, UK: Edward Elgar Publishing, 316–337.

Moore, Michael (2016): https://michaelmoore.com/trumpwillwin/.

Mounk, Yascha (2017). The People vs. Democracy: Why Our Freedom Is in Danger and How to Save It, Cambridge, Mass.: Harvard University Press.

Mudde, Cas/Kaltwasser, Cristobal Rovira (2017): Populism: A Very Short Introduction. New York: Oxford University Press.

Müller, Jan-Werner (2017): What Is Populism? London: Penguin.

Murray, Charles (1984): Losing Ground. American Social Policy, *1950–1980*, New York: Basic Books.

Norris, Pippa (1999): Critical Citizens: Global Support for Democratic Government, New York: Oxford University Press.

Norris, Pippa (2011): Democratic Deficit: Critical Citizens Revisited, New York: Cambridge University Press.

Norris, Pippa (2017): "The Conceptual Framework of Political Support," in: Sonja Zmerli/Tom W. G. van der Meer (eds.): Handbook on Political Trust, Cheltenham, UK: Edward Elgar Publishing, 19–32.

Norris, Pippa/Inglehart, Ronald (2019): Cultural Backlash: Trump, Brexit, and Authoritarian Populism, New York: Cambridge University Press. https://obamawhitehouse.archives.gov/the-press-office/2016/01/12/re-marks-president-barack-obama-%E2%80%93-prepared-delivery-state-union-address.

Oshinsky, David M. (2005): A Conspiracy So Immense: The World of Joe McCarthy, New York: Oxford University Press.

Patterson, Thomas E. (2019): How America Lost Its Mind: The Assault on Reason That's Crippling Our Democracy, Norman, OK: University of Oklahoma Press.

Perlstein, Rick (2001): Before the Storm : Barry Goldwater and the Unmaking of the American Consensus, New York: Hill and Wang.

Pew Research Center (2015): Beyond Distrust: How Americans View Their Government. Online www.pewresearch.org.

Pew Research Center (2017): Public Trust in Government Remains near Historic Lows as Partisan Attitudes Shift. Online www.pewresearch.org.

Pew Research Center (2019a): Trust and Distrust in America. Online www.pewresearch.org.

Pew Research Center (2019b): Why Americans Don't Fully Trust Many Who Hold Positions of Power and Responsibility. Online www.pewresearch.org.

Postel, Charles (2007): The Populist Vision, New York: Oxford University Press.

Rauch, Jonathan (2016): "How American Politics Went Insane," in: The Atlantic, July/August 2016, www.theatlantic.com/magazine/archive/2016/07/how-american-politics-went-insane/485570/.

Rosefielde, Steven (2017): Trump's Populist America, Hackensach, NJ: World Scientific Publishing.

Rossiter, Clinton (ed.) (1961): The Federalist Papers. Hamilton, Madison, Jay, New York: Penguin.

Reckwitz, Andreas (2019): Das Ende Der Illusionen. Politik, Ökonomie Und Kultur in Der Spätmoderne, Berlin: Suhrkamp.

Saez, Emmanuel/Zucman, Gabriel (2019): The Triumph of Injustice, New York: W.W. Norton.

Schaller, Michael/Rising, George (2002): The Republican Ascendancy: American Politics, 1968-2001, Wheeling, Illinois: Harlan Davidson.

Seeßlen, Georg (2017): Trump. Populismus als Politik, Berlin: Bertz und Fischer.

Simms, Brendan/Laderman, Charlie (2017): Donald Trump: The Making of a Worldview, New York: Tauris.

Skocpol, Theda/Williamson, Vanessa (2012): The Tea Party and the Remaking of Republican Conservatism, New York: Oxford University Press.

Stiglitz, Joseph R. (2012): The Price of Inequality: How Today's Divided Society Endangers Our Future, New York: W.W. Norton & Company.

Sunstein, Cass R. (2017): #Republic: Divided Democracy in the Age of Social Media, Princeton: Princeton University Press.

Tocqueville, Alexis de (1990), Democracy in America. II vols, New York: Vintage Classics.

Tooze, J. Adam (2018): Crashed: How a Decade of Financial Crises Changed the World, New York: Viking.

Trump Acceptance Speech, 21. 7. 2016, www.vox.com/2016/7/21/12253426/donald-trump-acceptance-speech-transcript-republican-nomination-transcript.

Trump-Rally in Pueblo, CO, 3. 10. 2016. https://factba.se/transcript/donald-trump-speech-pueblo-co-october-3-2016.

Trump-Rally in Grand Junction, CO, 18.10.2016, AP Archive, https://www.youtube.com/watch?v=ijD2VZ86_tI.

@realDonaldTrump, 12.12.2013, https://twitter.com/realDonaldTrump/status/411247268763676673?s=20.

@realDonaldTrump, November 27, 2016, http://fulltranscripts.com/donald-j-trump/tweets/2016/11/27/realdonaldtrump-november-27-2016.

@realDonaldTrump, 25.01.2017, https://twitter.com/realDonaldTrump/status/824227824903090176?s=20.

Uslaner, Eric M. (ed.) (2018): The Oxford Handbook of Social and Political Trust, Oxford: Oxford University Press.

Warren, Mark E. (2017): "What Kind of Trust Does a Democracy Need? Trust from the Perspective of Democratic Theory," in: Sonja Zmerli/Tom W. G. van der Meer (eds.): Handbook on Political Trust, Cheltenham, UK: Edward Elgar Publishing, 33–52.

Wills, Garry (1999): A Necessary Evil: A History of American Distrust of Government, New York: Touchstone.

Wolff, Michael (2018): Fire and Fury: Inside the Trump White House, London: Little Brown.

Wright, Robin (2017): "Is America Headed for a New Kind of Civil War?" in: The New Yorker, August 14, 2017, https://www.newyorker.com/news/newsdesk/is-america-headed-for-a-new-kind-of-civil-war.

Zmerli, Sonja/van der Meer, Tom W. G. (eds.) (2017): Handbook on Political Trust, Cheltenham, UK: Edward Elgar Publishing.

Waning Trust in (Scientific) Experts and Expertise?

Recent Evidence from the United States and Elsewhere

Martin Thunert

"People in this country have had enough of experts," pro-Brexit UK government minister Michael Gove famously proclaimed just weeks before 52.4% of British voters decided to leave the EU on June 23, 2016, defying the warnings of economists, analysts, and other professional forecasters. Similar warnings could be heard several months later on the other side of the Atlantic Ocean before Donald Trump won the Electoral College vote to become the 45th president of the United States. Expertise, it seemed, had become toxic. Shortly thereafter, a book-length study by Anthony Nichols announced the "death of expertise" (Nichols 2017). To be sure, a trend of declining trust has been underway across the western world for many years, even decades, as survey evidence attests. It is not so much the case that interpersonal or generalized trust has declined, but what has eroded—especially in the US—is the credibility of members of the political class—especially elected representatives and the people around them—and members of the news media. This chapter intends to find out whether this decline in trust really extends to experts and expert bodies, and why or why not. In a first step, I will briefly define what is meant by the terms "expert" and "expertise," then look back to a time when, allegedly, expertise was universally trusted. This paper's second part will examine whether there is empirical proof that trust in experts and expertise is really declining. After weighing the available evidence—largely in the form of opinion polls and experimental studies—reasons for a possible crisis of expertise are discussed. Finally, some very tentative evidence and arguments are presented regarding the way the global coronavirus/Covid 19 epidemic has recalibrated the role of experts and their reputation in the US and elsewhere.

Expertise and its alleged "Golden Age"

The "expert" appears in pre-modern times in the role of the bearer or carrier of specialized knowledge (Rexroth and Schröder-Stapper 2018). The origins of modern expertise can be traced back to the second half of the 17th century, when scientists and merchants first established techniques for recording and sharing facts and figures. The expert's position in society results from an interplay of external and his/her own attributions of specialist knowledge. Today, an expert has specialist knowledge for which he/she is credentialed through academic degrees and activities, as well as memberships in relevant scientific and academic organizations, both nationally and internationally. In contrast to the pure scientific specialist, the expert shares his/her knowledge with non-specialists. Political decision-makers, who in most cases are not experts themselves, are a key audience of expert consultation, but so is the general public. Specialists become experts not by talking to each other, but by being approached by courts, political bodies, or the media—and thereby the wider public—for their specialized knowledge in their subject area.[1] The non-ideological, non-political, and almost technical character of their subject matter expertise is illustrated by the German term "Sachverständige."[2] As historians of expertise like Caspar Hirschi have shown, the term *Sachverständige* was first used for expert witnesses appearing before courts of law, as well as in purely technical matters like the certification of road-readiness for automobiles, etc. (2018: 29). Later on, it was extended to expert witnesses in parliamentary hearings and advisory councils.

When and Why Expertise Was Trusted

The very notion of waning trust in expertise suggests that there once was a time in the not-so-distant past when the public trusted experts—a proverbial "Golden Age" in the relationship between experts, the public, and those

---

1   A similar point is made by Rexroth, when he states that one should only speak about experts and expertise where their specialist knowledge is passed on within the framework of social institutions and is therefore institutionally established (quoted from Rexroth/Schröder-Stapper 2018: 12).

2   The online dictionary Leo offers the following translations: technical expert, person with a specialist knowledge, authorized expert, official expert, authority on a subject, even referee.

who govern. According to business researcher and consultant Rachel Botsman, trust in the course of human history has evolved in three basic stages (2017). Local trust or interpersonal trust prevailed in premodern times when people lived in small communities and everybody knew everybody else. In the modern age, with industrialization and urbanization, people had to develop institutional trust so that they could trust complete strangers running governments, corporations, legal institutions, as well as the global frameworks and norms for international trade, commerce, and finance. It is therefore not a coincidence that the heyday of the industrial age—especially the decades following the end of World War II—are often described as something akin to a golden age of expertise; especially in the Nordic countries. As Lundqvist and Petersen have shown, the development of the Nordic model of the welfare state would not have been successful and enjoyed wide public acceptance without the successful interplay between knowledge-based actors in the civil service, external experts, politicians, and institutions (2010). Between the late 1950s and the 1970s there was enormous optimism—in the United States and elsewhere—regarding the social role of experts helping governments to think better and to solve problems. In the mid-1960s, the belief in the predictability of social conditions that had already arisen in the New Deal era of the 1930s had reached a peak. With confidence in expertise, there was hope for de-ideologization and the rationalization of politics (see Bell 1960).

However, there are important voices among contemporary sociologists of science questioning the narrative of an alleged golden age. Perhaps we have wrongly described the past in this regard, contend the German sociologists André Kieserling and Simone Rödder (2019). In their opinion, it cannot be assumed that the authority of scientific experts was universally recognized in practically every field of human life 50 or 60 years ago. Historians like Richard Hofstadter claimed that "anti-intellectualism" and a "paranoid style" have been fundamental traits in US political history (1965). But even if the golden age argument is too nostalgic, there is no denying that, in the US, it was the space race in particular that gave science expertise a big boost during the 1960s and 1970s. In addition, there is ample case study evidence—e.g. from the field of social science, including the field of international relations—that in the second half of the 20th century in the US, there was at least a productive relationship between the political class and policy-makers on the one hand, and experts and their expert bodies on the other (see e.g. Desch 2019, Drezner 2017) At that time, public trust in government and the media was much higher than today. As Daniel Drezner notes, "the national security advisors who dominated the 1960s and 1970s—Walt Rostow, Henry Kissinger, and Zbigniew Brzezinkski—all began their careers as academics" (2017:79). When surveys like the National Election Study began asking about trust in government in 1958, about three-quarters of Americans trusted the federal government to do the right thing almost always or most of the time. These very high trust levels began to erode during the 1960s. The decline continued in the 1970s with, for example, the Watergate scandal, but even then the numbers of those expressing trust stayed around 30% in the late 1970s. Since 2010, trust levels for government and the media have never reached above the 20% mark in the US (Pew 2017:1).

Disenchantment about the role of (technocratic) expertise set in at the same time because of and during the war in Vietnam, the nuclear arms race, and the social upheavals of the 1960s, and came predominantly from the progressive/left-leaning side of the political aisle. "Progressive" criticism of the technocratic rule of experts chipped away at the idea of a US government—under the Democratic administrations of Kennedy and Johnson—run by the "best and brightest." It was the very involvement of "scholar-experts" in many, if not most, policies of the day, which generated criticism from left-leaning intellectuals like Noam Chomsky or C. Wright Mills (Drezner 2017: 80–81). As a consequence, scientific experts in the US turned inward, and a large amount of policy-relevant expertise outside the natural and medical sciences moved from universities to think tanks in the 1980s and thereafter (Medvetz 2012).

Ironically, and perhaps paradoxically, the current trouble with trust in expertise became most intense just when the notion of the "knowledge society" became the distinguishing marker for the period beginning in the late 1990s. The knowledge society became a double-edged sword as far as trust in expertise is concerned. On the one hand, the public within knowledge societies expects politicians and public institutions to act rationally and rely on relevant knowledge, as expressed in the notion of evidence-based decision-making. But in a knowledge society, experts and their expertise touch many more areas in the lives of citizens than before; for example, in questions of education or nutrition. This creates more opportunities for discomfort with experts, because many of them seem to contradict each other—especially outside the fields of the core natural sciences. During the heyday of trust in experts, expertise was much more limited, being essentially an affair between experts and decision-makers in government and the corporate world.

But in order to avoid the technocratic pitfalls of the era of planning optimism in the 1960s, the knowledge society continued producing and relying
on ever more experts. The foundational idea for the knowledge society was
that expertise could be democratized—not just by producing more experts
and areas of expertise, but by erasing the boundary between expert knowledge shepherded over by certain credentialed individuals and expertise as a
joint public good in a society with much higher levels of education and new
groundbreaking technologies, such as the internet. If, in a knowledge society,
information is a public good to which all people have access, any individual
may also serve as a creator of knowledge and receive credit as an expert. As
Americans became better educated, they also became increasingly confident
in their own opinions, even though their actual subject matter expertise might
not have increased. While conservative defenders of technocratic expert rule
like Tom Nichols (2017) diagnosed the "death of expertise" in the US, Rachel
Botsman or Financial Times columnist Gillian Tett, citing the same technological drivers of a knowledge society, recognized a diffusion of trust into
different spheres of expertise. Through the digital revolution at the beginning
of the 21st century, we are witnessing a devolution of trust from large and
anonymous institutions to individuals—not to individuals on the local level,
to individuals that one knows in person like in the pre-modern age, but to
individuals in digitally generated peer groups and on the internet.

Michael Gove was by no means the first senior politician of a government
of an OECD state who was critical of this new and broader type of expertise.
As Lundqvist and Peterson (2010: 9–10) show, then Danish Prime Minister
Anders Fogh Rasmussen, who later became Secretary General of NATO, said
in his 2002 New Year's Speech:

> We do not need experts and arbiters of taste to decide things for us. In recent
> years, a veritable wilderness of governmental councils and committees and
> institutions has shot up everywhere.... There is a tendency towards a "tyranny
> of experts" which runs the risk of suppressing free popular debate. The Dan-
> ish population must not accept admonishing fingers from so-called experts
> who think that they know best. Experts are fine when it comes to conveying
> actual knowledge. But when it comes to making personal choices, all of us
> are experts.

Rasmussen's quotation reveals a fundamental problem underlying the relationship between expert cultures and society. A traditional understanding of
expertise is non-controversial, as it always refers to experts like rocket sci-

entists, civil engineers, or heart surgeons, where virtually everybody agrees that one should not have a say in certain things without expertise. But an expanded understanding of expertise—which is addressed by Rasmussen as personal choices—concerns questions of morality or lifestyle, where the idea of expert review can quickly become undemocratic.[3] Because this distinction is not always made, it is not really surprising that scholars like Tom Nichols or Salvatore Babones—both self-described conservatives—arrive at completely different conclusions regarding the role of experts in a modern knowledge society. While Nichols bemoans the death of expertise (2017), Babones (2018) blames the populist backlash against expertise—as expressed in the quotes by Rasmussen and Gove, or the victory of Donald Trump and Vote Leave in 2016—as a consequence of an anti-democratic power grab by a class of largely liberal-technocratic experts who seek to replace the vibrant unpredictability of democratic decision-making with a creeping authoritarianism of liberal-progressive technocracy. However, as the following section will show, the larger publics of the United States and other western countries seem to display a somewhat more relaxed point of view regarding trust in expertise. There is, perhaps, a crisis of expertise, but no linear decline in trust.

Studying Epistemic Trust in Experts and Expertise in the early 21st Century

At first glance, the thesis regarding the decline of trust in experts—or, in its more pointed version, as the alleged "death of expertise"—seems plausible, as it is confirmed in the United States by innumerable forms of anecdotal evidence. From a broader empirical point of view, however, the situation is somewhat more complicated, since time series data spanning a longer period are more readily available on questions of generalized trust, as well as trust in political institutions, the media, business elites, churches, the military, etc., whereas surveys on trust in science, the scientific community, experts, and knowledge-based actors are more sporadic and were often carried out unevenly. Rigorous statistical analysis on trust drawing on General Social Survey (GSS) data from 1974 to 1994 conducted by political economists Alberto

---

3   One of the editors, Günter Leypoldt, has helped me to develop this argument.

Alesina and Eliana La Ferrara (2002) somehow confirms the "golden age" hypothesis insofar as they found "a lot of variation across types of institutions. The highest degree of confidence is attributed to relatively 'impersonal' categories like 'medicine' and the 'scientific community.'" (Alesina and Ferrara 2002: 216–17) The lowest level of trust they found was towards institutions like organized labor, Congress, the media, and the federal executive branch. In addition, they found that the variables displaying the highest positive correlation with trust in people are confidence in the scientific community (ibid. 217). Nearly 20 years later, a national survey by the Pew Research Centers, conducted March 24–29, 2020 among 1,013 US adults, found that more than three years into the Trump administration, larger shares of Republicans than Democrats express favorable opinions of eight of 10 government agencies included in the survey—at the top, two agencies that are expert-based and play a crucial role during the Coronavirus pandemic of 2020: the Centers for Disease Control and Prevention, and the Department of Health and Human Services (Pew 2020c).

From surveys like GSS, which study interpersonal trust and trust in "neighboring" social institutions (neighboring to expertise and science), two conclusion for the early 21st century can be derived: firstly, within most of the countries of the developed world—primarily represented by the member states of the OECD—there is a decline in trust values; secondly, this loss of confidence is more pronounced in the United States than elsewhere. Ever since the beginning of the 21st century, the United States has been an outlier among the world's richer countries in terms of generalized trust. Among the 30 member states of the OECD in 2008, the United States ranked fourth for median household income, but was the 10th least trusting country, with only 48.7 percent of Americans responding that, generally speaking, most people could be trusted.[4] With regard to the authority of scientific expertise and trust in experts, things are more complicated.

Longitudinal Measure of Epistemic Trust: Edelman Trust Barometer (ETB)

The Edelman Trust Barometer (ETB) relies on surveying thousands of people in 28 predominantly western countries including the US. Among other

---

4   Drezner 2017: 46–49 provides a good summary of this data.

things, ETB asks about trust in institutions—especially government and the media—and tackles the question of trust in expertise mostly in an indirect way. For example, two-thirds of people surveyed in 2016 in 28 countries for the 2017 Edelman Trust Barometer expressed low levels of trust in "mainstream institutions" such as business, government, media, and nongovernmental organizations. The Trust Barometer probes the credibility of technical and academic experts by comparing them with other sources of knowledge and information including the category of "a person like me." According to ETB, trust in institutions—especially government and the media—continued to decline from 2005 until 2017. For several years, this global survey also found disturbing trends in the attitude toward "experts," with "a person like me" increasingly considered to be on par, in terms of credibility, with a technical or academic expert. This result seems to confirm Nichols's notion that especially Americans express overconfidence in their own subject matter expertise. 59% of people surveyed would rather believe a search engine than a human editor, and more than half (53%) do not regularly listen to people or organizations with whom they disagree. But if Edelman's most current data is to be believed, the erosion of trust in experts has at least slowed down or halted, perhaps even reversed. In 2007, the Edelman Trust Barometer found that Americans trusted their peers (a "person like yourself") the most, and, in 2017, a "person like yourself" was seen as just as credible a source of information as a company or a technical or academic expert (60 percent), and far more credible than a CEO of a private corporation (37 percent) or a government official (29 percent). But after 2018, trust in technical experts has been up and has reached 60% in the US and even more globally (63%), with academic credibility at 61% (sitting well ahead of government at 35% and journalists at 39%), whereas trust in a "person like yourself" has dipped to an all-time low of 54% in ETB's history.

Pew Research Center Studies on Trust in Expertise

The Pew Research Center in 2019 explored links between institutional trust and interpersonal trust in US society.[5] In terms of interpersonal trust, about a fifth of adults (22%) display consistently trustful attitudes, and roughly a third (35%) express consistently wary or distrustful views. Some 41% hold mixed

---

5   The source of the following numbers is Pew 2019a.

views on core personal trust questions. The first notable, but not very surprising finding was that levels of personal trust are associated with race and
ethnicity, age, education, and household income. This finding is consistent
with what Alesina and Ferrara found nearly two decades earlier about the lack
of trust in very economically unequal and socially and racially heterogeneous
states of the US (Alesina and Ferrara 2002). The share of whites who show
high levels of trust (27%) is twice as high as the share of blacks (13%) and Hispanics (12%). The older a person is, the more likely they are to tilt toward more
trustful answers. The more education Americans have, and the greater their
household income, the greater the likelihood they are high on the personal
trust spectrum. Those with less income and education are markedly more
likely to be low trusters. The military enjoys "a great deal" or "fair amount"
of confidence among 83% of US adults, as do scientists (83%)—an important
component of the expert community.[6] Even "low trusters" show as much confidence in scientists as they show in the military (Pew 2019a: 6). These largely
supportive views stand in sharp contrast to the public's overall lack of confidence in elected officials and corporate leaders: 63% express little confidence
in elected officials, and 56% take a similarly negative view of business leaders.
Although supporters of the country's two main political parties hold similar
levels of personal trust, Democrats and those who lean Democratic are more
likely than Republicans and Republican leaners to express worry about the
state of trust in America.[7]

In a companion survey (Pew 2019b) on trust and mistrust in scientific
experts, 86% of all Americans expressed at least a fair amount of confidence
in scientists to act in the public interest. The proportion of Americans who
said that they have a great deal of confidence rose from 21% in 2016 to 35% in
2019. More specifically, the survey conducted in January 2019 of 4,463 adult age
Americans focuses on scientific experts working in three fields of research:
medicine, nutrition, and the environment. Beyond a generally positive view
of scientists in these fields, only 20% believe that scientists in America are
transparent about potential conflicts of interest (Pew 2019b: 14–16). Trust is
lowest vis-a-vis the transparency of environmental experts.

---

6   Not far behind are principals of K-12 public schools (80%) and police officers (78%).
    Confidence in journalists stands at 55%.
7   The partisan cleavage in most trust-related matters is a recurrent pattern to which we
    will return later.

In another finding, more Americans trust science practitioners like medical doctors or dieticians more than medical researchers or nutrition scientists (ibid. 33–34, 44–45). Most Americans of all stripes expressed that open public access to data and independent committee reviews would boost their trust in scientific expertise (ibid. 24–27). Distrust fueled by misconduct—especially performed by medical experts—is far a greater concern among black and Hispanic Americans than among white Americans (ibid. 23–24). While most Americans (63%) believe that the so-called "scientific method" of observing and collecting empirical evidence is fundamentally sound and 55% believe scientists' judgments are "based solely on the facts," as opposed to scientists being "just as likely to be biased" in their judgments as other people (44%), more Democrats than Republicans (including those who lean towards either party) are inclined to express confidence in both the scientific method and scientists' conclusions. 55% of Republicans believe that scientific experts are as biased as other people (ibid. 9–12). Interestingly, 64% of Republicans with high science knowledge say scientists are just as likely to be biased as other people, while 42% of Republicans with low science knowledge agree. In other words: knowledge of the scientific process is less important in judging an expert's susceptibility to bias than a partisan lens, a phenomenon for which Pew coined the term "motivated reasoning" (ibid. 12).

A similar study was conducted in the UK after Brexit. Inspired by the Gove-quote on experts, a YouGov survey in the United Kingdom taken eight months after the Brexit referendum between February 14–15, 2017 has tested how far the British public trusts different types of experts when they talk about their own fields of expertise (see YouGov:2017). Three possibilities were given: "trust," "don't trust," "don't know." The net "trust" score is the "trust" answers minus the "don't trust" answers (see Table 1).

Table 1: Trust in different types of experts

Type of Expert	Net Trust
Nurses	+77
Doctors	+74
Your own GP	+71
Scientists	+60
Historians	+61
Sports commentators	+22
Weather forecasters	+20
Nutritionists	+03
Civil Servants	-17
Economists	-19
Your local MP	-32
Politicians	-74

At 84%, the group of experts the public was most willing to trust was nurses. The opinions of doctors were almost equally trusted, at 82% for doctors in general and 80% for people's own General Practitioner. Scientists and historians also performed well, with 71% of people saying they trust them when they talk about their own areas of expertise. At the other end of the scale, politicians in general were the least trusted, with just 5% of people trusting them—although this does increase to 20% for people's own MP. Also coming off poorly were civil servants (26%) and economists (25%). The results show that Leave voters are less likely than Remain voters to trust every single type of expert listed. This trust gap was especially pronounced for certain types of experts: Leave voters are 21 percentage points less likely to trust economists than Remain voters, 20 points less likely to trust scientists and civil servants, and are even 15 points less likely to trust weather forecasters.

Survey research on trust in experts and expertise has shown that attitudes towards experts have changed, but there is no across-the-board, uniform decline of trust in expertise comparable to the decline of trust in other social institutions like government or the media. Even though it is evident that confidence in institutions associated with knowledge and learning was higher in the 1970s than it was in 2008 and 2012, for example, the most recent data by the Pew Research Center in the US and YouGov in the UK suggests that the decline in institutions that can be associated with "expertise" was less dramatic than the decline in trust in government or the media. However, most quantitative survey research on trust in expertise focuses on experts and expertise in medicine, the natural sciences, including the environment, as well as technical experts in engineering and computer science. Only the YouGov survey distinguished between scientists on the one hand and experts from the humanities (e.g. from history) or from the social sciences (e.g. political science, international relations, psychology etc.) on the other.

In an experimental large-scale study conducted in the UK and the US, a research team from Queen Mary University in London examined the responses of randomly chosen groups of people in both countries to social policy interventions in the form of "nudges," which were suggested either by scientists or by a government working group consisting of special interest groups from the social policy field and policy makers (Osman et al: 2018). The research team found that trust was higher for scientists than the government working group, even when the scientists were proposing fictitious nudges. According to the Queen Mary study, people trust scientific experts, who in this case were not natural scientists, but mostly social scientists like psychologists, far more than members of the political class.

Explaining the Trust/Distrust in Expertise Conundrum

One set of plausible explanations for these and other empirical findings usually revolves around the digital revolution. The Edelman findings seem to confirm what Rachel Botsman has written on distributive trust in the digital age. The internet and digital media have allowed people to distribute their trust over more sources of expertise and knowledge than before. A good deal of knowledge that people trust on the internet does not come from professional experts per se or directly from them, but often from reviews, recommendations, etc. by laypeople whose currency often is first-hand experience or by experts that count as practitioner experts as opposed to experts based on academic research. A similar observation was made by Financial Times columnist Gillian Tett: "At a time when we increasingly rely on crowd-sourced advice rather than official experts to choose a restaurant, healthcare and holidays, it seems strange to expect voters to listen to official experts when it comes to politics." While Tett described a shift from vertical axes of trust to horizontal axes, researchers like Rachel Botsman have called the same phenomenon "distributed trust." Distributed trust is facilitated and made possible by high-tech platforms, many of which (though not all) are run by the private sector. Distributed trust, triggered by the digital revolution, has clearly led to a relative decline of trust in unknown experts, especially as far as consumer choices and other decisions in the non-political world are concerned.

Media and truth researchers like Danish philosophers Vincent F. Hendricks and Mads Vestergaard reject the notion that experts have lost their trust entirely (2018 and 2019). Like Botsman and Tett, they tie the reduction of trust in facts, journalists, and experts to the digital dissemination of information, through which the opinions of experts are drowning in the general cacophony of the internet and social media. This favors a kind of news that is not just fake news, but mixed products of the true, half-true, and freely invented. And this kind of news is very well suited to inflate narratives by reducing complexity. The most recent drops in trusting a peer (a person like myself) can be explained by a certain disillusionment regarding the benefits of digitization and the knowledge economy.

Historians of science and expertise point out that an important characteristic of the expert and of expertise is the claim to independence. Caspar Hirschi suggests that this claim has two aspects: Independence means to have no economic interest in the object of the expert consultation and not to be exposed to any political influences in the advisory activity (Hirschi 2018: 30). If this independence is questioned, experts will become lobbyists, activists, or propagandists depending on the situation, which will at least damage their credibility. The slightest suspicion, valid or not valid, that members of the political class are exploiting their power for their own private interest, has severely damaged trust in governmental institutions. The Muenster Epistemic Trustworthiness Inventory (METI) project at the University of Münster in Germany seems to confirm that this could potentially happen with trust in experts and expert bodies as well. Many of the problems regarding trust in expertise revolve around issues of transparency and conflict of interest of experts and less about doubts about their credentialed knowledge. In the Queen Mary Study, people were ready to trust social policy interventions and recommendations by scientific experts more, even when these recommendations were fictitious and bordered on the absurd, rather than trusting actual recommendations by government working groups. An experimental study by a team of researchers at METI may help to understand why.

The objective of the METI team was to measure laypeople's ascriptions of epistemic trustworthiness to an expert and to determine the underlying dimensions of such epistemic trustworthiness. Epistemic trust in "unfamiliar" experts was measured in three dimensions: i. Expertise: knowledge about topic; ii. Integrity: adhering to scientific standards, iii. Benevolence: towards others and society. For experts ("scientific authors") to be rated high on the scale of epistemic trustworthiness, they needed to do well in the three characteristics of expertise, integrity, and benevolence. The results showed that if a scientific author was rated highly on one dimension, this led to a higher rating on other dimensions—especially between "integrity and benevolence." But when an expert was rated high on expertise alone, i.e. was seen as very knowledgeable, it did not lead to epistemic trustworthiness, unless the expert was rated high on integrity and benevolence as well. In other words, there are other and arguably more important dimensions in trusting an expert than credentialed knowledge about a subject matter. In short, knowing your stuff is not enough: an expert needs to be seen as honest (integrity) and good-hearted with empathy (benevolence) (Hendriks et al. 2015). Obviously, the groups of the Queen Mary study thought that the members of the government working group—which included experts from interest groups—were lacking the all-important qualities of integrity and benevolence.

A similar conclusion on the importance of the two latter qualities of experts is drawn by Canadian philosopher of science Maya J. Goldenberg, who studies "vaccine hesitancy," which can be understood as a cautious or critical stance towards vaccines. By some estimates, it is on the rise in many western countries including the US and Canada. According to Goldenberg, hesitancy of parents to vaccinate their children is not primarily driven by scientific illiteracy or online misinformation, but ,rather, by public mistrust of scientific institutions. The non-expert public takes the necessary leap of faith into such institutions only if they are confident that the experts therein are both competent and honest (Goldenberg 2019). Again, the perception of honesty/integrity and benevolence in addition to competence/knowledge are crucial criteria that experts—and scientific experts in particular—have to meet if they want to be trusted by the public. At the risk of over-interpreting the findings of the METI project and Ms. Goldenberg, it can be stated that major scientific questions can be derailed by issues of trust like the lack of expert integrity and expert benevolence: when experts and expert institutions engage in political self-dealing, media hype, professional hypocrisy, or public confusion, and general gullibility, they are risking the benefits of their actual scientific accomplishments.

The Changing World of Expertise and Expert Institutions: Lack of Transparency and the Perception of Undue Influence

Ideas Industry

It can be argued that especially in the US, the trustworthiness of experts has been challenged by changes in the world of expertise and expert bodies: over-confidence in their methods, arrogance, the politicization of expertise, and scandals pertinent to some expert bodies. Daniel Drezner argues that many experts and expert institutions outside the natural sciences are now part of an emerging "ideas industry" (2017). In the US, "ideas industry" public intel-lectuals, defined as experts "who are versed and trained enough to be able to comment on a wide range of public policy issues" (2017: 8) are being sidelined by "thought leaders." This more recent archetype is, according to Drezner, "an intellectual evangelist" (2017: 9). In Isaiah Berlin's distinction of knowl-edge actors, public intellectuals are foxes, who know a little something about many things, while thought leaders are hedgehogs, who know a lot about one thing and—as thought leaders—flog that one particular allegedly "big" idea to death. But public intellectuals are not only foxes, they are also critics and skeptics; they prioritize expertise and they are often pessimists. Thought lead-ers, on the other hand, are creators instead of critics— preachers rather than doubters—and they prioritize experience over expertise and tend to be op-timists (Drezner 2017: 9–10). Drezner emphasizes that these binary distinc-tions should not suggest that archetypes embody different kinds of people within the ideas industry, but rather roles and archetypes that a certain group of experts may assume at different times. Drezner's point is that the mod-ern marketplace of ideas has become an ideas industry and thereby benefits the thought leader more than the older types of public intellectuals. Several factors are responsible for this transformation. The erosion of trust in erst-while prestigious institutions has weakened the position of both academia and the traditional journalistic perches of public intellectuals. The polariza-tion of American politics has segmented that marketplace into distinct and separate niches, and the dramatic growth in economic inequality has made wealthy individuals and corporations into the primary buyers of "ideas," and thereby dominating the market—at least in the US, but perhaps worldwide (Drezner 2017: 11–12).

A similar distinction is made by the Swiss historian of expertise Caspar Hirschi (2019). "Expert preachers" are similar to thought leaders in that they are scientists who have achieved top researcher status in their discipline and then turn into public authorities to change the world with "big ideas" from within their research. Expert preachers do not specialize in generalizations, but rather generalize their specialization by applying the perspectives, methods, and norms of their discipline beyond its boundaries. Examples mentioned by Hirschi in the field of International Economics are scholars like Jeffrey Sachs, Joseph Stiglitz, and Paul Krugman; in Business Administration, Clayton Christensen; historians like Niall Fergusson; and psychologists like Jordan Peterson. Expert preachers, like thought leaders, push big, often contrarian ideas through outlets such as TED talks, social media blogs (especially YouTube), op-eds, a brand name, and the paid lecture/speaker circuit. In the US especially, they are supported by ideologically friendly private funders and/or housed in ideologically-driven think tanks. Expert preachers are very good at broadcasting ideas widely and reaching large audiences of people hungry for allegedly "new" thinking. In Hirschi's terminology, expert preachers sideline or even replace so-called "professorial/academic journalists," who are a crossover species between journalism and academia. Like public intellectuals, "Professorenjournalisten" and conventional academic experts are critiquing and expanding the public's understanding of a topic. Their preferred outlets were, and still are, "highbrow" periodicals in the US such as New Republic, Commentary, Dissent etc., and they often hold fellowships, professorships (of practice) at universities, academies, and governance schools.

Think Tanks

A major type of expert institution in the US and elsewhere is think tanks. When the think tank boom in the US started to take off in the1980s during the Reagan administration with the arrival of conservative advocacy think tanks, the integrity of the research findings of right-wing and libertarian think tanks—like the Heritage Foundation, the Cato Institute and even older ones like the American Enterprise Institute—was challenged and questioned by many academic scholars because of these think tanks' close ties to the US business community and to wealthy businessmen disguising as politically neutral philanthropic foundation chiefs. But towards the end of the Obama era, flagships of the centrist, center-left, and mostly prestigious academic think tank world of the "universities-without-students" type—like the Brookings Institution, the Center for Strategic and International Studies, the Atlantic Council, or the Center for Global Development—were also challenged, especially by investigative journalists from the New York Times, for murky influence peddling and being bought by foreign governments and self-declared progressive donors. The New York Times traced $92 million in donations from 64 foreign governments to 28 US think tanks between 2011 and 2014 (Lipton et al. 2014). To the surprise of many liberal-leaning readers of the Times, the money did not just come from the "usual suspects" like Qatar or the United Arab Emirates, but also from an established and adulated democracy like Norway. While think tank managers were quick to emphasize that the money from governments like Norway or even UAE would not compromise the integrity of their organization's research, an internal document from the Norwegian government, quoted by the Times, stated that "funding powerful think tanks is one way to gain such access" to Washington decision-makers, especially for a small country struggling to be heard in the Washington power game. The problem here is not that think tanks as expert institutions are ineffective with policy-makers, rather the contrary: the problem is one of trust—that the line between scholarly research by experts and lobbying by experts on behalf on their donors was completely blurred, and, thus, the credibility of think tanks as a genre undermined. This calls to mind that, as the Pew survey found, scientific experts were mostly distrusted for lack of transparency, including conflicts of interest (2019b).

But the loss of credibility due to insufficient transparency and undue influence are not the only problems of US think tanks. The public relations firm Cast from Clay (formerly We are Flint) focuses on studying think tanks in the United States and United Kingdom and their impact on public debate. In 2018, a large survey conducted by Cast from Clay found that half of Americans knew what a think tank is and slightly less than half of Americans surveyed knew what a think tank does. 20% of Americans said they trust what a think tank has to say, while 24% do not. [8] But despite this seemingly low trust score, the surprising result was that over 50% of Americans said that they do not know whether to trust think tanks or not. The public relations professionals of Cast from Clay did not interpret these scores as a devasting blow to think tanks' reputations and credibility, but rather as an opportunity to shape and forge the narrative around an expert institution—think tanks—about which most people did not have a fixed opinion. Experts—including experts in think

---

8   The 2018 study on US think tanks surveyed 2,007 American adults over the age of 18. The sample was nationally representative by age, gender, and region, according to the report. See Hashemi and Muller: 2018a.

tanks—might know a bunch of stuff—and that stuff might be important—but unless those facts and figures are perceived as honest and benevolent, they will fail to break free from the bubble they are in.

The Coronavirus Pandemic and Trust in Experts

During the first months of the Coronavirus pandemic (February to May 2020), it became clear that both policy-makers and large parts of the general public were increasingly turning to scientific experts, working either in academia or for government agencies, and trust in whom, as we saw earlier, has been slowly on the rise in recent years. Coronavirus has catapulted a particular group of experts—medical specialists, especially epidemiologists and virologists—into virtual celebrity status; nearly world-wide, but also in the United States. There are two medical specialists in particular, who both became the scientific expert faces of the White House Coronavirus Task Force[9] and its daily briefings with the president. The task force was established on January 29, 2020 and Deborah L. Birx was picked by Vice President Mike Pence to become the White House Coronavirus Response Coordinator. Another key member of the Task Force is Anthony Fauci, who has been the director of the National Institute of Allergy and Infectious Diseases since 1984. The 79-year-old Fauci has advised every president since Ronald Reagan. In order to have an impact on the behavior of US citizens during the crisis and to communicate their expertise successfully to a larger American public, Birx and Fauci needed the authority of expert government advisers on Coronavirus and could not just assume the role of talk show expert pundits in a highly polarized media environment. If polls are to be believed, Deborah Birx and even Anthony Fauci seemed to be successfully straddling a fine line. Zignal Labs, a media analysis company, studied 1.7 million mentions of Dr. Fauci across the web and TV broadcasts from Feb. 27 to March 13, 2020 and found that, through mid-March, he was mainly praised, and his comments were straightforwardly reported. Right-wing figures quoted Dr. Fauci approvingly or lauded him for his approving comments on shutting down travel to and from China, Zignal Labs said (New York Times 2020). As a matter of fact, Anthony Fauci, with

---

9   The group is a US Department of State task force that coordinates and oversees the Administration's efforts to monitor, prevent, contain, and mitigate the spread of the coronavirus disease (COVID-19).

78% approval, earned the highest approval rating for his handling of the response to the coronavirus, according to a Quinnipiac University national poll released on April 8, 2020 (Quinnipiac University:2020). Governors followed at 74% approval, while President Trump and Congress were below 50%, at 46% and 44% respectively. "In a country gripped by crisis and divided by partisanship, public opinion is united when it comes to Dr. Anthony Fauci," concludes the survey (ibid.). Governors collectively, and especially those who were following the recommendations of epidemiologists and virologists, have been winning widespread praise from the public for their handling of the coronavirus pandemic, often with the kind of bipartisan approval that has eluded both President Trump and those governors who pushed for a speedy reopening of their states (Washington Post 2020a). Three months into the Covid-19 pandemic, health experts like Anthony Fauci and Deborah Birx have won the trust competition with President Trump by a considerable margin. In addition, Americans in red and blue states are staying home at nearly exactly the same rates, as was recommended by most scientific experts. Another recommendation by experts, the wearing of masks, is supported by 80% of Americans (Washington Post 2020b). These results suggest the public is highly attentive and is listening to advice from medical experts.

A new national survey by Pew Research Center, conducted April 29 to May 5, 2020 among 10,957 US adults, and a new analysis of a national survey conducted April 20 to 26, 2020 among 10,139 US adults, confirm the trend of rising trust in medical and scientific experts since the beginning of the pandemic, but with some important caveats (Pew 2020a). The percentage of Americans with a great deal of confidence in medical scientists to act in the best interests of the public has gone up from 35% before the outbreak to 43% in the Pew April 2020 survey. Similarly, there is a modest uptick in public confidence in scientists in general, from 35% in August 2019 to 39% in May 2020. But public confidence in medical and scientific experts has turned upward only among Democrats, not among Republicans. Thus, the somewhat bi-partisan trust in chief medical advisors Birx and Fauci has not translated into a bipartisan increase of trust in medical scientists in general. "Among Democrats and those leaning to the Democratic Party, 53% have a great deal of confidence in medical scientists to act in the public interest, up from 37% in January 2019. But among Republicans and those who lean Republican, 31% express a great deal of confidence in medical scientists, roughly the same as in 2019 (32%). As a result, there is now a 22 percentage point difference between partisan groups when it comes to trust in medical scientists." (Pew 2020a:

5–6) Another finding from the Pew survey conducted after the outbreak of Covid-19 confirms a trend that was visible in the most recent edition of the Edelman Trust Barometer. When people were asked, who should have a say in policy decisions about scientific issues, a majority of U.S adults (55%) in 2020 say that public opinion (which equals the answer "people like me" in ETB) should not play an important role "because these issues are too complex for the average person to understand," while 43% think the public (= "people like me") should help guide such decisions. "The balance of opinion on this issue has shifted since 2019, when a Center survey found the majority (54%) said public opinion should play an important role in science policy decisions" (Pew 2020a: 13). Partisan political differences over the role and value of scientific experts have remained since the breakout, but on some issues, they have been slightly reduced. The Covid-19 outbreak may have further increased trust in scientists, medical experts, and medical professionals—both from its lows in 2016/17 and from the time prior to the outbreak of the pandemic—but it has not significantly reduced distrust between the Democratic and Republican camps in the US. Republican trust in medical experts and scientists is no higher in 2020 than it was in 2019, while among Democrats trust rose by 16% in medical experts and 9% in scientists. Beyond the sustained partisan divide, it is noticeable that the increase in trust in both medical experts and scientists in general between 2019 and 2020—prior and after the Covid-19 outbreak—has been more pronounced among men than among women, more among whites and Hispanics than among blacks, and slightly more pronounced among the millennial generation than among older generations. Among African-Americans, confidence in scientists in general has actually fallen by 2% between 2019 and 2020, while it has risen by 11% among Hispanics during the same time period. (Pew 2020a: 31)

Conclusion

This paper has advanced three main arguments: First, and at the risk of overgeneralization, it argued that a crisis of expertise has more than one origin: the deliberate spreading of doubts about the credibility and the benevolence of experts certainly does occur—especially in the US—but it can only undermine public trust in expertise if and when some experts and expert institutions in some fields have shown an undeniable lack of transparency or clear conflicts of interest. Deliberate attempts to undermine trust in experts exists, but the data seems to indicate that these attempts only succeed in those instances where and when bodies of expertise tend to violate the norms of transparency and benevolence. Secondly, there is a backlash against a perceived tyranny of expertise when technocratic expertise is perceived as intruding into lifestyle choices or into questions of morality and ethics. In this realm, distributed trust (e.g. in people like oneself) can become as high or even higher than trust in technical experts. Thirdly, and perhaps most importantly, empirical evidence has demonstrated that, in the US, public trust in experts and expertise has stopped its decline—which had started in the late 20th century and peaked during the years after the Great Recession of 2008—and shown signs of reversal since 2018. With respect to experts in the natural and medical sciences, the outbreak of the Coronavirus pandemic in the spring of 2020 has accelerated rising public trust in this area of expertise, even though these very experts are sometimes sidelined by those in government.

The recent rise in public confidence for scientific and medical experts is in stark contrast with that for other groups and institutions in the US. For example, confidence in the military has been stable over the same time period, and that for journalists has declined, and slipped even further since the outbreak of Covid-19 (Pew 2020b). Still, the sharp partisan divide revealed by the most recent numbers suggests that the politicization of expertise can be expected to continue in the US—and most likely elsewhere as well. Advising governments in an ongoing crisis like the current Covid-19 pandemic poses risks for scientists. The nature of a crisis like Covid-19 means that scientific work that would normally take months or even a year to conduct, had to be done in a matter of days. The Imperial College London modelling study of March 16, 2020, which seemed to have had a strong influence on changing government policy on the pandemic in both Britain and the United States, has been criticized for allegedly using an outdated computer model that predicted an outlandishly high number of casualties should governments fail to take drastic action.[10] The behavior of individual experts, especially when they acquire a quasi-official role, is taken into account when citizens evaluate their trust in scientific expertise. It can boost the public reputation of the scientists and their research teams, as we saw in the case of US Coronavirus Task Force members Deborah Birx and Anthony Fauci, but it can also undermine the public reputation of experts, as we witnessed in the UK, when the head scientists of the Imperial College modelling team, Neil Ferguson, was forced to resign

---

10   See https://www.ft.com/content/41e98ccb-a39c-4f88-b444-74d50a76c383.

from the UK government's Scientific Advisory Group for Emergencies (SAGE) in early May 2020, after it was revealed he had broken social distancing rules, which had been recommended by scientific advisers. A public advisory role puts a spotlight on experts and their personal background, whether they like it or not. One reason why Fauci enjoys (limited) bi-partisan support is that he restricts his scientific advice to his narrow field of expertise: public health. When he was asked whether schools or the economy should open, he declined to give a recommendation and said that he would not give advice about economic things, nor any advice about anything other than public health. Fauci and Birx are reasonably popular and trusted scientific experts, but they are not perceived as thought leaders or as members of the ideas industry.

However, rising trust in medical and scientific experts may not immediately solve the credibility crisis of other expert bodies such as think tanks or universities. To regain trust, expert bodies and expert institutions like think tanks or university departments have to regain trust in their integrity and benevolence rather than trust in their subject matter knowledge.

Works Cited

Alesino, Alberto and Elania La Ferrara (2002): "Who Trusts Others?," *Journal of Public Economics* 85 (2002) 207–234.

Babones, Salvatore (2018): *The New Authoritarianism. Trump, Populism and the Tyranny of Experts*, Cambridge: Polity Press.

Bell, Daniel (1960): *The End of Ideology: On the Exhaustion of Political Ideas in the Fifties*. Glencoe: The Free Press.

Botsman, Rachel (2017): *Who Can You Trust? How Technology Brought Us Together and Why It Might Drive Us Apart*, New York: Public Affairs.

Desch, Michael C. (2019): *Cult of the Irrelevant. The Waning Influence of Social Science on National Security*, Princeton: Princeton University Press.

Drezner, Daniel W. (2017): *The Ideas Industry*, New York: Oxford University Press.

Goldenberg, Maya J. (2019): "Vaccines, Values and Science," *Canadian Medical Association Journal, CMAJ* April 8, 2019 191 (14) E397–E398; DOI: https://doi.org/10.1503/cmaj.181635.

Hashemi, Tom and Muller, A (2018a): "Forging the Think Tank Narrative (USA): Credible but not Effective Communicators." *We are Flint report*, https://we

areflint.co.uk/foreging-the-think-tank-narrative-perceptions-usa/, June 25, 2018.

Hendricks, Vincent F. and Vestergaard, Mads 2018: *Postfaktisch: Die neue Wirklichkeit in Zeiten von Bullshit, Fake News und Verschwörungstheorien*, Munich: Blessing Verlag at Random House.

Hendricks and Vestergaard 2019: *Reality Lost. Markets of Attention, Misinformation and Manipulation*, Cham: Springer Open.

Hendriks, Friederike, Kienhues D, Bromme R. (2015): "Measuring Laypeople's Trust in Experts in a Digital Age: The Muenster Epistemic Trustworthiness Inventory (METI)" *PLoS ONE* 10(10): e0139309. https://doi.org/10.1371/jour nal.pone.0139309.

Hirschi, Caspar (2018): *Skandalexperten, Expertenskandale, Zur Geschichte eines Gegenwartproblems*, Berlin; Matthes & Seitz.

Hischi, Caspar (2019): "Warum nicht das Schlimmste verhindern?," *Frankfurter Allgemeine Zeitung* Nr. 1, 2.1.2019, p.N4.

Hofstadter, Richard (1965): *The Paranoid Style in American Politics, and Other Essays*, New York: Knopf.

Kieserling, André and Simone Rödder (2019): "Misstrauen ohne Folgen. Steckt die Wissenschaft in einer Vertrauenskrise?," *Forschung & Lehre*, Jg. 26, Nr.10, 898–899.

Lipton, Eric, Brooke Williams and Nicholas Confessore (2014): "Foreign Powers Buy Influence at Think Tanks," *The New York Times*, September 7, 2014, Section A, p.1.

Lundqvist Asa and Klaus Petersen (eds) (2010): *In Experts We Trust. Knowledge, Politics and Bureaucracy in Nordic Welfare States*, Odense:University Press of Southern Denmark.

Medvetz, Thomas (2012): *Think Tanks in America*, Chicago: UoC Press.

New York Times (2020): "Medical Expert Who Corrects Trump Is Now a Target of the Far Right," By Davey Alba and Sheera Frenkel, March 28, 2020 New York Times, https://www.nytimes.com/2020/03/28/technology/coronavir us-fauci-trump-conspiracy-target.html.

Nichols, Tom (2017): *The Death of Expertise. The Campaign Against Established Knowledge and Why it Matters*, Oxford: OUP.

Osman, Magda, Norman Fenton, Toby Pilditch, David Lagnado and Martin Neil (2018): "Whom Do We Trust on Social Policy Interventions?," *Basic and Applied Social Psychology*, P. 249–268 | Received 31 Oct 2017, Accepted 24 Apr 2018, Published online: 30 Jul 2018, https://doi.org/10.1080/019735 33.2018.1469986.

Pew Research Center (2020a): "Trust in Medical Scientists Has Grown in U.S., but Mainly Among Democrats," May, https://www.pewresearch.org/science/wp-content/uploads/sites/16/2020/05/PS_2020.05.21_trust-in-scientists_REPORT.pdf.

Pew Research Center, (2020b): "Americans' Views of the News Media During the COVID-19 Outbreak," May, https://www.journalism.org/wp-content/uploads/sites/8/2020/05/PJ_2020.05.08_Views-of-Media-Coronavirus_FINAL.pdf.

Pew Research Center (2020c): "Public Holds Broadly Favorable Views of Many Federal Agencies, Including CDC and HHS," April, https://www.people-press.org/2020/04/09/public-holds-broadly-favorable-views-of-many-federal-agencies-including-cdc-and-hhs/.

Pew Research Center (2019a): "Trust and Distrust in America," July, https://www.people-press.org/wp-content/uploads/sites/4/2019/07/PEW-RESEARCH-CENTER_TRUST-DISTRUST-IN-AMERICA-REPORT_2019-07-22-1.pdf.

Pew Research Center (2019b): "Trust and Mistrust in Americans' Views of Scientific Experts," August 2019.

Pew Research Center (2017): "Public Trust in Government Remains Near Historic Lows as Partisan Attitudes Shift," May, https://www.people-press.org/2017/05/03/public-trust-in-government-remains-near-historic-lows-as-partisan-attitudes-shift/.

Quinnipiac University (2020): "Fauci, Governors Get Highest Marks For Response To Coronavirus, Quinnipiac University National Poll Finds; Majority Say Trump's Response Not Aggressive Enough", April 8, 2020 https://poll.qu.edu/national/release-detail?ReleaseID=3658

Rexroth, Frank and Teresa Schröder-Stapper (Eds.) (2018): *Experten, Wissen, Symbole. Performanz und Medialität vormoderner Wissenskulturen*, Berlin/Boston: DeGruyter/Oldenbourg.

Tett, Gillian (2016): "Why we no longer trust the experts," *The Financial Times*, July 1, 2016, https://www.ft.com/content/24035fc2-3e45-11e6-9f2c-36b487ebd80a.

Washington Post (2020a): "Ipsos coronavirus employment survey, April 27–May 4, and May 15, 2020", https://www.washingtonpost.com/context/washington-post-ipsos-coronavirus-employment-survey-april-27-may-4/4bd8dd8b-1257-4d5f-b3c1-0af6c38f060d/?itid=lk_inline_manual_2.

Washington Post (2020b): "May 5–10, 2020 Washington Post-University of Maryland poll," https://www.washingtonpost.com/context/may-5-10-2020-washington-post-university-of-maryland-poll/722b3348-4f59-4b35-9fa0-2f9eb4ac76c0/?itid=lk_inline_manual_2.

YouGov (2017): "Leave voters are less likely to trust any experts – even weather forecasters," https://yougov.co.uk/topics/politics/articles-reports/2017/02/17/leave-voters-are-less-likely-trust-any-experts-eve, full results: https://d25d2506sfb94s.cloudfront.net/cumulus_uploads/document/w5uik0fcsy/InternalResults_170215_TrustExpertise_W.pdf

Shifting Meridians of Global Authority
Who Is Pushing in Which Direction, and Why?

Florian Böller and Sebastian Harnisch

Introduction

There is wide variation in the authority structures upholding the current international order, ranging from institutional authority in international organizations and courts, to authority held by states and transnational networks (Alter et al. 2018; Bogdandy et al. 2010; Peters/Schaffer 2013). What factors induce some leading actors and institutions to accept the withering of authority, while others stand up and resist authority transformation, is an open question. It appears to be certain, however, that the dramatic foreign policy shift during the Trump administration has undermined the traditional authority of the United States as a guardian of the liberal world order. Indeed, the Trump administration has attempted to overhaul the rules and principles of the international order that its predecessors established and nurtured to "strike better deals" for a significant minority among the current polarized American electorate (Jervis et al. 2018).

One of the distinct features of the authority of the U.S. global leadership role lay in the self-limitation of its material power by adhering to the universal norms, rules, and institutions within a liberal world order (Ikenberry 2001, 2011). And because authority is a relational concept, establishing rules-based relations between a leader and followers, U.S. authority hinged on the continuous willingness of subordinate actors to support America's course (Bennett et al. 1997). Today, however, there is considerable evidence that international support for U.S. leadership among key audiences, its allies and partners, their societies and businesses, or tolerance by rivals and enemies, is diminishing (Wike et al. 2017; Shapiro/Pardiijs 2017).

We contend that these strains on U.S. authority have been at work for some time. They arise from several distinct but interconnected sources: First, and most notably, over the past three decades international institutions have gained considerable authority for themselves, resulting in a substantial politicization of international authority in general (Zürn et al. 2012). Second, and relatedly, domestic institutions in liberal democracies, including the United States, have displayed variant but limited capacities to cope with the cultural and economic discontents of the liberal world order, most dramatically after the Global Financial Crisis (GFC) in 2008. From a longer-term perspective, the spread of post-modern value systems, including a greater approval of diverse lifestyles, has evoked a cultural backlash in many industrialized countries, while economic pressures for businesses and employees, especially after 2008, have encouraged populist movements, parties, and politicians, to protect "the people" from abusive internationalized elites (Inglehardt/Norris 2016). Third, and more recently, strains in U.S.-led institutions, most notably its alliance system, have been exacerbated by the unintended consequences of expanding the geographical scope of U.S. authority through failed liberal interventions in Afghanistan, Iraq, and Libya (Anderson et al. 2008; Wickett 2018). Fourth and very much related to the previous points, there is also a growing contestation and opposition towards central tenets of the liberal order, such as free trade, democracy, and liberal values, in non-Western countries and by their respective governments (Acharya 2017, 2018; Mounk/Foa 2018). Rising nationalism in both China and Russia, as well as various forms of populism in Europe, Asia, and Latin America inform strategies to frustrate democratic expansionism and bolster authoritarianism abroad (Tansey 2016; Weyland 2017).

In our reading, America's turn towards populism under Donald Trump and the demise of the bipartisan internationalist consensus in the U.S. are thus manifestations of a larger trend: unfettered forces of globalization and the costs of U.S. authority expansion have corroded the authority of U.S. leadership and the liberal international order itself both in America, the West, and in many non-Western societies.

From a theoretical perspective, we argue that authority in international relations is constantly transformed on two levels: first, at the level of the state, where modern state authorities were made and are remade through war, trade, and other peaceful exchanges. Second, at the level of inter-state authority, where state authorities' and other entities' foreign policies, such as those of the EU, have reconfigured international authority, resulting in various distinctive configurations of legitimate statehood, rightful state actions, and institutional practices of interstate relations (Dunne/Reus-Smit 2017).

There are, of course, different incarnations of authority and domination in inter-state relations, i.e. distinct forms of relational hierarchies in international relations over time (Zarakol 2018). Some of these appear to be compatible with the current liberal order. But some of them are clearly not—for example, those which are primarily based on domination and military coercion because they violate the principle of authority production through self-determination on the state level. As a consequence, we argue that domestic shifts in authority production, i.e. towards illiberalism or authoritarianism, will impact the re-production of international authority.

How different powers choose to relate to the waning U.S. authority, and what kind of hierarchical order emerges through respective "relational shifts" is the focus of our undertaking. We presume that analyzing how and why authority is transformed on the domestic level is essential to better understand the course of new authority patterns on the international level.

Much of the debate about the demise of the liberal order so far has focused on the extent of the decline and the causes that have brought it about.[1] Will the Trump administration destroy the U.S.-led order to make good on its promise to "make America great again?" Or, in turn, is the sustainment of global diversity, liberal and illiberal alike, a prerequisite for reconstructing American democracy at home? Is China committed to the open trading order that seemed to have served large chunks of its society so well, or is it predestined to dominate the Asian region (and how much beyond) (Johnston 2019)?

These are important questions. In this chapter, however, we are focusing on the causal mechanisms that transform authority relations on the domestic level and which, in turn, shape a country's foreign policy towards authority relations on the international level. We contend that the current theoretical debate about the nexus between national and international authority ascription is biased towards systemic trends shaping domestic authority relations, e.g. in a "second-image reversed"-type of argument (Gourevitch 1978). By focusing on the interaction between systemic trends, globalization, and domestic trends such as populism, domestication, and economization, our chapter adds a new perspective to the debate.

The analysis proceeds in three steps. First, we explore different concepts of authority and their nexus with respective international orders. We argue

---

1   Cf. Acharya 2018, Böller et al. 2018; Ikenberry 2018, 2017; Lake 2018; Nye 2017; Risse 2006.

that authority is a hierarchical relationship that hinges on the recognition of subordinate states and other actors such as transnational non-governmental groups. Domination, in turn, is also a hierarchical relation. But it primarily relies on threats and punishments to alter the behavior and/or disposition towards the superordinate state, thereby establishing international orders without significant institutions.

Taking these two concepts as a baseline against which the transformation of the current order can be gauged, the second section introduces four mechanisms of domestic authority transformation (politicization, domestication, populism, and economization) that are related to or caused by globalization, and that inform respective foreign policy choices to support, contest, or dissent from the current liberal order. The final section examines the distinct patterns of foreign policy choices, ranging from support to opposition or (re-)creation of a new order.

Authority, Domination and the Emergence of International Order

International relations scholars have long debated to what extent, in which context, and why the supposed anarchy between states is layered by rules, principles, institutions, and other manifestations of social relations. Different concepts, such as hierarchies (Lake 2007; Clark 2017; Zarakol 2018), hegemony (Keohane 2005; Hurrell 2007), international status (Paul/Larson/ Wolforth 2014; Bially Mattern 2005) or international society (Bull/Watson 1984; Dunne/Reus-Smit 2017) seek to explain material differentiation and/or social stratification of international orders, as well as the resulting manifestations and contestations in that order.

Structuralist accounts of international order and authority foreground the relative positioning of actors in a system according to their material attributes. Geopolitical thinkers posit that powerful states create and sustain international orders that privilege themselves over others. International order, in this sense, entails international legal regimes and institutions only so far as they reduce the costs of governing for the most powerful states, such as in theories of hegemonic stability (Lake 1993). Or the order may be manipulated to the benefit of the hegemon by increasing the number of constitutive entities, so as to weaken a rising opponent, for example through competitive decolonization (Hager/Lake 2000). Contestation towards order, or revisionism as it is preferably called in the realist tradition, is then reduced to the struggle for power and supremacy between dominant states, while lesser powers and non-state actors are bound to endure what they must (Davidson 2006).

Other "structuralist materialists" stipulate that the distribution of economic prowess, i.e. production capacity, vis-à-vis other classes and powers does instill distinct foreign (economic) policy strategies in states: economic supremacy upholds liberal trade orders in which free trade principles favor the hegemon over lesser powers. In turn, multicentric economic systems increase competition between great powers and spur control over lesser powers' economic resources (Wallerstein 1980). Contestation, then, ensues when lesser classes and powers in the periphery challenge unequal trade and treaties with the center in order to limit or end their dependency on the latter (Stephen 2014).

Defining Authority

These two examples of structural mechanisms related to material differentiation among states pertain to hierarchical systems. They rely—not exclusively but mainly—on domination by more powerful vis-à-vis subordinate actors. The major difference of these types of hierarchies from those based on authority is the aspect of social recognition. Authority, in our reading, generates a specific form of social hierarchy: one which rests on the recognition of power towards the bearer of authority (Weber 2014; Lake 2010; Hurd 1999; Sennett 2008; Furedi 2013).

Following the conceptualization of Zürn et al. (2012: 83–88), we find that authority is constituted by two layers of recognition: First, actors may grant authority towards other actors or institutions in general, if they believe that these bearers of authority produce a necessary common good for all actors within the order. Here, authority is grounded on the expectation of a specific expertise or capability that obliges the authority to deliver the good or assume a responsibility necessary to uphold the order. Second, subordinate actors recognize authority because they trust that a specific set of rules, norms, and institutions presents a rightful order.[2] This second layer refers to the traditional reading of authority as the legitimate exercise of power.

---

2   As Krieger (1977: 259) stipulates, "(i)ndeed, we may say that, if obedience is the counterpart of power, trust is the counterpart of authority."

Thus, in both international and domestic relations, various actors can only articulate a claim for authority. This claim entails a particular demand. It seeks to implement rules and norms and create institutions which aim to preserve the former. Within these authority relations, both actors, those who are able to claim authority and those who are bound to follow, need to accept these rules and norms, and they need to regularly take part in its institutions to uphold the order. Within institutionalized relationships, actors who successfully claim authority are able to generate rules and norms that are perceived as legitimate and/or necessary within a given order by the other actors.[3] Through interactions within this set of rules, norms, and institutions, there emerges a specific system of authority that produces compliance by participating actors. That way, authority also serves as a mechanism of social control (Hurd 1999). At the same time, systems of authority create (permanent) inequalities, both in terms of material distribution as well status and other social ascriptions; for example, the rights and responsibilities of different actors within the order (Clark 2017: 251). However, subordinate actors will accept this stratification as long as the leader also sufficiently obeys the rules and principles he established. Self-restraint is thus a significant factor to retain legitimacy in authority relationships (Lake 2010: 588; Deudney 2007).

It is important to note that authority will seldom be undisputed or uncontested. Nor will the specific order created by this authority pertain to all actors on a global scale (Reus-Smit/Dunne 2017: 37). It is thus an empirical question as to how far-reaching and expansive a particular claim to authority is.

International Authority as a Relational Concept

The feature of recognition and assent by subordinate actors recasts authority as a distinct form of hierarchy (Bially Mattern/Zarakol 2016: 627). Thus far, research on international hierarchies has primarily focused on power, status, and questions of the superiority of one actor compared to others. It includes authoritative rule and domination without the specific characteristics of legitimacy, such as accountability, transparency, participation, expertise, etc. In contrast to international authority, the concept of hierarchy is also more static, as it usually does not specify the corridor of acceptable actions that

---

3   In the words of Beetham (1991): "a given power relationship is not legitimate because people believe in its legitimacy, but because it can be justified in terms of their beliefs."

groupings of authority delimit. Hierarchies thus typically pertain across policy areas, whereas authority structures, such as those of international courts, can be highly circumscribed both in functional and temporal terms (Alter et al. 2018). It follows that authority relations are continuously re-evaluated and re-made by actors as they are subject to constant contestation, transformation, and decline, as well as expansion. It also follows that legitimization as a central source of authority varies over time and policy areas as the accountability, transparency, and participation in authority relationships waxes and wanes. Hence, as employed here, the concept of international authority focuses on agency interaction rather than systemic configuration to account for the transformation of a social order (see Bially Mattern/Zarakol 2016: 625).

Consequently, we theorize (international) authority as a relational term that posits distinct roles taken by actors within a hierarchical system (see Lake 2010): leaders uphold existing rules, norms, and institutions, and are able to (re-)define them, but also need to show self-restraint, i.e. accountability and openness towards participation of lesser powers in order to root the common purpose in the belief systems of followers. Followers recognize the order by either participating actively in establishing the set of rules, norms, and institutions, or by accepting them and acting accordingly. Spoiler states then seek to actively oppose existing authoritative structures while providing no distinct concepts themselves. Other actors may seek to replace the leader either by filling a leadership vacuum within existing systems of authority, contesting the legitimacy of the current leader, or by creating new authoritative structures.

The Nexus of International Authority and the Domestic Level

While the existing international order prescribes certain rules, accepted forms of behavior, and incentives for states to follow (or lead), the inter-state level is related to the domestic level in several ways: First, governments in leading states need to find domestic support for the costs of providing authority in the international arena to fulfill special responsibilities expected from them (Bukanovsky et al. 2012). This support can become contested if domestic coalitions dispute material gains or the normative value of existing hierarchical arrangements (Shils 1982: 95). Second, contestation may be represented through "transmission belts" (Moravcsik 1997: 528) on the international level, i.e. through responsive institutions. Here, the domestic feedback loop pertains to leaders as well followers whose societies are affected by international outcomes. Only as long as domestic audiences view this arrangement as legitimate, i.e. if it can be legitimated in terms of their own beliefs (Beetham 1991: 11), will they support the authority. Also, if actors perceive that an authority acts detrimentally to the common good of the domestic order, contestation towards an international authority may emerge (Zürn et al. 2012: 87). Third, the impact of international authority or the lack thereof on the domestic level may alter domestic institutions, societal cleavages, and economic relations (Gourevitch 1978). Certain domestic actors might be privileged by the rules and principles predicated by an international order. Disadvantaged groups will therefore have an interest in opposing existing arrangements and submit their demands within the domestic political system. Fourth, domestic societies, functioning as authority audiences, provide a reservoir of ideas and interests that can be uploaded through transnational movements to the international level, thereby transforming international authority through nongovernmental channels.

Gauging the degree of (international) authority is thus a nontrivial endeavor (Daase/Deitelhoff 2017; Simmerl/Zürn 2016). First, it involves the conceptual delimitation between dominance, legitimacy, and authority. Then it requires the empirical analyses of their mixture in existing international orders. Moreover, the interrelatedness between domestic and international authority relations necessitates a closer look at the social mechanisms forging them.

The Domestic Side of Authority Transformation: Politicization, Populism, Domestication, Economization

In the most general terms, authority is a relational form of power characterized by a range of supportive responses to an order. Legal authority, such as in international courts, rests on content-independent responses, which are not tailored to the recipient's interests (Alter et al. 2018). Political authority, such as the U.S. leadership authority, rests upon responses that are tied to a range of forms of recognition. Recognition itself can take various forms: input legitimacy pertains to the participation of subordinate actors in establishing the rules and norms delimiting the authority relationship between them and superordinate actors. Output legitimacy, in turn, is tied to the production of common goods, the provision of expertise, and accountability in providing that good by the superordinate actor. It follows that political authority is based both functionally and temporally on a much more regular and symmetrical relationship than legal authority.

Our analysis starts from the acknowledgment that international authority vested in international organizations and regimes, such as the International Criminal Court (ICC), and in the U.S. global leadership role are distinct, if intimately tied to each other. We argue that it is possible, if not probable, that some international authority structures may persist in the future without U.S. support, while others may not (Bower 2017).[4] In turn, we suppose that various foreign policy responses by other powers are tied to the politicizing effects of the authority of international institutions—such as the European Union in the case of Hungary—that were up to now supported by the U.S. but are not genuine effects of U.S. authority as such. As a consequence, we hold that it may be worthwhile to distinguish between politicizing effects of international institutions and U.S. authority because the former may have considerably larger audiences than the latter.

Politicization

Out of the four concepts, politicization of authority is the broadest. Following Zürn et al. (2012), politicization of authority refers to a demand for, or the act of, transporting authority relations and their impact into the field of politics, making previously apolitical authority relations political (Zürn et al. 2012: 73). As an analytical concept, politicization thus neither narrows the range of actors or their structural positioning to each other, nor should it be understood as a unidirectional concept, implicating support or opposition by one actor towards a fixed authority structure. Concerning the range of actors involved, politicization may encompass various societal actors but also parliaments, which re-politicize authority relations that may have been deemed legal authority relations before (see the section on domestication below). With regard to the direction of politicization of authority relations, the concept encapsulates both the contestation and the support of international authority. More specifically, as Zürn et al. (2012) suggest, authority relations imply two different layers of recognition: on the first layer, addressees recognize that

---

4   The International Criminal Court and the shifting U.S. position towards it is one of the more prominent cases in which international authority structures persisted although various U.S. administrations openly opposed its establishment and very existence (see Fehl 2012: 95).

authority is per se functionally necessary to achieve a certain public good. On the second layer, authority is recognized if acknowledged as legitimate in the context of a given stock of beliefs in a community (2012: 83).

For our purpose, we presume that contestation on the first layer, i.e. whether authority is considered legitimate per se, has other implications than contestation of consent on the second layer. Examples of politicization that affect elements of the hitherto existing order can be found across countries and policy fields. Recent studies show that political contestation increasingly affects foreign and security policies. Within the United States as well as within allied societies, military intervention decisions have become subject to partisan fights. Here, the old paradigm that politics "stops at the water's edge" seems no longer applicable (see Wagner et al. 2018; Böller/Müller 2018). In these cases, the sobering results of democracy promotion abroad through interventions in Iraq, Libya, and Afghanistan pertain to the first layer of authority regarding the production of common goods (i.e. security or democracy). Contestation by domestic actors regarding international trade agreements are then related to the perceived legitimacy deficit that concerns non-transparency, and the lack of opportunities to participate and voice concerns. These contestations, for example regarding the Transatlantic Trade and Investment Partnership (van Loon 2018), have made it increasingly difficult for executive actors within the liberal order to enhance and refine the liberal trade regime.

Domestication

Domestication can well be understood as a specific form of politicization, for it involves the deliberate effort by legislative and judicial branches to address the structural effects of international authority on the domestic separation of powers. Domesticating strategies originate from political actors, legislatures, and courts that seek to contain and re-direct the delegation of domestic competencies by executives to international institutions in a way to preserve the balance of power between the different branches of government (Harnisch 2006, 2009). Focusing on the German safeguards to preserve parliamentary and federal participation in European policy and the use of military force, Harnisch finds that both the Federal Constitutional Court, the Parliament (Bundestag), and the Federal Chamber (Bundesrat) sought to limit the federal government's autonomy to cede competences to the European Union and/or NATO by imposing procedural hurdles (such as 2/3 majority require-

ments or prior constitutive parliamentary consent for the deployment of German armed forces) and normative limits by imposing structural safeguarding
clauses, requiring a structural correspondence between Germany's constitution (domestic authority) and inter-state institutions, such as the EU or NATO
(international authority) (Harnisch 2009).

In the case of France, domestication has also narrowed the maneuver-
ing room of the French executive in pursuing an ambitious pro-integrationist
agenda in the European Union (Schild 2008). Arguably, domestication has also
amplified the German government's hesitancy to deploy its armed forces, resulting in German abstentions from U.S.-led coalition warfare in Iraq and
Libya, as well as numerous caveats in the Afghanistan campaign. Similarly,
after the 9/11 attacks (Harnisch 2015, 2011, 2004), the U.S. Supreme Court has
become more willing to intervene in and review presidential decisions curtail-
ing civil liberties, finding that some executive decisions were unconstitutional
(Breyer 2016).

While they are part of the long-term trend towards politicization of international authority, domestication strategies may respond to both instances of
U.S. authority and international authority assertion. In contrast to populism,
domesticating responses are oriented towards the status quo, since they are
rooted in the (dynamic) effort to re-balance the separation of powers of a
given constitutional system in interaction with an emerging international legal political order. Moreover, domesticating agents are few and they accept
the given political order, not the least because they are constitutive parts of
it. This does not mean that domesticating strategies may not transform international authority, as in the case of the German policy during the Eurozone
crisis (Harnisch/Schild 2014).

As the U.S. case shows, domestication processes may hinder the exercise
of a leadership role to maintain the current authoritative order. Already before Trump, domestic actors within the U.S. Congress sought to avoid the
delegation of authority to international bodies (for example, to the International Criminal Court) or blocked involvement in international regimes.[5] This

---

5   Examples include arms control treaties such as the Comprehensive Test Ban Treaty
     1999 and the Arms Trade Treaty 2013, or climate policies, regarding the Kyoto protocol
     1999 and the Paris agreement 2015. In each case, Republicans criticized these policies
     because they would interfere with U.S. national authority and either voted down the
     treaty or precluded its ratification in the Senate.

limited the ability of the U.S. to influence those institutions and allowed other actors to assume a more leading role (e.g. Europe regarding climate policies).

Populism

Among the different concepts of politicization of authority, populism takes pride of place insofar as different strains of populism challenge national as well as international authority on both levels, i.e. the necessity of authority *per se* and the authority in a particular community. Populism—defined here as a thin-centered ideology that considers society to be ultimately separated into two homogenous and antagonistic groups, the "pure people" and a "corrupt elite"—holds that politics should be an expression of the "volonté générale (general will) of the people" (Mudde 2007: 23) or a particular part of that people.[6]

The distinctive structures of populism shape how the transformation of domestic and international authority occur, as both levels are intimately connected. On the domestic level, populist leaders pretend to protect a selection of citizens—oftentimes representing only a fraction of society—from abusive elites, i.e. industrial monopolies, neoliberal takers, or corrupt government officials. Depending on the ideological trait of the underlying societal cleavage (racial, religious, economical), populism may comprise more inclusive groups, such as transnational working classes, or more exclusive groups, such as religious and/or ethno-nationalist communities. On the international level, some populists seek to safeguard "their people" from both domestic and foreign authorities' predatory strategies to "exploit, rape or rip their own people off." As a consequence, populist movements in Central and Eastern Europe do not contest but rather support the "America First" strategy of the Trump administration in order to legitimize their own struggle against the European Union's authority (Shapiro/Pardijs 2017). In turn, because Trumpian populism is a response to the structural growth of international authority, such as in the Dispute Settlement Body of the WTO, and the unintended consequences of U.S. authority assertion through liberal interventions—in particular after 9/11—it attacks central institutional pillars of both orders, such as the freedom of the press and the independence of the judiciary (national level), as well as the

---

6   This concept builds on Shils (1956), who believed populism to be an ideology of "popular resentment against the order imposed on society" by a ruling class with a monopoly of power and property.

U.S. alliance system and the liberal international economic order (international level).

Economization

Economization pertains to the transformation of political processes into market-oriented forms of governance, as well as to the dominance of economic rationales in democratic policy making (Lazzarato 2015: 67; Best 2017: 383). An important source of the economization effects on domestic systems is the enlargement of norms, principles, and institutions upholding free trade regimes after the end of the Second World War, and the growth of global economic interdependencies. Capitalism within Western societies and international regimes, such as the Bretton Woods institutions, GATT, WTO, and regional agreements (NAFTA, EU) served as core pillars of the international authority structures led by the U.S. By these means, this liberal order was recognized as producing wealth for a large share of the electorate in participating societies, while stabilizing income expectations through its rule-based institutional structure both in the leading nation, i.e. the U.S., as well as subordinate states (Goldin/Margo 1992; Ikenberry 2011: 333).

Domestically, coalitions emerged between producer interest groups and organized labor in Europe and free trade-oriented elites on both sides of the Atlantic that, backed by the financial and service industries in the U.S., supported the expansion of this liberal economic order (Bailey/Goldstein/ Weingast 2010). At the same time, social policies with different reach and form among Western countries were designed to cushion the detrimental effects of the capitalist order, to create what Ruggie termed "embedded liberalism" (Ruggie 1982, 1992).

More recently, the Global Financial Crisis (2008) and the Eurozone crisis (2010) have triggered substantial contestation and dissent by populist movements—for example, the "Tea Party" in the U.S.—with regards to core liberal principles and norms, such as the freedom of capital, goods, services, and persons. In Europe, governments sought to implement emergency responses to the sovereign debt crisis in several member states and craft new institutions to prevent a further deterioration of the Euro zone. However, as the resurgence of Euro-skepticism and the "Brexit" referendum show, the crisis deepened already existing societal cleavages and led to an overextension of domestic institutions that sought to attenuate economic risks. In the U.S., symptoms of the crisis—such as growing unemployment rates, mass default of private homeowners, and growing federal debts—fueled dissent among the electorate with regard to the prospects and core principles of the hitherto supported liberal order. In addition, the growing disparities in the distribution of wealth hampered the legitimacy of the order and nurtured doubts about the necessity of the authority of liberal economic institutions and policies (Tooze 2018).

While the GFC affected Western as well as non-Western states, it further accelerated the relative decline of the U.S. and its Western partners vis-à-vis emerging economies. President Trump's "America First" policies are attempting to externalize the negative effects of this relative decline of the U.S. economy (in particular the de-industrialization and resulting decimation of blue-collar jobs) that caused domestic conflicts and triggered fears within the U.S. working class. At the same time, Trump's course spurs the corrosion of the supporting role of the U.S. for the authority structure it created by violating core principles of that order (Carnegie/Carson 2019).

Populist economic policies can thus be interpreted as an antidote against the economization of international trade and financial policies that should have been held accountable for the outbreak of the GFC (Boucher/Thies 2019). Populists claim that their protectionist policies will shield workers' interests from the effects of neoliberal open market strategies through authoritative political decisions, whereas strategies of economization are meant to protect corporate interests from governmental interventionism through the introduction of market-principles, such as self-coordination among corporations themselves.

Overall, politicization, domestication, populism, and economization are significant mechanisms that link domestic politics and international authority. As Table 1 summarizes, these processes are intertwined, but also pertain to distinct functional levels with specific sets of actors and symptoms of crisis.

Grasping Foreign Policy Reactions to Shifting International Authority

Seen from a systemic perspective, the transformation of an international order sets in motion a realignment of role taking by other actors. However, as the previous section outlined, the concrete cues received by subordinate states are refracted through the processes that shape the authority production on

Table 1: Mechanisms of domestic impact of authority change

Mechanism	Functional level	Agency and antagonism	Symptoms of Crisis	Dynamics between levels and mechanisms
(1) Politicization	Society and Political institutions	Parties, societal groups	Break-up of bipartisan liberal consensus	Politicization (1) may fuel populism (2) and informs domestication strategies (3)
(2) Populism	Society	Elite v. public	Mistrust	Lack of transparency and blocked responsiveness of institutions (3) increases level of mistrust (2)
(3) Domestication	Political institutions	Government v. parliaments	Executive dominance	Attempt to provide governance of global economy (4) largely via executives (e.g. Euro crisis) increases de-parliamentarization (3)
(4) Economization	Economy	State v. corporations	Lack of control	Misallocation of wealth and growth (4) fuels populism (2)

the domestic level: politicization, populism, domestication, and economization.

Leadership transformation thus creates a window of opportunity for other actors to introduce their own claims for authority and pursue changes to the existing rules, norms, and institutions in accordance with their own ideas. In this case, actors need to possess alternative concepts of rightful rule that contrast to the status quo. These actors will thus adapt their foreign policy decisions accordingly and seek leading roles for themselves through the introduction of new rules, norms, and institutions that were not deemed acceptable before.

There might also be actors who, despite leadership transformation, are interested in preserving existing authority structures because their governments and/or societies profit from the existing order, value its normative principles, or because they are unwilling or unable to introduce new authority claims. It follows that these actors will be pressed to take on roles which stabilize existing rules, norms, and institutions.

If authority structures disintegrate and previous rules and institutions break down without being replaced by new authority relationships, then (some) actors might seek to hedge against the resulting insecurity (as a vacuum of leadership and authority emerges). This way, even actors who are interested in upholding the status-quo will be forced to adapt their respective roles to the changing international circumstances.

Accordingly, as a first approximation to gauge variant types of foreign policy reactions to shifting global authority, we can differentiate between two dimensions (see Table 2). The first dimension concerns the question of whether actors are interested in upholding or challenging the status-quo of the rules, norms, and institutions that have been guaranteed by the reigning authority and have structured the previous order. The second dimension requires us to examine whether the actors are willing and/or able to assume a leading role by advancing claims of authority for themselves.

Table 2: Typology of foreign policy reactions to authority change with tentative examples

		Willingness to lead	
		Leader	*Follower*
Positioning towards status quo authority	*Status quo orientation*	France	Germany
	Transformative orientation	China	Russia

Conclusion

To sum up, we argue that it takes the convergences of two authority processes to stabilize international authority relationships: one within states, in particular within the leading states to legitimize and effectuate an executive branch to extract enough resources to sustain a global leadership role; and second, one (or more) authority relationships between states, to legitimize special responsibilities and duties between leading and following states. As both processes have come under significant pressure in the United States and between the U.S. and international institutional authorities and lesser states, the current liberal international order is bound to be substantially transformed.

Here we have focused on the social mechanisms through which the effects of the transformation of international authority are refracted within the domestic authority structures. We contend that the four mechanisms (politicization, domestication, populism, economization) are all geared towards finding new equilibria between international and domestic authority structures. It is fair to suggest that some of the mechanisms are more transformational in kind and degree than others: Politicization may contest a new international authorities' impact upon domestic authority so as to uphold given domestic authority relationships, as in judicial rulings to limit an executive autonomy vis-à-vis its own or other citizens in the "war against terrorism." Or politicization may instill transformation on the domestic and international level as non-governmental actors use international authority so as to effectuate change in domestic authority structures. Domestication, in turn, is more conservative, as it seeks to preserve a given domestic authority structure. However, it may do so by projecting one's own domestic structures onto international institutions, such as in the case of the German Bundesbank model being transposed onto the European Central Bank structures. Populism, on the other hand, is a distinct transformational mechanism as it seeks to recalibrate both domestic and international authority structures towards the need of an (imagined) oppressed people that has been betrayed by its elites. Economization has proven to be no less transformational in the sense that it puts the interests of corporate actors first vis-à-vis governmental regulations, favoring market forces as regulatory instruments rather than governmental or administrative oversight.

Works Cited

Acharya, Amitav (2017): "After Liberal Hegemony: The Advent of a Multiplex World Order," in: *Ethics & International Affairs* 31:3, 271–285.

Acharya, Amitav (2018): The End of the American World Order, London: Polity Press.

Alter, Karen/Helfer, Laurence R./Madsen, Mikael Rask (eds.) (2018): *International Court Authority*, New York: Oxford University Press.

Anderson, Jeffrey/Ikenberry, G. John/Risse, Thomas (eds.) (2008): *The End of the West? Crises and Change in the Atlantic Order*, Ithaca: Cornell University Press.

Beetham, David (1991): *The Legitimation of Power*, Atlantic Highlands (NJ): Humanities Press International.

Bennett, Andrew/Lepgold, Joseph/Unger, Danny (1997): *Friends in Need: Burden Sharing in the Persian Gulf War*, New York: St. Martin's Press.

Boucher, Jean-Christophe/Thies, Cameron G. (2019): "'I Am a Tariff Man': The Power of Populist Foreign Policy Rhetoric under President Trump," in: *The Journal of Politics* 81:2, 712–722.

Best, Jacqueline (2017): "Security, Economy, Population: The Political Economic Logic of Liberal Exceptionalism," in: *Security Dialogue* 48:5, 375–392.

Baily, Michael/Goldstein, Judith/Weingast, Barry R. (2010): "The Institutional Roots of American Trade Policy: Politics, Coalitions, and International Trade," in: Jeffrey Frieden/David A. Lake/J. Lawrence Broz (eds.), *International Political Economy: Perspectives on Global Power and Wealth*, New York: W.W. Norton, 422–442.

Bially Mattern, Janice (2005): "Why 'Soft Power' Isn't So Soft: Representational Force and the Sociolinguistic Construction of Attraction in World Politics," in: *Millennium: Journal of International Studies* 33:3, 583–612.

Bially Mattern, Janice/Zarakol, Ayse (2016): "Hierarchies in World Politics," in: *International Organization* 70:3, 623–654.

Bogdandy, Armin von/Wolfrum, Rüdiger/Bernstorff, Jochen von/Dann, Philipp/Goldmann, Matthias (eds.) (2010): *The Exercise of Public Authority by International Institutions. Advancing International Institutional Law*, Heidelberg: Springer.

Böller, Florian/Hagemann, Steffen/Opitz, Anja/Wilzewski, Jürgen (Hg.) (2018): *Die Zukunft der transatlantischen Gemeinschaft. Externe und interne Herausforderungen*, Baden-Baden: Nomos.

Böller, Florian/Müller, Marcus (2018): "Unleashing the Watchdogs: Explaining Congressional Assertiveness in the Politics of US Military Interventions," in: *European Political Science Review* 10:4, 637–662.

Bower, Adam (2017): *Norms Without the Great Powers International Law and Changing Social Standards in World Politics*, New York: Oxford UP.

Breyer, Stephen (2016): *The Court and the World. American Law and the New International Realities*, New York: Vintage Books.

Bukanovsky, Mlada et al. (2012): *Special Responsibilities. Global Problems and American Power*, New York: Cambridge University Press.

Bull, Hedley/Watson, Adam (eds.) 1984: *The Expansion of International Society*, Oxford: Clarendon Press.

Carnegie, Allison/Carson, Austin (2019): "Reckless Rhetoric? Compliance Pessimism and International Order in the Age of Trump," in: *The Journal of Politics* 81:2, 739–746.

Clark, Ian (2017): "Hierarchy, Hegemony, and the Norms of International Society," in: Timm Dunne/Christian Reus–Smit (eds.), *The Globalization of International Society*, Oxford: Oxford University Press, 248–264.

Daase, Christopher/Deitelhoff, Nicole (2017): "Opposition und Dissidenz in der Weltgesellschaft – Zur Rekonstruktion globaler Herrschaft aus dem Widerstand," in: Christopher Daase/Nicole Deitelhoff/Ben Kamis/Jannik Pfister/Philip Wallmeier (Hg.), *Herrschaft in den Internationalen Beziehungen*, Wiesbaden: Springer VS, 1–28.

Davidson, Jason (2006): *The Origins of Revisionist and Status-Quo States*, Basingstoke: Palgrave MacMillan.

Deudney, Daniel (2007): *Bounding Power: Republican Security Theory from the Polis to the Global Village*, Princeton: Princeton University Press.

Dunne, Tim/Reus-Smit, Christian (eds.) (2017): *The Globalization of International Society*, Oxford: Oxford University Press.

Dunne, Tim/Reus-Smit, Christian (2017): "The Globalization of International Society," in: (Dunne, Tim/Reus-Smit, Christian, eds.), *The Globalization of International Society*, Oxford: Oxford University Press, 18–42.

Fehl, Caroline (2014): *Living with a Reluctant Hegemon: Explaining European Responses to US Unilateralism*, Oxford: Oxford University Press.

Furedi, Frank (2013): *Authority: A Sociological History*, Cambridge: Cambridge University Press.

Goldin, Claudia/Margo, Robert A. (1992): "The Great Compression: The Wage Structure in the United States at Mid-Century," in: *Quarterly Journal of Economics* 107:1, 1–34.

Gourevitch, Peter (1978): "The Second Image Reversed: The International Sources of Domestic Politics," in: *International Organization* 32:4, 881–912.

Hager Jr, Robert P./Lake, David A. (2000): "Balancing Empires: Competitive Decolonization in International Politics," in: *Security Studies* 9:3, 108–48.

Harnisch, Sebastian (2004): "German Non-Proliferation Policy and the Iraq Conflict", in: *German Politics* 13:2, 1–34.

Harnisch, Sebastian (2006): *Internationale Politik und Verfassung: Zur Domestizierung des sicherheits- und europapolitischen Prozesses der Bundesrepublik Deutschland*, Baden-Baden: Nomos.

Harnisch, Sebastian (2011): "Deutschlands Rolle in Afghanistan: State-Building Dilemmata einer Zivilmacht," in: Klaus Brummer/Stefan Fröhlich (Hg.), *10 Jahre Deutschland in Afghanistan*, Wiesbaden: VS Verlag, 223–252.

Harnisch, Sebastian (2015): "Deutschlands Rolle in der Libyenintervention. Führung, Gefolgschaft und das angebliche Versagen der Regierung Merkel," in: Marianne Kneuer (Hg.), *Standortbestimmung Deutschlands: Innere Verfasstheit und internationale Verantwortung*, Baden-Baden: Nomos, 85–123.

Harnisch, Sebastian/Schild, Joachim (Hg.) (2014): *Deutsche Außenpolitik und internationale Führung. Ressourcen, Praktiken und Politiken in einer veränderten Europäischen Union*, Baden-Baden: Nomos.

Hurd, Ian (1999): "Legitimacy and Authority in International Politics," in: *International Organization* 53:2, 379–408.

Hurrell, Andrew (2007): *On Global Order: Power, Values, and the Constitution of International Society*, Oxford: Oxford University Press.

Ikenberry, G. John (2001): *After Victory. Institutions, Restraint, and the Rebuilding of Order after Major Wars*, Princeton: Princeton University Press.

Ikenberry, G. John (2016): "The Rise, Character, and Evolution of International Order," in: Orfeo Fioretos/Tulia G. Falleti/Adam Sheingate (eds.), *The Oxford Handbook of Historical Institutionalism*, Oxford: Oxford University Press, 658–675.

Ikenberry, G. John (2017): "The Plot Against American Foreign Policy," in: *Foreign Affairs* 96:2, 1–7.

Ikenberry, G. John (2018): "The End of Liberal International Order?", in: *International Affairs* 94:1, 7–23.

Ikenberry, G. John (2011): *Liberal Leviathan: The Origins, Crisis, and Transformation of the American World Order*, Princeton: Princeton University Press.

Inglehart, Ronald F./Norris, Pippa (2016): Trump, Brexit, and the Rise of Populism: Economic Have-Nots and Cultural Backlash, Cambridge: *Harvard Kennedy School Faculty Research Working Paper No. 26*.

Jervis, Robert/Gavin, Francis J./Rovner, Joshua/Labrosse, Diane N. (2018): "Introduction," in: (Jervis, Robert/Gavin, Francis J./Rovner, Joshua/Labrosse, Diane N., eds.), *Chaos in the Liberal Order: The Trump Presidency and International Politics*, New York: Columbia University Press.

Johnston, Alistair Ian (2019): "China in a World of Orders. Rethinking Compliance and Challenge in Beijing's International Relations," in: *International Security* 44:2, 9–60.

Keohane, Robert O. (2005): *After Hegemony: Cooperation and Discord in the World Political Economy*, Princeton: Princeton University Press.

Krieger, Leonard (1977): "The Idea of Authority in the West," in: American Historical Review 82:2, 249–70.

Lake, David A. (2017): "Domination, Authority, and the Forms of Chinese Power," in: *Chinese Journal of International Politics* 10:4, 1–26.

Lake, David A. (1993): "Leadership, Hegemony, and the International Economy: Naked Emperor or Tattered Monarch with Potential," in: *International Studies Quarterly* 37:4, 459–89.

Lake, David A. (2007): "Escape from the State of Nature: Authority and Hierarchy in World Politics," in: *International Security* 32:1, 47–79.

Lake, David A. (2009): *Hierarchy in International Relations*, Ithaca (NY): Cornell University Press.

Lake, David A. (2010): "Rightful Rules: Authority, Order, and the Foundations of Global Governance," in: *International Studies Quarterly* 54:3, 587–613.

Lake, David A. (2018): "International Legitimacy Lost? Rule and Resistance When America Is First," in: *Perspectives on Politics* 16:1, 6–21.

Lazzarato, Mauricio (2015): "Neoliberalism, the Financial Crisis and the End of the Liberal State," in: *Theory, Culture & Society* 32:7–8, 67–83.

Moravcsik, Andrew (1997): "Taking Preferences Seriously: A Liberal Theory of International Politics," in: *International Organization* 54:4, 513–553.

Mounk, Yascha/Foa, Roberto Stefan (2018): "The End of the Democratic Century: Autocracy's Global Ascendance," in: *Foreign Affairs* 97:3, 29–36.

Mudde, Cas (2007): *Populist Radical Right Parties in Europe*, Cambridge University Press

Nye, Joseph S. (2017): "Will the Liberal Order Survive? The History of an Idea," in: *Foreign Affairs* 96:1, 10–16.

Paul, T.V./Larson, Deborah/Wohlforth, William (eds.) (2014): *Status in World Politics*, New York: Cambridge University Press.

Peters, Birgit/Karlsson Schaffer, Joan (2013), "The Turn to Authority Beyond States," in: *Transnational Legal Theory* 4:3, 315–335.

Risse, Thomas (2006): "The Crisis of the Transatlantic Security Community," in: Ingo Peters (ed.), *Transatlantic Tug-of-War: Prospects for US-European Cooperation*, Berlin: LIT, 111–142.

Ruggie, John G. (1982): "International Regimes, Transactions, and Change: Embedded Liberalism in the Postwar Economic Order," in: *International Organization* 36:2, 379–415.

Ruggie, John G. (1992): "Multilateralism: The Anatomy of an Institutions," in: *International Organization* 46:3, 561–598.

Schild, Joachim (2009): "Die 'Domestizierung' französischer Europapolitik," in: Deutsch-Französisches Institut (Hg.), *Frankreich-Jahrbuch 2008*, Wiesbaden: VS Verlag, 29–49.

Sennett, Richard (2008): *Autorität*, Berlin: Berlin Verlag.

Shapiro, Jeremy/Pardijis, Dina (2017): *The transatlantic meaning of Donald Trump: a US-EU Power Audit*, Brussels: European Council on Foreign Relations.

Shils, Edward (1982): *The Constitution of Society*, Chicago: Chicago University Press.

Shils, Edward (1956): *The Torment of Secrecy*, New York: Ivan R. Dee.

Simmerl, Georg/Zürn, Michael (2016): "Internationale Autorität. Zwei Perspektiven," in: *Zeitschrift für Internationale Beziehungen* 23:1, 1–38.

Stephen, Matthew D. (2014): "Rising Powers, Global Capitalism and Liberal Global Governance: A Historical Materialist Account of the BRIC Challenge," in: *European Journal of International Relations* 20:4, 912–938.

Tansey, Oisín (2016): *The International Politics of Authoritarian Rule*, Oxford: Oxford University Press.

Tooze, Adam (2018): *Crashed: How a Decade of Financial Crises Changed the World*, London: Allen Lane.

Van Loon, Aukje (2018): "Diverging German and British Governmental Trade Policy Preferences in the Transatlantic Trade and Investment Partnership (TTIP) Negotiations," in: *Journal of Contemporary European Studies* 26:2, 165–179.

Wagner, Wolfgang/Herranz-Surrallés, Anna/Kaarbo, Juliet/Ostermann, Falk (2018): "Party Politics at the Water's Edge: Contestation of Military Operations in Europe," in: *European Political Science Review* 10:4, 537–563.

Wallerstein, Immanuel (1980): *The Modern World-System, Vol. 2: Mercantilism and the Consolidation of the European World-Economy, 1600–1750*, New York: Academic Press.

Weber, Max (2014): *Wirtschaft und Gesellschaft: Grundriss einer verstehenden Soziologie*, Tübingen: Mohr Siebeck.

Weyland, Kurt (2017): "Autocratic Diffusion and Cooperation: The Impact of Interests vs. Ideology," in: *Democratization* 24:7, 1235–1252.

Wickett, Xenia (2018): *Transatlantic Relations: Converging or Diverging?*, London: Chatham House.

Wike, Richard/Stokes, Bruce/Poushter, Jacob/Fetterolf, Janell (2017): *U.S. Image Suffers as Publics Around World Question Trump's Leadership*, Washington, DC: Pew Research.

Zarakol, Ayse (ed.) (2018): *Hierarchies in World Politics*, Cambridge: Cambridge University Press.

Zürn, Michael/Binder, Martin/Ecker-Ehrhardt, Matthias (2012): "International Authority and its Politicization," in: *International Theory* 4:1, 69–106.

Trust and the City
Analyzing Trust from a Socio-Spatial Perspective

Ulrike Gerhard, Judith Keller, Cosima Werner

> "That's where the trust issues come in, because if people say to someone in the Lower 9thWard [neighborhood in New Orleans affected by Hurricane Katrina]: Oh, don't worry, we'll replace your house somewhere else. There's no trust that that is gonna happen, right? No, there is no trust. Historically, no reason to trust."
> *MA Sheehan, Lower 9th Ward Homeownership Association, New Orleans 2018*

Introduction

Transformations of (authority and) trust manifest themselves in space, especially in urban space. As the quote by homeownership association's representative Sheehan illustrates, flourishing urban development relies on trust. It is here, on the neighborhood level, where trust relations matter (e.g., for buying or building a home, for feeling at home in a neighborhood) or where the erosion of trust creates anger and fear (e.g., failing public housing policies, the destruction of homes to make room for new developments, the policing of public spaces). These daily urban encounters of residents, citizens, and other actors tell us about recent societal, economic, and political transformations affected by the shifting meanings of trust in US society. We therefore suggest exploring different urban dimensions of trust by developing trust as a socio-spatial concept. Furthermore, we argue that trust relations are essential to understand the recent evolutions and transformations of the city.

Urban Studies have emerged into a major discipline that analyses societal changes from a broad theoretical and empirical agenda. It has become a massive interdisciplinary endeavor to understand globalization, the transformation from an industrial to a post-industrial society, and the increasing capitalization of culture and society. Trust, however, has seldom been used as a conceptual lens to understand urban developments. Even more so, it has hardly ever become a methodological tool to analyze recent developments in the city. So, while we outline trust as a socio-spatial concept by applying two quintessential urban geographic rationales to trust —the relational and the mobile—in the first two sections of this essay, we then suggest that scholarship needs more empirical accounts of the struggles, practices, and representations of trust in US cities. Subsequently, we detail related themes that help to grasp empirically the urban dimension of trust. These themes—cities as imaginative spaces, cities as social spaces, the temporal dimension of urban development, and the meaning of home and housing as spatial fixations—do not constitute a comprehensive list of research areas, but they are drawn from different long-term research projects that seek to understand recent struggles and increasing inequalities within US cityscapes. We contend that these issues are among the most important challenges that cities have been facing over the last decades. We therefore suggest that trust can help to conceptualize these issues in a profound manner and, vice versa, that the urban geographic perspective helps to better conceptualize trust in US society.

Relationality and Mobility as Geographic Concepts to Understand Trust

Trust can never exist by itself (Luhmann 1989). It emerges through relations to other objects: to persons (relationships, friendships, communities, etc.), to contexts (time frame, political systems, nation states, etc.), and to places (homes, cities, etc.). Without trust (in any of its possible definitions, see Gerhard/Keller 2019), there would not be any relationship nor bonding, just as any clear delineation would be impossible. As much as trust is relational, there is no absolute meaning, understanding, or measurement of trust. "How much" trust exists in governments, for example, is difficult, if it is even possible to answer (see, for example, Hartmann 2020). Most often, this problem is circumvented by the use of terms such as decreasing trust, which is then categorized as distrust. Distrust, however, is not the opposite of trust, but its "functional equivalent" that always comes along with it (Luhmann 1989). It is, in simple words, a prerequisite for developing trust relations.

To comprehend the complexity of trust as a relational entity, an understanding of the different concepts of space is helpful. Following Lefebvre's metatheory of three dialectically linked dimensions (also: moments or formants) of the production of space (Lefebvre 1991 [1974]), geographer David Harvey (1973; 2006) identifies a tripartite division in the nature of space. Besides a mere *absolute* space defined by boundaries or mathematic equations that exists independently of matter, he distinguishes between *relative* and *relational* spaces. *Relative* space is demarcated and explained by the relationship between objects and only exists because objects exist and relate to each other (Harvey 2006). This type of space, for example, emerges through flows of people, things, and capital. *Relational* space, in contrast, is contained in objects in the sense that "an object can be said to exist only insofar as it contains and represents within itself relationships to other objects" (Harvey 1973: 13). *Relational* space, in this sense, can be demarcated by immaterial human desires, linguistic attitudes, or political opinions. It emerges from interactions, processes, practices between different actors or objects which bear these relationships within them. Foucault argues in the same direction, but with his own distinct conceptual terminology, when he writes, "we do not live inside a void that could be colored with diverse shades of light, we live inside a set of relations that delineates sites which are irreducible to one another and absolutely not superimposable on one another" (Foucault 1986: 23).

The definition of relational space helps to describe trust, namely the *understanding* of another person (or institution, or object) as being trustworthy, which is established due to their mutual (or even shared) relationship. Consequently, we argue that trust plays out in relational space: Its relationality constitutes a certain space as much as it is constituted by it. Urban theorist Edward Soja's critical contributions add another helpful term here: the concept of *Thirdspace* (Soja 1996). Following Lefebvre's ideas on the production of space, Soja argues that the real (*first space*) and the imagined (*second space*) cannot be separated any longer; they have become one, as in *third space*. The usefulness of these different concepts for discussing trust from an interdisciplinary perspective can be illustrated by looking at the treatment of charismatic trust in this volume. It contains a spatial sense of authority, meaning the orientation and setting of an object in a certain landscape that shapes values, norms, or a so-called "vertical resonance" (Rosa 2016, 457ff). The assumed relationships between object and surrounding landscapes connect the actors and thus produce relational places which we need to analyze and understand.

Studying relationality, however, is quite a challenge. How can we analyze trust in specific spaces (e.g., neighborhoods, cities) if they only exist through their relations to others, as nodes within networks? The locality debate or the discourse of relationality vs. territoriality in the field of geography offers a starting point here. Massey (1991), for example, demands a "global sense of place" and suggests that specific places have to be analyzed as dynamic spaces that are embedded in a broader context of networks and flows. These spaces are constituted by their relations to other places or scales as much as they are unique places and can be studied as such. We therefore can use specific places as "exemplars" for the understanding of broader contexts and processes (Massey 1993). McCann and Ward (2010) further develop this dialectic relationship by emphasizing the simultaneous nature of relationality (the global) and territoriality (the local, the urban, etc.). They suggest the concepts of "mobile urbanism" or "mobile policies" that emerge from the dual existence of circulating knowledge and embedded policies (177ff.). In this sense, policies are shaped by fixity and flows at the same time; both of which need to be researched.

This is what the (new) mobilities paradigm, mainly developed by Cresswell (2006) and Sheller (2014), emphasizes poignantly and which becomes crucial also for the understanding of trust. Since trust changes over time and space, possesses different meanings in relational contexts, and develops from stage to stage, its manifestations are fluid and historical. The mobilities paradigm outlines that we not so much need to focus on specific places but rather on the landscapes, routes, lines, and spaces in between them. We can look at flows (e.g., residential movements, evictions) and developments (e.g., planning cultures, housing policies) and try to understand what they signify, how fast they develop, and what changes they cause (e.g., among residents, in the neighborhood, on the larger urban scale). This holds especially true in an interdisciplinary and temporal context, as stressed by Sheller and Cresswell.

There has been a rapid growth in attention to mobilities across the humanities and social sciences since the turn of the millennium. This perspective underlines how the experience of globalization is in myriad ways defined through ever-increasing mobility: ranging from the concrete transportation systems enabling the flows of people negotiating everyday urban and global mobilities to the movement of capital and socio-economic classes into urban habitats; from the manufactured goods and hazardous wastes carried across logistics networks to the diffusion of urban governance policies, practices, and ideas; and from the dynamics of those migrating by choice to those fleeing (or being left behind) in the face of war, natural catastrophes, or conflicts. Far from simply being a "marker of an era" or a "neutral means to an end," mobilities are deeply meaningful and embodied, gendered and racialized, bound up in social, cultural, and political struggles from the local to the global (Culver 2016). Mobilities thus directly relate to trust relations in the city. It is here where social interaction coincides on a micro scale. Cities themselves are "theaters of social interaction" (Mumford 1937), in which conflicts as well as co-operation among various actors proceed. Trust then can be a mobile phenomenon that links the different groups, actors, entities, and places. It is fluid and changeable, but also offers stability, authority, and reliability.

We can therefore consider the erosion of trust or the emergence of distrust as a sign of mobility, or better: immobility. Cresswell (2012), in his second report on mobilities, presents "stuckness" (649) and fixity as important aspects of mobility. It can be man-made (e.g., racial profiling in cities) but also natural (e.g., volcano eruptions, hurricanes), causing human responses or policies that then stop mobility and cause stillness. Such frictions illustrate the severe vulnerability and injustice that is inherent in the global urban spaces we produce. They are thoroughly incorporated into our mobility practices. Evictions, for example, are such a form of mobility: They trigger an involuntary movement, ending the fixity of the place called home. Yet, as a consequence, families are stuck in spaces of homelessness; the loss of home fixes them in a space of social marginality. We are going to discuss evictions as one urban dimension of trust in more detail in the latter part of the paper. We first, however, turn to outline trust as a socio-spatial concept with the help of relationality and mobility in order to analyze and understand transformations of trust in the city.

Trust as a Socio-Spatial Concept

Trust, first of all, is always embedded in a specific, local context. Being aware of the simultaneity of relationality and territoriality, trust relations depend on involved actors, political contexts, historic conditions, as well as social and cultural environments. In cities, we find social ties between landlords and renters, between public housing agencies and public housing applicants, or between municipal governments and private investors (public private partnerships), all of which form a unique environment for trust relations to develop. The relational spaces between them change, also over time. This is to show that context and time frame matter and can never be generalized: public housing estates tell a different story about trust relations than do condo buildings or suburban homes. As one example in urban development, public housing projects were widely espoused as a cure for social ills during the 1950s and 1960s, before they quickly merged into symbols of squalor and neglect. But not in every city or neighborhood: While some lasted only a few decades, others provided homes for generations of mainly African American families. Thus, the very specific locality of these public housing estates has to be taken into account when analyzing what spaces of trust are produced here. Depending on the surroundings, trust developed in different forms or, quite the opposite, has been severely damaged.

This, secondly, leads to the conceptualization of trust as being a highly contingent, context-bound phenomenon, as described by the mobilities paradigm. Trust does not follow rules, it cannot be planned or predicted—although most rational choice theories aim to do just this. It manifests itself in relationships between human beings (ongoing dyads, groups, and collectives), but not of isolated individuals. Or—following the rationale of the mobilities paradigm—trust is the line that connects two entities. Trust therefore contains different emotional, behavioral, and collective components that need to be acknowledged. It represents a complex social reality (Lewis/Weigert 1985) that penetrates the whole institutional fabric of society and therefore needs to be analyzed with the use of a comprehensive, and, most importantly, an interdisciplinary approach.

Thirdly, trust is not an intrinsic resource or an act that is always conscious, but emerges as a habitualized practice in daily lives and experiences. Therefore, it is closely related to social practices. According to Hartmann (2011), trust can only manifest itself in practices, with the practices again evoking trust (or reliability). If residents, for example, are used to go to a convenience store in their neighborhood, despite how high the prices are or how dangerous the trip is, the store itself and its surroundings become a relational, social space that offers reliability, shelter, social contact or, in contrast, fear and loneliness (Werner 2017). It is through those everyday practices of visiting the store (or routines, rhythms, see Cresswell 2012) that the social reality and thus relational space is being produced.

Fourthly, trust is a term, a discourse, and a social practice under continuous change. Due to certain eruptions, residents alter their behavior or political programs change (e.g., new public housing acts, the opening or closure of a store or restaurant in the neighborhood). People are then not eligible to live in certain buildings anymore, they do not receive food stamps any longer, or they are evicted from their homes. Consequently, trust relations have to be reconfigured as new people move in and out of the related space, changing the network of trust relations and thereby the urban fabric. This holds true also for planning laws and urban narratives (e.g., the ideal of a homeowning democracy; the demonization of certain streets or neighborhoods as being dangerous, derelict, or ghetto spaces) which depend on public discourses, media attention, and architectural vogues that shape urban place-making (Busse 2019). Cities also function as imaginative spaces that are represented by literary texts, poems, music, film, or street-art and gain a specific meaning that strongly depends on shifting relations of trust. So, it is not so much the physical, absolute space of buildings and streetscapes, but more specifically the relational space that is being produced through trust relations.

We finally argue that the eruptions, shifts, practices, and movements that constitute these relational spaces need to be investigated empirically. Only then can we understand the role trust plays in urban development. Trust as a socio-spatial concept frames our empirical investigations by looking at different urban dimensions of trust. In doing so, another trust-related concept will come to light: authority. It helps to institutionalize trust relations. For example, housing agencies serve as an authority implementing urban development. Authority therefore also helps to understand implicit power relations between different agents on the urban scale.

The Urban Dimension of Trust

The urban context is the sphere where trust relations epitomize in space. While cities are specific, absolute spaces defined by boundaries and physical buildings, they are also relative and relational, hence an adequate arena for studying social transformations of trust. They are expressions of modern society that is increasingly described as urban society. So, it is in this context in which trust relations function like the gearwheels or lubricating oil of societal relations. Since we understand Urban Studies as an interdisciplinary endeavor, we not only study the temporal development of cities, but also how cities function as social spaces, arenas for political fights, and as the material which sparks our imagination. By analyzing these different urban arenas, we show that urban space is permeated by trust relations. We call this the urban dimension of trust. Without trust, the urban as a theater of interaction evaporates. Trust relations are not only formed between different urban actors (mostly dealt with in urban geography) but are also a vital component in the representation of cities as utopian, trustful social spaces in fiction, which will be depicted in the next chapter.

Cities as Imaginative Spaces:
The Cultural Representations of Trust in the City

We all have them in our minds: the images of the grand metropolises of our times. There is the glamorous New York City with the promise of an anything-goes urban lifestyle; there is Paris where lovers walk along the Seine while in the background the Eiffel Tower is glistening in the night sky; there is the progressive spirit of Singapore where the global elites touch ground; or, there is the ever-welcoming Rio de Janeiro with the open arms of the Redeemer and the joy of Carnival. Cities have never been mere physical, absolute places made of bricks, cement, and tons of asphalt—they have always also been the places we imagined them to be. Images of cities travel across and around our globe in the form of books, movies, TV shows, and, most importantly these days, social media. Cities become cultural representations and aesthetic experiences for global audiences with no physical connection to them other than the book they are reading or the Instagram account they are following. These texts, scripts, and images produce a second layer to an already existing cityscape; a layer that is made out of the fictional material that feeds our imagination. The city is thus not only New York, but the glamorous Sex-and-the-City-universe and, at the same time, the place where Betty Smith's Francie is coming-of-age and James Baldwin's Sonny plays the most beautiful blues and someone wants to have Breakfast at Tiffany's. So, while cities still are specific places with a specific locality, they are also global icons relating places, people, and things to each other. In the Harveyan sense, cities are truly *relational spaces* in that they can be understood only in their relations to other places and, vice versa, are constituted by those relations (Harvey 1973). This relational character is reflected in the images and texts, which, in some way or another, are all representations of the city. The city as a *third space* is not merely a mute backdrop to our imaginaries; it is simultaneously constituting of and constituted by them. Thus, as trust relations are strongly reflected in cityscapes, they are taken up and interlaced into cultural artefacts of all kinds. Fictional texts, for example, are one source of this cultural representation of trust as they reflect in what ways changing notions of trust have shaped urban society over the centuries.

American cities, both as specific localities and global icons, play a key role in popular culture, reflecting on trust as a "formant" of urban space. Cities have become cultural authorities, providing in many cases a continuity and stability which seems to have been lost in so many other aspects of US-American society. For decades, therefore, works of fiction reflected trust in the progressive American city and its promise of endless opportunities. One might think of Fitzgerald's classic *The Great Gatsby* or Sinclair Lewis's *Babbitt* who captured like few others the spirit of the "Roaring Twenties" and its trust in constant progress. "*I like the way the City makes people think they can do what they want and get away with it,*" says Viole(n)t in Toni Morrison's novel *Jazz* (1992: 8) when describing how she fell in love with New York after coming North during the Great Migration. There are millions of stories of those who left their homes in the countryside behind, trusting in an image they had of a city that would provide them with a better future (often only to find that a city is not a place where one should trust easily). On the flip side, the city has always been portrayed as a dreary and dangerous place, where, in a sphere of distrust and anonymity, each individual fights for her own survival. Ralph Ellison's *Invisible Man* is roaming the streets of New York all by himself, remaining unnamed and invisible to the world, while hard-boiled detectives in novels by Dashiell Hammett, Raymond Chandler, or James Ellroy fight off gangsters and femme fatales, never trusting anyone but themselves. Here the theme of the city as an "anonymous jungle" and the general attitude of mistrust have shaped an entire genre (Most 2006; Schmid 1995).

Yet, as cities change, so does the material that tries to capture their unique spirit and characteristics, as well as notions of trust and distrust on the urban scale. The concept of mobilities might be helpful here to understand those transformations. The positivity and excitement about change ("growth is gospel in America," Muller 2012: 303), which seemed to be omnipresent in the early 20th century, is long gone. The promise of endless liberties, riches, and opportunities has been replaced by a more sober picture: skyrocketing rents, evictions, homelessness, a fragile infrastructure, and a skyline which stands more than anything for an unpopular finance service sector. People have grown distrustful of cities as mere "growth machines" (Wilson 2018), embodied by big investors moving into their cities, powerful real estate businesses, creative city agendas, as well as municipal and national governments who fail to find effective ways of creating a more egalitarian and inclusive city. Nowadays, we find works of fiction, such as Nathan McCall's novel *Them*, discussing gentrification and displacement in such ways that they could be interpreted as a root of distrust into urban development. Other novels address the 2008 financial crash and the subsequent American housing crisis, the tough reality in public housing projects, or the bankruptcy of cities such as Detroit. In her graphic novel *Creation*, Sylvia Nickerson takes a tour through a Rust Belt city which is simultaneously in decline and being upgraded by bohemians who find the shabby-chic inspirational. While her main protagonist, an artist, is endlessly searching for an affordable place to stay, two worlds collide: the young artist is confronted with the proximity of homelessness and severe poverty to her own life overshadowing her upward mobility. The dark images reflect those contradictions and an atmosphere of distrust so typical of the Noir genre. Similarly, natural and human catas-trophes are treated as events which end mobility and cause stuckness in (and of) cities. For example, since 2005, Hurricane Katrina and its aftermath have been the subject of many works of fiction and non-fiction (e.g., Dave Eggers: *Zeitoun*; Tom Piazza: *Why New Orleans Matters* or *City of Refuge*) as well as documentaries and TV shows (e.g., Spike Lee: *When the Levees Broke*; David Simon und Eric Overmyer: *Tremé*). They all have one motif in common: as the city drowned, so did people's trust in their government and a post-racial America.

Here a new image of the city is constituted: one which tries to incorporate the harsh realities of American urban society into the fabric of our real-and-imagined cityscapes. It is thus necessary to analyze those texts and images to find what they tell us about trust and distrust in American urban society, and how those notions have shifted over the years. While in geography we believe that it is crucial to do in-depth studies of places—observing and interviewing people as well as participating in everyday city life—we support the idea that this can go hand in hand with an analysis of the cultural representation of those places in literature, film, music, and the visual art.

Cities as Social Spaces: Daily Urban Practices on the Neighborhood Level

The field of Urban Studies researches social spaces and neighborhoods, but the corresponding theories barely analyze trust explicitly. However, it is only with a clear analytic focus on trust relationships that certain innovative research projects can be undertaken—for example, in C. Werner's ongoing project on convenience stores in impoverished neighborhoods in the cities of Chicago and Detroit. While the analysis of texts and images allows a broad perspective on American cityscapes, this ethnographic project focuses on the microscale of the neighborhood. The ethnographic methods help to explain the social significance of these small-scale food stores in marginalized urban quarters, opening up new meanings of trust. These dynamics need to be emphasized more strongly in the constitution of social space. In the fore-ground are the everyday constitutions of the customers in relation to their life-worlds. To depict trust in practices not only highlights shifts of practice but also the hidden multidimensionality of trust. Therefore, trust can be conceptualized with the help of a praxeological approach (Hartmann 2011).

Trust determines the sphere of agency (*Handlungsspielraum*) in which peo-ple can move because they are trusted. The boundaries of this sphere become tacit knowledge but also emerge as rules and laws (Schatzki 2002). Boundaries convey unspoken expectations on the part of the person who has determined the sphere of agency: A person anticipates the trusted person to move within the given framework. If these limits are crossed, this usually harms trust and promotes the development of distrust. Let us illustrate this with an example from a Chicago store.

A regular customer tries to secure an income with occasional activities through the sale of stolen goods, used clothing, and single cigarettes. She finds her clients in the street, near the store. Sometimes she goes to the store to talk to friends or to warm up until she is asked to leave. On her last visit, she complains that she is starving. The employee is on the phone ordering some food for himself from the nearby eatery. Out of an empathetic gesture, he orders an additional dish for her—his treat. Just as he has placed the order, he catches her stealing some pastries from the store. Accompanied by loud words of disappointment, she is expelled and banned from the store forever. The employee immediately cancels her order.

The example illustrates that rules and laws define the sphere of agency, such as theft, as a punishable offense. It also demonstrates that a general un-derstanding guided the employee's action: that if you are caring and generous to someone, the person will not turn against you. He did not expect that the customer would steal from him in the same moment he is taking care of her. She crossed a legal boundary, but more so, she triggered emotions of disap-pointment. Her crossing these boundaries was not only punished by banish-ing her from the store, but by distrusting her from then onwards. She is no longer trustworthy. She risked being caught and has thus not only lost the trust that was placed in her, but has also forfeited the convenience store as a relational space for social (and economic) interaction.

Another example illustrated by an interview quote from a female resident shows the extent to which trust can affect individual mobility practices within the neighborhood. The interview has been conducted in the social space surrounding the store and reveals the following situation:

> [My son] didn't really have no fear [as a child]. But now, you kinna gotta little fear because of the violence that's going on. You know, and they don't care. It could be seven in the morning; it will be two in the evening, three in the evening. You know, when my son was probably in 2nd grade, you could let them walk to the school and back home. Versus now, we don't trust things like it used to be during that time. [...] So it's been a figure from 20 something years up until ... You just can't hide. You got to go out here and circulate, you know 'cause you gotta go to work, you gotta go pay bills, you gotta go to the grocery store. So you just try to be careful and act like as I say: Keep God on your side. An accident will cover you in blood out here". (female resident, Chicago 2017)

Goffman (1963) uses the term "unfocused interaction" (97), alluding to the fact that, while the public interactions between strangers take place in physically close space, they keep their social distance through "polite estrangement" (Giddens 1991: 81). One acknowledges strangers, maybe with a brief greeting, a nod, or a smile, but rarely anything beyond that. This practice allows people to assess situations in public spaces and behave accordingly. As a rule, people can trust that others will act according to this restraint. We experience it in everyday life: we have to screen situations for familiar patterns to decide whether to trust strangers. However, the female Chicago resident reveals that the conditions she used to be familiar with no longer apply. Continuous and even arbitrary violence shook her general appreciation of the neighborhood and her openness to judge everyday situations. The underlying assumption in the selected statement would be that children "normally" go to school alone because they need to have no fears in their neighborhood. Nobody would want to do them any harm as even strangers are entrusted with this shared set of believes. Some residents, however, such as those involved in gangs, break the norm of "polite estrangement" by using violence. In the full-length interview, she reports that the violence she has been exposed to in her lifeworld has changed the way she moves around. She is now afraid of passing through the neighborhood for her daily errands. If she had the choice, she would stay at home. This situation stresses the mobile and relational character of trust. Trust relations in the neighborhood change due to the practices of its residents, while the atmosphere of distrust changes the mobility practices of the residents. This female resident doubts that political agendas and police actions can cope with the high level of violence in the neighborhood; only faith in higher authorities (in this case, God) seems to offer some respite.

Both examples show that the sphere of agency is both opened and limited by trust. The formulation of trust can be seen in the practices of "entrusting" (Baier 1986: 236). People trust each other not to endanger the well-being of others and not to abuse loyalty; and they expect the corresponding behavior. Also, trust must be bound to a subject who assesses whether the person is trustworthy or the situation familiar. The focus on trust and practices therefore identifies new dynamics and interactions in the study of social spaces and facilitates an understanding of why practices are carried out in a specific way.

The Temporality of Urban Development and Planning

Over the past decade, trust has gained attention as a decisive factor in urban planning (Mössner 2010; Lobeck/Wiegandt 2019). While trust is seldom analyzed conceptually, it is acknowledged as a necessary ingredient for the urban network to function, e.g. in neighborhood planning, urban mobility politics, or participatory planning processes. We argue, however, that trust should not only be a catchword on developers' agendas but has to be theoretically grounded and that its workings have to be analyzed in actual planning processes (Gerhard/Keller 2019). Trust here works not so much on the interpersonal scale, as in the convenience store discussed above, but rather on the institutional scale: it is placed in city planning departments of municipal and national governments or in private developers and corporations, which fulfill a quasi-institutional role. Often this form of trust is said to be one characteristic of modern societies, which tends to embed trust in institutions (Luhmann 1989; Giddens 1991). Yet, the idea of trust in city planning is by no means only a modern phenomenon. Similarly to the city as an imaginative space, cities have always been spaces of utopia. Some well-known examples are hundreds, even thousands of years old: Aristotle discusses urban citizenship in his *Politics* while Augustine examines Christian values in city life in his *The City of God*. One of the most productive periods for urban utopias was the late 19th century when, due to industrialization and mass urbanization, the cities were on the verge of collapse. Overcrowding, unsanitary conditions, air pollution, epidemics, and many other pressing issues needed to be addressed. Daniel Burnham proposed the *City Beautiful*, Benjamin Ward Richardson *Hygeia*, the city of health, and Ebenezer Howard the famous *Garden City*. They all believed that they could change the way people behaved and form better and healthier citizens merely through design (Hall 1988).

This top-down, bureaucratic understanding of planning did not change in the decades following the so-called Progressive Era. Planners such as Frank Lloyd Wright and Le Corbusier assumed an authority and arrogated a level of trust for themselves which seems almost disconcerting in our neo-liberal age. Having said this, we too have to question the trust we place in city planning agendas and wonder who is claiming authority here and how those actors legitimize the trust placed in them. Buzzwords such as "creative," "smart," "green," and "mixed-income" are thrown around like confetti, often presupposing an almost blind trust because, who would oppose a more sustainable and inclusive city (Swyngedouw 2007). This matter-of-fact attitude of city planners has come to its limits in recent decades. Too often those mega-projects seem to come at a price which fewer and fewer urban citizens are willing to pay: rising rents, displacements, traffic congestion, etc. Grass root activism therefore increasingly opposes large redevelopment projects, claiming the need of citizen involvement in urban planning policies (Jacobs 1961).

In Washington, D.C., for example, the public housing project Barry Farm is being torn down and redeveloped as a mix-income neighborhood. While the project could not be stopped, activists were able to demand a historic marker on the grounds of Barry Farm's extraordinary importance to the civil rights movement and black culture in the capital. In September of 2019, they organized a history walk through the, by then, half-way torn down project, telling the stories of civil rights leaders as well as ordinary individuals who have recently lost Barry Farm as their home; the event ending with a concert of Barry Farm's own go-go band (*see photo 1*). With their actions, the activists were able to postpone the further demolitions until a suitable solution was found. Another example is Amazon's search for the new site of their headquarters. That New Yorkers were able to reject such a huge corporation has gained worldwide media attention in 2019 (Kort/Postinett 2019; Goodman 2019). Even though Amazon promised to bring many jobs to the city while following an equitable development plan, people distrusted their intentions. It would have been likely that the jobs created would not have benefited those who need them so badly but rather the highly skilled professionals who move to the city for the jobs, putting even more pressure on the housing market (Schröder 2018). These examples show that in order for people to trust in city planning they need to be given a chance to voice their opinions and participate in the planning process. If people feel like decisions are being made for them and that those decisions are not for their own good, a wave of distrust is set off which can cause entire projects to fall. Yet, institutional trust should also not be understood as a one-way street. Trust as a relational entity has to work reciprocally. While citizens trust in municipal governments and city planners to work out highly complex plans and to come to wise decisions, those representatives should return the trust placed in them by respecting the needs expressed by the communities.

Photo 1: #DontEraseBarryFarm—That is the message of Barry Farm's own Go-Go-Band (The Junk Yard Band) playing after the History Walk on Sep 7, 2019

(Photography: Judith Keller 2019)

As a consequence of this, we should perhaps seriously rethink the relationship of trust and city planning. Maybe it is not enough to only focus on the trust relations of planning institutions and residents. Rather, trust should be understood as an entity which is present from the very beginning and not merely a goal to work towards. The city itself should be understood as a space in which trust is constantly working between people and institutions. It is a relational phenomenon that cannot be understood in isolation, but only in light of those interactions and their spatial dimension. Again Lefebvre (1991 [1974])'s trichotomy of *The Production of Space* helps to understand that trust is perceived, conceived, and *lived* in space. As Hollis (2013) points out, trust in the city becomes a functional entity if we plan spaces which "allow us to be ourselves" and "behave and interact in trusting ways" (192). The work of Klinenberg (2018) supports this point. He analyzes the positive impact of social infrastructure—spaces of social interaction—in times of crisis and finds that people in neighborhoods with libraries, playgrounds, neighborhood parks, etc. fare better because they have built up a network of trust relations; in other words, the necessary social capital to survive. Trust then is not only the necessary ingredient for urban planning to work smoothly, but for the city to become a lived space and a home.

Fixity and the Fight for Urban Space: Home and Housing as Spaces of Trust

In the opening quote, MA Sheehan talks about the absence of trust in New Orleans's Lower 9th Ward. Literally cut off from the rest of the city by a canal, the neighborhood has always been disadvantaged and passed over. Little has been invested in its infrastructure, retail, and public transport accessibility. Tragically, this also left the Lower 9th Ward most vulnerable when Hurricane Katrina made landfall in August of 2005. The neighborhood's proximity to the canal was fatal. When its levees broke, the suddenness of the breach swept away entire houses and trees, burying the Lower 9th Ward under ten feet of water. People had to camp on their roofs with no help in sight—they were stuck for days. Yet, while Katrina prominently showed how a highly mobile urban society can instantly collapse into stillness, the residents of the Lower 9th Ward were not only physically stuck in place, but had been stuck economically, socially, and politically long before Katrina hit.

The Lower 9th Ward is exemplary for African American neighborhoods and other communities of color all over the United States. Almost all of them have a long history of discrimination, segregation, and displacement. Institutionalized racism in the form of Red Lining, the denial of federal housing loans, school segregation, defunding of supermarkets and retail, police surveillance and brutality, etc. has kept an entire social group in a state of perpetuate marginality. Many people are both figuratively and literally stuck in place, as stressed by the new mobilities paradigm. In many cases, those neighborhoods are very isolated, having little relations to the rest of the city as canals, rivers, or highways separate them. If public transport is available, it is often heavily underfunded and thus scarce and unreliable. Yet, the stuckness refers not only to the actual mobility practices within the city, but also to the limited housing options. Even if families are working towards moving to other parts of the city, they often experience discrimination on the housing market. Many landlords do not house people of color in the first place or check their criminal histories and credit scores which then disqualifies them. The severe poverty and the lack of any economic potential in those neighborhoods excludes many people from the for-profit housing market. They depend on public housing or landlords which are willing to take their Section 8 housing vouchers.[1] Yet, many African Americans not only have trouble finding housing, but have experienced displacement and eviction for decades. African American communities are depicted as blight or slums in order to justify their removal (Wacquant 2008). They have to make room for highways, high risers, or, these days, mixed-income developments. Then, people are displaced, resulting in a constant form of forced mobility as they are being moved from one disposable place to the next (Desmond 2012). The African American urban experience has thus been one which led many people to distrust those institutions which are supposed to secure an inclusive urban society. They have been failed so many times that there is "historically, no reason to trust," to put it in MA Sheehan's words. While the situation in New Orleans might be especially grave due to the most recent history of Hurricane Katrina and its aftermath, it still reflects the general distrust towards institutions by a substantial part of American urban society.

It has already been mentioned that many people in those neighborhoods depend on public housing. The trust relationship between the state as a provider of housing and public housing residents is a very special one. The state here assumes the responsibility to provide its most vulnerable citizens with decent housing. The first generation of public housing was initiated by government funds during the New Deal Era with the National Housing Act of 1934 and the Wagner-Steagall Housing Act of 1937 (Gottesdiener 2013). Those

---

1   Refers to the Section 8 of the Housing Act of 1937. It establishes that the state pays rental assistance to private landlords in order to support low-income families.

pieces of legislation helped many poor, working-class families who had been passed over by the for-profit housing market. The aforementioned Barry Farm in Washington, D.C.'s Southeast quadrant was built back then and was thus one of the oldest public housing projects in the United States. In the beginning, Barry Farm and similar projects—not yet high risers that turned into vertical ghettos, but neat row houses with a lot of green space—were seen as a success. Yet, starting with the Nixon presidency, funds for public housing were constantly cut and, at the same time, many white Americans left the cities, subsidized by the loans they were offered for a suburban home. What happened next is a well-known story: many projects collapsed under the weight of gang wars, drugs, violence, and other social issues, iconically captured by the pictures of the demolition of Pruitt-Igoe (Bristol 1991). Barry Farm has a similar story. Since the project was built in the 1930s, it has been lacking many amenities, and so, in the 1960s, civil rights activists fought for it to be remodeled (Schoenfeld 2019). From then onwards, Barry Farm received no further investments. Later, when the decision was made to tear down the project, its signs of serious neglect where held against its residents and thus their removal framed as the only logical consequence.

However, in contrast to public opinion and stereotypes, public housing, including Barry Farm, was and still is a necessity, and sometimes a success. Many people do not only find a home here but also a community which supports them. There are many urban residents who need public housing because they cannot afford rent from their (minimum) wage or because they are physically or mentally impaired and cannot work. Public housing is their safety-net, and yet, they witness how it is underfunded, torn down, and replaced by mixed-income developments. The trust they placed in their government is broken as they find themselves stigmatized, discriminated against, and moved around cities like a disposable entity, instead of being helped when in desperate need of a place to call home. In 2018 and 2019, this was also the fate of the Barry Farm residents. Many tried to resist the redevelopment of their community, but in the end, they were evicted, and their community torn apart (*see photo 2*). Those who were lucky and found a new home in one of the District of Columbia's other projects have learned that they should not think of themselves as out of harm's way. As one of the residents told us in an interview, she is afraid that her new home, the Kelly Miller-LeDroit Apartments, are next on the Housing Authority's list:

You think, you would consider it home but the whole time they [DC Housing Authority] don't (...). All of a sudden, they tell you: well, this was supposed to be temporary; or this is, you know, not fit for you to live. So, now we have to tear it down and do it all over again. And then they send you some place that might be worse or that they gonna come for shortly down the line, and you'd be doing it all over again." (former resident of Barry Farm, Washington, D.C. 2019)

And it is millions of Americans who feel this way: the uncertainty on the housing market and the few prospects for government aid leave many fearing that they are next to be swallowed by the massive wave of displacements, evictions, and foreclosures that rolls over the United States (Desmond 2016). There is no trust that the housing market or their government is going to show any mercy.

This very tense situation on the housing market is a root cause of poverty. Access to decent housing is in most cases the first step out of these deprived conditions towards self-sufficiency and participation in public life. If people are stuck in a perpetuate state of marginality, they cannot fight for what is naturally theirs: a "Right to the City." In the Lefebvrian sense, this entails more than merely housing; it is the right to partake in city life and to create and form the city as one desires (Lefebvre 2016 [1968]). As Munoz (2018) stresses, the Right to the City cannot be claimed if home and housing do not provide a safe sphere. People need the security of home in order to experience a form of empowerment that enables them to become activists and to fight for a more egalitarian urban society. As participatory observations of the activists fighting for urban space in New Orleans's Lower 9th Ward and Washington, D.C.'s Barry Farm have shown, it is the experience of home and the attachment to place which gives the activists not only strength but also a purpose.

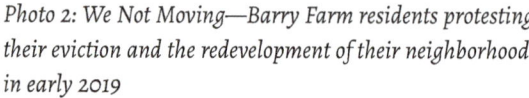

Photo 2: We Not Moving—Barry Farm residents protesting their eviction and the redevelopment of their neighborhood in early 2019

(Photography: Judith Keller/Ulrike Gerhard 2019)

Conclusion

These examples from a range of US American cities document how trust as a socio-spatial concept works on all scales of urban space. It could be on the micro scale of the neighborhood between residents, but also on larger scales between investors and buyers or between citizens and municipal governments. As long as trustful relationships are maintained, cities function as social spaces. This paper argues that these trust relations are best described in terms of relationality and mobility, two concepts coming mostly from geography: If mobility and relationality are interrupted or suspended, be it by a natural disaster, an investment-friendly landlord, or a hungry shoplifter, trust ends. This affects general trust in urban space as well: The city no longer represents a safe space and a home (as often portrayed, for example, in fiction). This can be best observed when we look at the formation of urban space. If we detail cities not merely as absolute spaces, but as relative and relational entities, then we can understand the emotional, social, and economic meanings of trust relations in cities.

Trust as a socio-spatial concept sheds light on urban spaces that emerge through the stories told, the social ties developed, or the trauma experienced collectively. As shown by the different case studies, trust relations become prevalent not only in the planning and building of physical urban space, but also shape the daily practices of people living within them and the images which influence their behavior and attitude towards urban space. By looking at these case studies we learned that visions as much as realities of cities change over time and are sometimes expressed by new political agendas, or by changing tastes or socio-economic conditions. Trust relations, therefore, are never stable or consistent, but changeable und fluid. They develop around conflicts and crises, as much as they (try to) provide stability and the feeling of security.

While the empirical details touched upon in this paper are important, this article is only the beginning of a larger research endeavor on the shifting meaning of authority and trust in US American urban society. As a result, we suggest extended research on different cities to gain further insights into the specific relationality and mobility of trust. We portrayed four relevant urban dimensions of trust in this paper. This list, however, can easily be extended by further themes or topoi. Questions of surveillance and policing, for example, are highly relevant not only in US American cities—often sparked there by racial profiling and other discriminatory practices—but confront urban society in many parts of the world. This directly relates to different forms of trust relations: from the interpersonal (between residents) over the institutional (police presence), to the loss of trust in the state as a trustworthy authority. Also, mass media have a strong influence on trust relations in cities as they shape public discourses and thereby impact perceptions of urban space. And, finally, having suggested mobilities as a helpful paradigm for understanding trust in cities, we see mobility itself telling us a lot about trust: investments into driverless cars, for example, will only be successful if people trust the new technology. Trust and technology in cities, therefore, is a topic worthy of in-depth research. With these (and other) examples in mind, our way forward is to argue for a framework that uses trust as a socio-spatial concept to analyze urban space. This space, being absolute, relative, and relational, is formed through social relations as much as it influences it. If we understand those urban processes, we can come to a new understanding of trust. Relationality and mobility help to conceptualize trust as a socio-spatial entity, yet they also reflect back on the concept of trust itself.

Works Cited

Baier, Andrea (1986): "Trust and Antitrust," in: *Ethics* 96(2), 231–260.

Bristol, Katherine G. (1991): "The Pruitt-Igoe Myth," in: *Journal of Architectural Education* 44(3), 163–171.

Busse, Beatrix (2019): "Patterns of Discursive Urban Place-Making in Brooklyn, New York," in: Viola Wiegand/Michaela Mahlberg (eds.), *Corpus Linguistics, Context and Culture*, Berlin: de Gruyter Mouton, 13–42.

Culver, Gregg (2016): "Moving forward or taking a stand?: Discourses surrounding the politics of Wisconsin High-Speed Rail," in: *Mobilities*, 11(5), 703–722.

Cresswell, Tim (2006): *On the Move. Mobility in the Western World*, New York & London: Routledge.

(2012): "Mobilities II: Still," in: *Progress in Human Geography* 36(5), 645–653.

Desmond, Matthew (2016): *Evicted. Poverty and Profit in the American City*, London: Penguin.

(2012): "Disposable Ties and the Urban Poor," in: *American Journal of Sociology* 117(5), 1295–1335.

Foucault, Michel (1986): "Of Other Spaces," in: *Diacritics* 16, 22–27.

Gerhard, Ulrike/Keller, Judith (2019): "'My home is my castle'—über die Rolle von Vertrauen im Wohnungsbau. Ein Blick auf US-amerikanische Städte," in: *Forum Wohnen und Stadtentwicklung* 6, 300–304.

Giddens, Anthony (1991): *The Consequences of Modernity*, Cambridge: Polity Press.

Goffman, Erving (1982): *Interaction Ritual—Essays on Face-to-Face Behavior*, New York: Pantheon Books.

Goodman, J. David (2019): "Amazon Pulls Out of Planned New York City Headquarters," *The New York Times*, https://www.nytimes.com/2019/02/14/nyregion/amazon-hq2-queens.html (accessed March 16, 2020).

Gottesdiener, Laura (2013): *A Dream Foreclosed. Black America and the Fight for a Place to Call Home*, Westfield, NJ: Zuccotti Park Press.

Hall, Peter (1988): *Cities of Tomorrow*, Malden, MA: Blackwell Publishing.

Hartmann, Martin (2011): *Die Praxis des Vertrauens*, Berlin: Suhrkamp.

Hartmann, Martin (2020): *Vertrauen. Die Unsichtbare Macht*, Frankfurt: S. Fischer.

Harvey, David (2006): "Space as a Keyword," in: Noel Castree/Derek Gregory (eds.), *David Harvey: A Critical Reader*. Malden, Oxford, & Carlton: Blackwell, 270–294.

(1973): *Social Justice and the City*, Baltimore: Johns Hopkins University Press.

Hollis, Leo (2013): *Cities Are Good for You. The Genius of the Metropolis*, London: Bloomsbury.

Jacobs, Jane (1961): *The Death and Life of Great American Cities*, New York, NY: Vintage Books.

Klinenberg, Eric (2018): *Palaces for the People. How Social Infrastructure Can Help Fight Inequality, Polarization, and the Decline of Civic Life*, New York: Crown.

Kort, Katharina/Postinett, Axel (2019): "Amazon scheitert an New York," *Handelsblatt*, https://www.handelsblatt.com/unternehmen/handel-konsumgueter/absage-des-milliardenprojekts-amazon-scheitert-an-ne-w-york/23989136.html (accessed March 16, 2020).

Lefebvre, Henri (1991 [1974]): *The Production of Space*, Oxford & Malden: Blackwell.

(2016 [1968]): *Das Recht auf Stadt*, Hamburg: Edition Nautilius.

Lewis, J. David/Weigert, Andrew (1985): "Trust as a Social Reality," in: *Social Forces* 63(4), 967–985.

Lobeck, Michael/Wiegandt, Claus-Christian (2019): "'Can't buy me trust'—zur Rolle des Vertrauens in der Stadtentwicklung," in: *Forum Wohnen und Stadtentwicklung* 6, 289–294.

Luhmann, Niklas (1989): *Vertrauen: ein Mechanismus der Reduktion sozialer Komplexität*, Stuttgart: Enke.

Massey, Doreen B. (1993): "Questions of Locality," in: *Geography* 78(2), 142–149.

(1991): "A global sense of place," in: *Marxism Today* (June), 24–29.

McCann, Eugene/Ward, Kevin (2010): "Relationality/Territoriality: Toward a Conceptualization of Cities in the World," in: *Geoforum* 41(2), 175–184.

Morrison, Toni (1992): *Jazz*, London: Chatto & Windus.

Mössner, Samuel (2010): *Integrierte Stadtentwicklungsprogramme—eine "Vertrauens-Konstellation": Beispiele aus Frankfurt a. M. und Mailand*, Kiel: Selbstverl. des Geographischen Inst. der Univ. Kiel.

Most, Glenn W. (2006): "Urban Blues: Detective Fiction and the Metropolitan Sublime," in: *The Yale Review* 94, 56–72.

Muller, Edward K. (2012): "Building American Cityscapes," in: Michael P. Conzen (ed.), *The Making of the American Landscape*, New York and London: Routledge, 303–328

Mumford, Lewis ([1937] 1996): "What is a city?" in: Richard T. LeGates/Frederic Stout (eds.), *The City Reader*, London & New York: Taylor & Francis, 92–96.

Munoz, Solange (2017): "Urban Precarity and Home: There Is No 'Right to the City,'" in: *Annals of the American Association of Geographers* 108(2), 370–379.

Rosa, Harmut (2016): *Resonanz: eine Soziologie der Weltbeziehung*, Berlin: Suhrkamp.

Schatzki, Theodor (2002): *The Site of the Social—A philosophical account of the constitution of social life and change*, University Park, PA: Penn State Univ. Press.

Schmid, David (1995): "Imagining Safe Urban Space: The Contribution of Detective Fiction to Radical Geography," in: *Antipode* 27, 242–269.

Schoenfeld, Sarah (2019): "The History and Evolution of Anacostia's Barry Farm," *D.C. Policy Center*, https://www.dcpolicycenter.org/publications/barry-farm-anacostia-history/ (accessed March 16, 2020).

Schröder, Thorsten (2018): "Queens kann einpacken," *Zeit Online*, https://www.zeit.de/wirtschaft/unternehmen/2018-11/amazon-hauptsitz-new-york-queens-onlinehandel-protest (accessed March 16, 2020).

Sheller, Mimi (2014): "The New Mobilities Paradigm for a Live Sociology," in: *Current Sociology Review*, 1–23.

Soja, Edward W. (1996): *Thirdspace. Journeys to Los Angeles and Other Real-And-Imagined Places*, Malden: Blackwell.

Swyngedouw, Erik (2007): "Impossible 'Sustainability' and the Postpolitical Condition," in: Rob Krueger/David Gibbs (eds.), *The Sustainable Development Paradox. Urban Political Economy in the United States and Europe*, New York and London: The Guilford Press, 13–40.

Wacquant, Loic (2008): *Urban Outcasts: A Comparative Sociology of Advanced Marginality*, Cambridge & Malden: Polity Press.

Werner, Cosima (2017): "Convenience Stores als Soziale Orte im US-amerikanischen Ghetto—Ein ethnographischer Feldbericht," in: Ulrike Gerhard et al. (Hg.): *Geographie der Extreme* HGG-Journal 31, 2016/2017. Heidelberg, 13–23.

Wilson, David (2018): *Chicago's Redevelopment Machine and Blues Clubs*, Cham: Palgrave Macmillan.

"We must trust that look of hers"
William Dean Howells's Urban Theory of Trust and Trustworthiness in *A Hazard of New Fortunes* (1890)

Margit Peterfy

American distrust of the city goes back to the very beginnings of the nation, and is probably most famously voiced by Thomas Jefferson in his *Notes on the State of Virginia* (1785):

> The mobs of great cities add just so much to the support of pure government, as sores do to the strength of the human body. It is the manners and spirit of a people which preserve a republic in vigour. A degeneracy in these is a canker which soon eats to the heart of its laws and constitutions.

Jefferson's vividly phrased abhorrence of "great cities" is closely tied up with his distrust of government, which we see expressed even more durably in his machinations to designate the site of the nation's then new capital away from the existing major urban centers, New York and Philadelphia (Wills 2002; Conn 2014; Boehm/Corey 2017: 13). Most of the canonical American writers of the nineteenth century (from Emerson to Dewey) harbored similarly anti-urban attitudes, with some exceptions such as Walt Whitman's vision of an urban utopia of flamboyant and harmonious co-existence. But, all in all, anti-urbanism remained the dominant ideology among the major American writers and thinkers of the nineteenth century (White 1961).

This said, many Americans, whether of old stock or recently immigrated, did not shun cities throughout the long nineteenth century.[1] On the contrary: the city that will be the "scene" of this essay, New York, had about 60,000

---

1   In their 2017 study on America's urban history, L.K. Boehm and S H. Corey write in their "Introduction": "The history of the American city is in many was the history of the United States. Although the agricultural tradition of rural America has left an indelible mark on the physical and cultural landscape, the United States is essentially an urban nation,

residents in 1800 and 600,000 by 1860 and, by 1900, Manhattan alone had 2.2 million residents (Conn 2014: 14).[2] Of course most of these city-dwellers did not see themselves as ideological or intellectual advocates for the advantages of cities or urban life-styles; they "just" moved there with various motivations. There has been so much emphasis on the squalid working and living conditions of the—objectified—"Other Half" (Riis 1890) that we tend to forget that, during these years of explosive urban growth through migration, even poor and underprivileged city-dwellers were intelligent, self-interested agents, who arguably chose the city over the countryside because it afforded them opportunities, however meagre, that they could not find elsewhere. The fact that they were lied to and criminally exploited (as vividly described in Upton Sinclair's *The Jungle*, published in 1906), was not a problem of the "mobs" feared by Jefferson, but the result of governmental negligence, fraud, and political corruption steeped in economic egotism. Adding insult to injury, some "theoreticians" of the urban poor, such as, for example, the leader of the Social Gospel movement, Josiah Strong, called these city dwellers an "insolent rabble," or compared them, following a wide-spread nativist, anti-immigration impulse, to "cannibals in some far off coast" (Strong 1885: 129; see also Boyer 1978, Boehm/Corey 2017: 141–182).[3]

Given the anti-urban stance among nineteenth-century literary commentators on city life, William Dean Howells (1837–1920) stands out as an exception and as one of the first observers who attempted to (re-)present a more comprehensive and also more detailed social view of New York just before 1900 (Kaplan 1986; Bramen 2000; Puskar 2018). This paper will argue that the novel *A Hazard of New Fortunes* (1890) can be read as a reflection on trust and trustworthiness with respect to the momentous changes in urban institutional and political conditions in the metropolis of New York just before 1900. In this, I will focus both on trust (as a relational attitude) and trustworthiness

---

and has been so for a much longer period and to a greater degree than is generally acknowledged" (Boehm/Corey 2017: 1).

2   In percentages, the changing ratios are even more striking: in 1800 94 % of Americans lived in rural areas; by 1900 this number declined to 50 % (Conn 2014: 13–14).

3   Even reformers with deep sympathy for the plight of the urban poor and with an earnest wish to help, were often not able to see that their help took on the form of moralistic control and social engineering, disrespecting the dignity and individuality of their "wards," especially when the persons to be "reformed" were foreigners, or of a different religious persuasion (Boyer 1974:ix; Kaplan 1986: 69–70).

(as a condition of the trustee), thus following Russell Hardin, who writes: "Poets, playwrights, and novelists get the issue right, but academics often miss … the causal connection that trustworthiness begets trust" (Hardin 2002: 28).

William Dean Howells as Social Commentator

It is important to point out that my reflections on Howells's understanding of trust relationships in American urban society rest specifically on references in his novel *A Hazard of New Fortunes*. The terms "trust" and "distrust" appear there again and again in a range of contexts, also in implicit references to trustworthiness, reliability, risk, expectation, and social justice. The centrality of the topic reveals itself in the closing sentence of the novel—a classically "foregrounded" position in any literary work. Here, the remark "Well, we must trust that look of hers" appears as a comment on a fleeting urban encounter—a point I will come back to later. The statement seems to be typical of the open endings in Howells's novels (Wetzel-Sahm 1995), but when we take trust to be one of the main motives of this work, it provides thematic closure, harking back not just to other moments in the novel, but also to the title that references a concept often understood to be a necessary element of trust: hazard, in the sense of risk (Skyrms 2008).

But before the actual analysis of *A Hazard of New Fortunes* (1890), Howells's own trustworthiness as a reliable and insightful commentator on trust needs to be established. As in many of his almost forty other novels, he made use of a literary aesthetic that he had developed throughout his long and successful career as a novelist, critic, editor, and social commentator. He called this new mode "democracy in literature" and "realism" and saw its superiority above older literary traditions in its openness to a whole set of new topics and experiences that he summarized in the category of the "common sense" or "everyday" life (Howells 1891: 9–10). Much has been written about the success or failure of his efforts in terms of various interpretations of "realism" (with respect to style, philosophy, literary sociology, economy, institutional theory), [4] but this discussion is only relevant here concerning his more inclusive stance towards topics and themes that he felt should be part of his fiction, or rather of literature in general (Trachtenberg 1982: 184–190). He has been criticized for

---

4   For a recent research overview and bibliographic essay see Ernst/Matter Seibel/
     Schmidt 2018: 1–34 and 29–31.

having a limited perspective, but this does not invalidate his observations; as Simon Blackburn writes: "It is a big step from the omnipresence of perspective to the omnipresence of illusion. You and I see the world from literally different points of view, but on the face of it we can each be right about what we see" (Blackburn 2005: 87).

That Howells did not question the soundness of his perception as such, did not mean that he was naïve when it came to problematizing the meaning of all that he saw. In fact, this epistemological uncertainty is at the center of his attitude towards the notion and meaning of trust in his A *Hazard of New Fortunes*. According to Georg Simmel, we are dealing with the phenomenon of trust when we are in a position or partial knowledge and control; both complete ignorance and complete knowledge preclude the notion of trust (Simmel 1908/1992: 393.) Philosophical definitions of trust since Simmel have been developed in manifold directions, but trust is often described as something that we only become aware of when we notice its absence, or when we feel that our trust has been betrayed (Hartmann 2020: 68). In a *Hazard of New Fortunes*, Howells describes various crises of trust in a way that also support Ute Frevert's identification of trust as an "obsession" of the modern period (Frevert 2013). Howells was concerned with such crises of trust just as he was deeply worried about the state and development of American society as a democracy during the last decades of the nineteenth century. His exceptional, but unsuccessful attempt in 1887 to save the anarchists of the Haymarket Affair from the death sentence is probably his most public and principled case of political activism,[5] but he was an incessant commentator on American politics, both in his public and his private writings (Goodman/Dawson 2005: 279–287; Konrad 1986). Since the close relationship between democracy and trust has been shown extensively in research on the latter,[6] this chapter will extend that connection in the sense that Howells's literary notion of "democratic art" deserves credit for recognizing the relevance of trust relationships in late 19th century American society—in particular, urban society.

---

5   Howells was the only American writer who petitioned until the last minute against the death sentences for the anarchists; not one of his friends (who included Twain, Garland, Hale, Norton, Higginson, Lowell, Whittier, etc.) endorsed his protest (Goodman/Dawson 2005: 281).

6   The number of collections discussing the role of trust in democracies is daunting; for a useful recent overview see "What Kinds of Trust Does a Democracy Need? Trust From the Perspective of Democratic Theory," by Mark E. Warren (2017).

Howells's talent and reliability as an observer of the American scene was prominently recognized including by his friend, Henry James, who wrote in an open letter: "Stroke by stroke and book by book your work was to become for this exquisite notation of our whole democratic light and shade and give and take in the highest degree documentary, so that none other, through all your fine long season, could approach it in value and amplitude" (Henry James, "A Letter to Mr. Howells" 1912, reported in Cady and Cady 1983: 233). James's compliment about Howells's powers of documentary observation echoes the latter's own self-image: "It makes me think that my strongest faculty, after all, may have been an art of seeing and hearing everything. I am sure I c'd not invent half as many things, thoughts, ideas, as I can remember" (February 9, 1890; quoted in Goodman/Dawson 310).

Throughout the novel, the observations and remarks on trust and the conditions of trustworthiness appear on various narrative levels: within conversations between characters, in dramatic interior monologues, or as authorial comments. It is striking that Howells repeatedly voiced his concerns about contemporary America by referring to faith and trust, but also distrust. Thus, he wrote to Henry James in 1888: "[America] seems to me the most grotesquely illogical thing under the sun. I should hardly like to trust pen and ink with all the audacity of my social ideas; but after fifty years of optimistic content of 'civilization,' and its ability to come out all right in the end, I now abhor it, and feel that it is coming out all wrong in the end, unless it bases itself anew on a real equality" (quoted in Trachtenberg 1982: 200). Soon after, he writes to his father in a slightly more optimistic mood in 1890 about his "faith in the grand and absolute change, sooner or later" and "the change that must come in favor of truth and justice" (quoted in Konrad 1986: 220). Between the overwhelming pessimism of the quotation from 1888, and the more positive outlook he conveys to his father, lies Howells's publication of his novel *A Hazard of New Fortunes* in 1890.

Though decidedly not autobiographical, *A Hazard of New Fortunes* is inspired by Howells's own move to the city of New York in the year 1889. The novel's protagonist, Basil March, a writer and literary journalist (but, again, not an avatar of Howells), and his wife, Isabel, decide to relocate from Boston to New York. They experience the urban environment and make new acquaintances: Dryfoos, a rich "capitalist;" Lindau, a German-American "anarchist/socialist;" Alma, a female artist; Miss Vance, a philanthropist—all of whom are trying to find their bearings in New York. Howells, as a public intellectual and literary historian (Melzer 2003; McGrath 2012), uses them to construct a web of trust-related case studies, from which three urban topics seem to evolve: (1) trust in the city of New York and the development of a modern urban environment; (2) big business and the question of trustworthiness; and (3), trustworthiness of women, or "gender trust," referring to the changing role of women in modern urban society. These themes demarcate areas that were important for Howells's own, often ambivalent, attitude towards the future of the United States as a social experiment. Indeed, Howells's optimism (or, sometimes, pessimism) is closely related to his own ability to trust and his expectation of others, while it is also at the center of his poetics of realism of everyday life, when he explicitly writes that "the time is coming, we trust, when each new author, each new artist, will be considered, not in his proportion to any other author or artist, but in his relation to human nature, known to us all" (Howells 1887: 154).[7]

From a theoretical perspective, all three areas are directly related to questions of trust, but not all in the same way. As Geoffrey Hosking has argued,[8] the definitions of trust and trustworthiness can be placed on a continuum defined by two coordinates, thick versus thin, and strong versus weak. The thick-thin distinction refers to the *kind* of contact the trustor and trustee have: a close contact based either on extensive knowledge (thick), or a relationship that is based on superficial contact (thin). The strong-weak distinction points to the degree of vulnerability the trustor exposes herself to (Hosking 2016: 47). The sort of trust that is required to support the "routine coordination relationships" that are the necessary foundation of a functioning urban society are increasingly located in large part at the strong, thin corner. Impersonal (strong, thin) trust appears in complex social institutions such as banks, police, urban planning agencies, complex government services, etc. without which large modern cities not only could not function, but never would have come into being in the first place. Hosking notes that this sort of trust is "ever more prevalent in our social life today" (ibid. 47).

---

7   When Howells reprinted this text in his collection *Criticism and Fiction* (1891), he changed the "we trust" to "I hope." His reasons for this could not be established so far.

8   Hosking's analysis goes back to Tilly (2009), but arguably also as far as Hume, who developed what we would now recognize as the distinction between social coordination projects (thin trust) and cooperation projects (thick trust), framing the development of complex society in terms of the former, in the analytical framework of his *History of England* (Sabl 2012: 21–42).

A Hazard of New Fortunes takes us to the scene of New York at an early phase of the dynamic changes to which Hosking refers. To characterize Howells as a pioneering "literary sociologist" of trust relationships[9] does not require us to see him as a systematic theoretician of trust. Also, the following reflections cannot claim to give a comprehensive view of the treatment of trust in the entirety of his oeuvre—this would require a project of a much larger scope. What a novel like *A Hazard of New Fortunes* can add to our understanding of a new urban modernity on the one hand, and of trust and trustworthiness on the other, lies in the fact that it is a text written by an exceptionally perceptive observer, who delivers a "good-faith" contemporary description of open-ended social developments in a rapidly expanding metropolis. In literary theory, Catherine Elgin talks about narratives as "thought experiments," in which authors creatively—not just empirically, but also making use of *poesis*—create scenarios that self-referentially theorize their observations (Elgin 2007) and thus can be linked to a specific type of literary epistemology (Davies 377–379). Additionally, as Hardin and others have pointed out, literature has always been a great semantic field to discuss trust, and trustworthiness (Hardin 2002: 28; Hartmann 2020: 94–95).[10]

Trust in the City

A Hazard of New Fortunes is one of the first novels to present New York as a modern urban environment, displaying aspects of infrastructure, housing, socioeconomic observations, and even "what may be the first Italian restaurant in all of American fiction" (Puskar 2018:491). Howells, remaining true to his convictions as a documentary realist, records details that strike him as surprising, noteworthy, or simply novel developments.[11] Given the large number

---

9   Howells's special position and signature status as a sociologically inclined actor in the literary field of late nineteenth-century American literature is convincingly presented by Florian Sedlmeier as an idiosyncratic position in which "Howells imagines the societal function of both criticism and literature in a way that constructs literature, and most prominently, the novel, as always already contingent upon the shifting configurations of the social" (Sedlmeier 2018: 86).

10   Dietmar Schloss's contribution to this volume points in a similar direction.

11   Some of Howells's remarks, especially about the "picturesqueness" of poor, ethnic areas of the city have been rightly criticized as signs of his bourgeois, white, middle-class perspective (Kaplan 1986: 72, Puskar 2018: 496).

of studies on urban reform, sociology, and history of American cities in the Progressive Era and beyond,[12] one might wonder what Howells's novel could possibly contribute to the debate. But, as already argued, it is exactly his *literary* point of view that promises new insights into the emotional and cultural development of trust relationships in American cities; Howells's eye and ear for seemingly insignificant details (as admired by Henry James) provide valuable and so-far untapped sources for scholarly research.

Cities cannot function without a complicated and carefully calibrated set of trust relationships. In *A Hazard*, there are several aspects of the urban environment that could be related to notions of trust and distrust, but I will concentrate on a few aspects related to public transportation in New York. As argued elsewhere in this volume, mobility—and immobility—are closely connected with trust relationships on various levels (see Gerhard/Keller/Werner in this volume). Howells's approach to the implications of urban mobility exhibits two features: a realistic, documentary style, and also a literary/figurative technique, which allows him to express atmosphere, mood, and emotions; resulting in a tapestry that includes both straightforward description and symbolic action. In particular, as I will argue later, in the case of the issue of mobility and trust it provides a heuristic tool for the examination of "strong thin trust" (following Hosking's categories), but also of a frequently discussed distinction between trust and reliance (or trustworthiness and reliability) as Hartmann (2020: 104) would put it. One suggested empirical distinction between the two is that if we trust something or someone, that trust can be "betrayed," while if we rely on something, although we expect that it functions in a specific way, we are not emotionally involved if it does not (Baier 1986). Annette Baier's explication of this distinction is that, in the absence of "goodwill" on the part of the trusted person or institution, we can talk only about reliance. But since the presence or absence of this goodwill in the trustee is not always traceable, I suggest a distinction based on the feelings and attitudes of the trustor. Following up on the thoughts of Karen Jones in her article "Trust as an Affective Attitude" I will show how, in *A Hazard*, the positive feelings and optimistic expectations of the novel's protagonists influence their perception of New York's transportation system as trustworthy—or not.

---

12   The first wave of what we consider sociological publications on the American metropolis started shortly after the Civil War, when the American Social Science Association (ASSA) was established in Boston and influenced the whole course of urban studies, even beyond its dissolution in 1912 (Boehm/Corey 2017: 168).

New York had grappled with traffic management problems all through the nineteenth century, and various approaches were proposed to help develop effective means of mass transportation for a rapidly growing population (Cheape 1980). In 1880, the Census Bureau recognized that New York had become something new—a metropolis (ibid.: 20)—and thus presented essentially different, and more complex, problems of urban management. Beside the practical question of moving a large number of people to and from work, urban reformers thought they had also to address less tangible aspects of transport management beyond simple infrastructure; e.g. the prevention of disease and crime, but also the wish for order and control (Boyer 1978). By 1889, when Howells moved to New York, there was an extensive system of elevated tracks in place (Cheape 1980: 32–40). The "El" or "L" roads were important for the development of New York, but they were often the target of severe criticism: the trains were dirty, loud, and the streets underneath them were thrown into all-day shade. Since the system in any given area was privately run by a local monopoly, the owners did not feel compelled to make improvements: the local transit facilities made money anyway.

When the protagonists in *A Hazard* first arrive in the city, they are not aware of any of this, and they are thoroughly fascinated with the El. It becomes part of the experience of New York as a place providing a sense of freedom and also an optimistic, progressive environment: "At Third Avenue they took the Elevated, for which she [Isabel March] confessed an infatuation. She declared it the most ideal way of getting about in the world" (79). Later, they arrive at Grand Central Station, where they look down on the tracks and, observing the trains waiting to leave, they fall into a similar rapture:

> They had another moment of rich silence when they ... looked down upon the great night trains lying on the tracks dim under the rain of gas-lights ... . What forces, what fates, slept in these bulks which would soon be hurling themselves north and west and south through the night! ... The Marches admired the impressive sight with a thrill of patriotic pride in the fact that the whole world perhaps could not afford just the like (80).

This mix of excitement about, and admiration for, the technological and organizational "affordances" of the *American* transportation system, quite explicitly expressed in terms of emotional involvement, can be characterized as an attitude full of trust in institutional structures and not merely a reliance on them: trust that the system works, that it is effective, safe, and that it is there for the public who do not need to worry about it, but rather can simply rely on it. However, there is more than just a sense of reliability in this comment: "The attitude of optimism is ... in terms of a distinctive, and affectively loaded, way of seeing the one trusted" (Jones 1996: 4). The Marches even connect this to their patriotism, pride, and a cradled feeling of community. But, as we will see, this kind of "affective" trust towards New York's transportation system will fade and finally almost disappear in the course of the novel—a development, which is, of course, carefully orchestrated by Howells.

When we are still at the beginning of the March family's life in New York, the couple also comments on the fact that the elevated trains afford glimpses into the living rooms of New York residents: "He said it was better than the theatre, of which it reminded him, to see those people through their windows; [...] what suggestion, what drama, what infinite interest!" (*A Hazard*: 79).[13] It seems odd that Basil and Isabel March do not show any compunction about peering into other people's lives, but the significance of the scene lies also in the way the inhabitants offer themselves up for this "performance." To call this "trust" would be overstating the degree of agency involved, but the Marches do not notice any active signs of "distrust" (in the form of curtains, etc.) either. The speed with which the train moves past these windows seems to insulate the inhabitants from the potential of real intrusion, while the voyeuristic impulse of the travelers parallels Howells's conviction regarding the importance of ordinary life as the subject of democratic art. The atmosphere of this quintessentially urban scene contradicts notions of the metropolis as a place characterized by distrust and taciturnity. Compare, for example, Georg Simmel's much more threatening description of encounters in a metropolis in his "Großstädte und das Geistesleben":

> If we had to respond with the same number of internal reactions to the continuous external contacts as in a smaller city ... we would be completely atomized internally and come to a wholly inconceivable mental condition. It is partly due to this psychological circumstance, and partly to the right not to distrust, which we feel in the face of ephemeral elements of the life in a metropolis, that we are forced to be reserved. (Simmel 1803/1995: 122–3, my translation)[14]

---

13   Amy Kaplan criticizes the Marches for looking into poor peoples' lives, but it is clear that the "El" does not just go past poor apartments; what the Marches see is middle-class life. (Kaplan 1986:70).

14   In the original German: "Wenn der fortwährenden äußeren Berührung mit unzähligen Menschen so viele innere Reaktionen antworten sollten, wie in der kleinen Stadt, ... so

Simmel does not just describe distrust as an essential attitude in the city, he even talks about a "right to distrust."[15] His position could not be further from the attitude of the Marches, who feel a sense of acceptance and an exhilarating connection to the city; to its system of transportation and its inhabitants. Whenever March takes the El, he ponders over his fellow passengers on the train: "He found the variety of people in the car as unfailingly entertaining as ever. He rather preferred the East Side to the West Side lines, because they offered more nationalities, conditions, and characters to his inspection" (*A Hazard* 197). There might be some objectification, but there is never a sense of distrust or discomfort, as mentioned by Simmel in his account of life in a metropolis. March also notices the "numerical subordination of the dominant race" (ibid. 198), in other words, the growing cultural and ethnic diversity of the city. At the same time, he does not connect these observations to any kind of explicit political statement: "he did not take much trouble about this"(ibid. 199). His interest is rather personal: "what these poor people were thinking, hoping, fearing, enjoying, suffering; just where and how they lived; who and what they individually were—these were the matters of his waking dreams" (ibid. 199). In this, he anticipates Simmel's own conclusions about the interplay of various influences and "powers" in a city: "To the extent that such powers are organically present in the roots as in the crown of social life in its entirety ... it is not our task to accuse or to forgive, but alone to understand" (Simmel 1903/1995: 131, my translation).[16]

As already mentioned, Basil March (and, indirectly, Howells) has been criticized for the limitations of his middle-class background. But one episode shows that his interest is genuine and that he is capable of real empathy.

---

würde man sich innerlich völlig atomisieren und in eine ganz unausdenkbare seelische Verfassung geraten. Teils dieser psychologische Umstand, teils das Recht auf Misstrauen, das wir gegenüber den in flüchtiger Berührung vorüberstreifenden Elementen des Großstadtlebens haben, nötigt uns zu Reserve."

15   It is interesting to note here that research about the current political situation in the US also contradicts Simmel and his association of cities with distrust. In a research paper by Will Wilkinson of the Niskanen Center, titled "The Density Divide: Urbanization, Populization, and Populist Backlash" from June 2019, it is argued that it is not urban diversity that creates distrust, but spatial segregation, https://www.niskanencenter.org/wp-content/uploads/2019/09/Wilkinson-Density-Divide-Final.pdf (accessed April 12, 2020).

16   "Indem solche Mächte in die Wurzel wie in die Krone des ganzen geschichtlichen Lebens eingewachsen sind, ... ist unsere Aufgabe nicht, anzuklagen oder zu verzeihen, sondern allein zu verstehen."

When he walks through one of the poorer parts of the city, he witnesses a dramatic scene on the street, which he does not entirely understand, but which he is able to recognize as an event that is typical of what gives life in a city a specific atmosphere:

> March understood the unwillingness of the poor to leave the worst conditions in the city for comfort and plenty in the country when he reflected upon this dramatic incident. ... A small town could rarely offer anything comparable to it and the country never. He said that if life appeared so hopeless to him as it must to the dwellers in that neighborhood, he should not himself be willing to quit its distractions, its alleviations, for the vague promise of unknown good in the distance somewhere. (202)

Howells's observations are an indirect commentary on the programs of reformers who thought of themselves as the "ethical elite" and whose vision of a perfectly managed urban world took the form of social engineering based on their own set of values and norms, "with objective standards of social control" and plans forged above the heads of individuals (Boyer 1978: 149, 176 ff.) These reformers would never have identified with the tastes of the "disorderly" poor as March does.

The Marches go regularly on long walks, during which the city appears as "huge, noisy, ugly, kindly" (339), and when Isabel March reminisces about Boston's "intellectual refinement of the life they had left behind them," her husband answers that "it was very pretty, but he said it was not life—it was death in life" (339). Finally, on the occasion of one of her returns to Boston, also Mrs. March recognizes the sullen faces in the horsecars as the "Puritan mask, the cast of a dead civilization" and she "sighed to think that less than a year of the heterogeneous gayety of New York should have made her afraid of it" (*A Hazard* 342). Ms. March is not afraid anymore of the "heterogeneous gayety" of New York, which can be translated into the positive statement: Ms. March began to see the heterogenous gayety of New York as a trustworthy environment—nothing to be afraid of.

The spontaneous affection for, and comfortable trust in, the city's institutions begins to change when Basil March becomes more aware of some aspects of the city, including the workings of its transportation system. He starts to notice and comment upon the chaotic system of elevated trains. The way they cut through the cityscape fills him with a sense of foreboding, with a "vague discomfort." After the enthusiasm of his first encounters with the elevated trains, he now perceives the struggle between the established architecture and the messy system of the elevated railroad, as an "absence of intelligent, comprehensive purpose in the huge disorder" resulting in a "chaos to which the individual selfishness of the railroads must always lead" (*A Hazard* 200). The railroads are, of course, not capable of selfishness, and, thus, the butt of the criticism must, in fact, be human beings and the institutions and businesses run by them. March's aesthetic unease translates into social anxiety and foreshadows the climax and catastrophe of the novel, when public and private storylines converge and bring about chaos, violence, and death—in a complete antithesis to the earlier "gay" exuberance of the city.

This decisive turn is closely related to a labor crisis in New York. Modeled on the 1889 strike of the employees of the Atlantic Avenue Railroad (Cudahy 2002: 152), Howells culminates his novel with some tragic events around a streetcar strike. The strike is about a loss of wages that affects about six thousand drivers and conductors (of horse-drawn streetcars). Beaton, a minor, rather unattractive, character in the novel, has no sympathy for the strikers:

> Beaton felt a sudden turn of his rage toward the men whose action would now force him to walk five blocks and mount the stairs of the Elevated station. "If you'd take out eight or ten of these fellows," he said, ferociously, "and set them up against a wall and shoot them, you'd save a great deal of bother." (*A Hazard* 450)

The character's reaction unequivocally reveals him to be a cynical, self-involved, and cruel person, whose anger about having to walk "five blocks and mount the stairs" is enough to provoke such a violent reaction. The policeman Beaton is talking to does not take up the suggestion, but it is clear that his role is to survey the scene and keep order: "On the other side of the street Beaton could see another officer sauntering up from the block below. Looking up and down the avenue, … he saw a policeman at every corner. It was rather impressive" (*A Hazard* 451). The system of surveillance presented here is adapted to the long, straight grid of streets of midtown Manhattan.

Whereas Beaton is annoyed, because inconvenienced, Basil March is actively drawn to the situation and is "very curious about the strike, whose importance, as a great social convulsion, he felt people did not recognize" (*A Hazard* 457). He has read about violent outbreaks between the strikers and the police, but when he starts walking the streets, he does not experience anything of the sort: "[A] car laden with policemen came down the track, but none of the strikers offered to molest it. In their simple Sunday best, March thought them very quiet, decent-looking people, and he could well believe that they had nothing to do with the riotous outbreaks in other parts of the city" (*A Hazard* 458). The reference to the looks and the clothing, and the overall habitus of the protesters is not accidental and is part of a general source of epistemological anxiety in *A Hazard of New Fortunes* that is related to trust and distrust: The question of how much of what is "visible" affords a reliable foundation for future action; in other words, how far can one "trust" one's own impressions.

In a situated response to exactly this theoretical conundrum, the state of affairs changes abruptly, chaotically; the car, which March has meanwhile mounted, is stopped by a tumult between strikers and the police. He is astonished to see a "tall, old man, with a long white beard, who was calling out to the police: 'Ah yes, Glup the strikers—gif it to them! Why don't you co and glup the bresidents that insoalt your lawss'"? (470)[17] The man, Lindau, is a German anarchist/socialist and an old friend of Basil March (more about Lindau in the next sub-chapter). Lindau's criticism is systemic and characterized by a deep distrust of the whole organization of American business life, including the organization of transportation in the city. The alternative to the system of countless private companies would be an arrangement founded upon public interest and organization, leading to reliable services (cf. March's earlier unease about the "selfish railroads"). Lindau is clubbed so severely that he dies later, but his death is paired with another casualty: the (more or less) accidental shooting of a young man, Conrad, who naively approached the scene of violence with the intention of arguing for a peaceful resolution of the conflict. Before he even can say a word, he is hit by a bullet coming from a policeman.

With respect to our discussion of trust, we see here a disintegration on various levels: the spontaneous and affective trust of the March couple in the city's institutions, but also on the level of the organization of transportation infrastructure; a typical instance of a trust relationship that is strong (the importance of mobility) and thin (the general reliance of a system), according to Hosking's terminology (2016: 47).

---

17   Howells tries to reproduce the German accent of Lindau—an accepted means of "realistic" dramatic characterization around 1900, which was also used for other accents, most notably for the rendering of African American vernacular expression (cf. Redling 2006).

"Merchant princes, railroad kings, and coal barons": The (Un)Trustworthiness of Big Business

As already mentioned in the introductory part of this essay, Howells became deeply skeptical about the political development of the United States during the last decades of the nineteenth century. Although he had profited from having written the campaign biography for the Republican president Hayes in the 1870s, fifteen years later he dismissed both the Republican and the Democratic parties and started on his own campaign for social reform. He took to Tolstoy's ideas, whom he first read in 1885, but, in his native context, was more influenced by Henry George's theories on the taxation of land and by Laurence Gronlund's popular American re-interpretation of Marx's theories in *The Cooperative Commonwealth* (1884). The influence of these thinkers appear also in *A Hazard of New Fortunes* (Arms 1939), tailored to the overall experience of the March family in New York.[18] From the perspective of theories of trust and trustworthiness in modern democracies, it is important to emphasize that the character constellations and plot twists invented by Howells are only possible in an urban setting. The triangulation, for example, of a beautiful old-money socialite, a poor German anarchist, and a troubled young man looking for his place in life is only realistic in the metropolis, where chance encounters are nothing out of the ordinary.

Howells creates a character constellation that allows him to play out a conflict between a "socialist" and a "capitalist": On the one hand, Lindau, an elderly German exile of the 1848 revolution, with radical socialist tendencies, and, on the other, Dryfoos, the wealthy owner of a gas-field, of the same generation as Lindau but with "typical" modern American persuasions concerning business practices. While Lindau had participated in the Civil War and lost an arm in battle, Dryfoos "had an old rankling shame in his heart for not having gone into the war" (*A Hazard* 372). The sacrifice that Lindau had made for the country, in fact giving the proverbial arm for it, is an important marker for his trustworthiness. As Basil March puts it: "He lost a hand in the war that helped to save us and keep us possible, and that stump of his *is character enough for me*" (*A Hazard*: 163; my emphasis).

---

18   Howells's political views in the 1880s were still developing, which allows us to view *A Hazard* as a thought experiment. His most explicit exposition of his socialist views appears in his later, utopian novel *Travelers from Altruria* (1895).

The go-between who arranges for contact between Lindau and Dryfoos, is Basil March, who had known Lindau from his youth. Their reunion about thirty years later in the novel is firmly situated in an urban setting,[19] in a restaurant, where March accidentally comes across his former friend and German teacher. Whereas their earlier, pre-Civil War friendship flourished in the environment of a small-town printing shop, resembling an idyllic American, democratic version of an old-world private education, the relationship in New York is dominated by the social gap between the two: the younger man a successful editor of a magazine, firmly anchored in a middle-class existence versus the old and frail Civil War invalid, who rejects his government pension out of principle and makes a meagre living as a painter's model.

March is shocked to see that his former friend lives such a lonely life full of deprivation and decides to help Lindau by offering him a freelance position as a translator and reviewer of foreign literature. March delivers his proposition in person, and they start a conversation about the question of the causes of poverty and inequality. For Lindau, it is clear where the problem lies: "those boor millionaires that hadt to steal their money," and continues ("in German," therefore without the accent-markers):

> Not the most gifted man that ever lived, in the practice of any art or science, and paid at the highest rate ... could ever *earn* a million dollars. It is the landlords and the merchant princes, the railroad kings and the coal barons (the oppressors to whom you instinctively give the titles of tyrants)—it is these that *make* the millions, but no man *earns* them (*A Hazard*: 207).

Lindau's interpretation of the economic developments in the USA points not just to his own distrust, but also to a general distrust felt by the public; after all, the associations he invokes (the one he leaves out is the "robber baron") are not Lindau's inventions but were in general usage. The distrust of "big business" started long before the successful campaign of anti-trust legislation (Sherman-Act of 1890) and has continued as an undercurrent in the public perception of American economic life long after that (Orbach/Rebling 2012). A systematic analysis of this economic aspect is beyond the scope and ambition of this paper, but the question of the trustworthiness of "big business" and "monopolies" was a live—and yet undecided—issue on the minds of the

---

19   March is being asked by his fellow editor: "What did I tell you about meeting every man in New York that you ever knew before?" (*A Hazard*: 99).

American public when Howells wrote *A Hazard of New Fortunes*. The 1888 illustration in *Harper's Weekly* expresses the distrust towards big business, and, in particular, of the so-called, and somewhat ironically designated, "trusts."[20] These are represented as a giant octopus, reaching for Justice, who is only half-blind, and uses its one open eye to kill the scorpion of anarchism. The caricature can be taken as a backdrop to Lindau's radical convictions, and, in a larger sense, to Howells's unsuccessful activism for the sake of the Haymarket anarchists in 1886:

The exchange between March and Lindau now turns towards that "mark" of Lindau's character, his missing hand, which is the proof of Lindau's trustworthiness. March effuses about Lindau's sacrifice: "And I don't believe there's an American living that could look at that arm of yours and not wish to lend you a hand for the one you gave us all" (*A Hazard*: 209). But Lindau rejects March's slightly sentimental suggestion:

> Lindau smiled grimly "You think zo? I wouldn't moch like to drost'em. I've driedt idt too often." He began to speak German again, fiercely: "Besides, they owe me nothing. Do you think I knowingly gave my hand to save this oligarchy of traders and tricksters, this aristocracy of railroad wreckers and stock gamblers and mine-slave drivers and mill-serf owners? No; I gave it to the slave." (*A Hazard*: 209)

March reacts to this with "a look of pain," but, as it turns out later, still does not understand Lindau. He idolizes his former teacher, but thereby turns him into a symbol: a hero of the Civil War and an American patriot, although Lindau

---

20   A straightforward synonym for a trust in this sense, is conglomerate, combination, or monopoly, but only in the US, and only since 1882, when the first large trust of this kind was created, the Standard Oil Trust. The term "trust" rapidly gained an independent existence and both approving, and disapproving language users created its meaning as simply a business corporation that controlled a certain field of business. The specific American usage also becomes obvious in that that legislation against it is called Anti-Trust law in the US, whereas, in British and European legal contexts, the synonymous term is Competition Law (Orbach/Rebling 2012). The term had, however, little to do with its original usage: "It is important at the outset to state the nature of a "trust." The term is an unfortunate one, since it is in no respect descriptive of the subject at issue. A trust is in general simply the case of one person holding the title of property, whether land or chattels, for the benefit of another, termed a beneficiary. Nothing can be more common or more useful. But the word is now loosely applied to a certain class of commercial agreements and, by reason of a popular and unreasoning dread of their effect, the term itself has become contaminated" (Dwight 1888: 592).

Figure 1: *"Crushing the Scorpion of Anarchy, But Sparing the Octopus of Monopoly"*

Harper's Weekly, January 21, 1888. (Quoted in Orbach/Rebling 2012: 615)

had told him earlier that he did not feel "American" ("What gountry hass a poor man got, Mr. Marge?"). March fails completely to engage the actual Lindau's politics. Their exchange sets up an explicit contrast in their understanding of the (trust) relationship between citizens and business. Lindau sees this as essentially predatory. When March claims that any American would be happy to "lend [Lindau] a hand for the one you gave us all," his response is summarily dismissive, and is explained by a lack of trust in the people who support the current system.

Interestingly, in spite of his supposed intellectual credentials, March does not counter, is not able to counter, Lindau with any sort of argument about why trust is to be expected. The only response he can provide is naive patriotism (essentially: Americans, simply because they are Americans, are decent—trustworthy—people). Howells, the author of the novel as a thought-experiment, clearly understands this: he is endorsing neither March's unreflective naivete, nor Lindau's incoherent radical leftism that dismisses the Americans in the street by confusing them with their institutional oppressors. Rather, Howells draws our attention to the reasonable synthesis of these two extremes, which recognizes that money, the law, and financial institutions in fact *embody* the necessary basic levels of trust required for a city based on economic expectations to function. As Geoffrey Hosking writes: "Money and financial institutions underpin the *minimal* trust necessary to the never ceasing human activity of trade in goods and services. ... This is the basis of capitalism" (Hosking 2016: 196).

The key here is the word "minimal." As the further developments in the novel make clear, especially the ending, Lindau's distrust is not a solution, but it is similarly clear that in the eyes of Lindau, March is not trustworthy either. When March enlists Lindau's services for the magazine, he realizes from the beginning that Lindau would find it impossible to accept a salary if he knew that it came from Dryfoos, the capitalist, "who had got his money together out of every gambler's chance in speculation, and all a schemer's thrift form the error and need of others" (*A Hazard* 211). But March just glosses over this, and thus effectively betrays his friend's trust. To make matters worse, March organizes a dinner at Dryfoos's house, where Lindau is also invited. Since both Dryfoos and Lindau are convinced of the rightfulness of their positions, there is no polite, non-committal conversation, and once Dryfoos learns about Lindau's radicalism, he insists on dismissing him from the magazine. March, however, refuses to do so, and is ready to resign himself, when Lindau turns up at his doorstep and returns the money he was already paid: "It iss not hawnest mawney... I feel as if dere vas ploodt on it" (*A Hazard* 402).

The idiomatic personification of the money as "honest" needs to be seen here in the larger context of Lindau's trust in American society. Since the money is of course only a synecdoche for a system that Georg Simmel first characterized as trust-based, this kind of trust can also involve an additional element of faith that "can vary in strength and importance" (Möllering 2001: 406). For Lindau, his lack of trust in the "system" does not allow him to make any compromises; his trust, or distrust, is fundamental (religious connotation intended). Additionally, the association with "blood" foreshadows the tragic ending of the novel.

The description of the situation, in which Lindau and Conrad die, is told from an omniscient perspective:

> The officer lifted his club, and the old man threw his left arm up to shield his head. Conrad recognized Lindau ... and he was going to say to the police-man: "Don't strike him! He's an old soldier! You see he has no hand!" but he could not speak, could not move his tongue. The policeman stood there; he saw his face; it was not bad, not cruel; it was like the face of a statue, fixed, perdurable—a mere image of irresponsible and involuntary authority. Then Conrad fell forward, pierced through the heart by that shot fired from the car. (*A Hazard* 470).

The specifics leave no doubt that both Lindau and Conrad are victims of random violence. At the same time, the symbolism of the scene is striking: Lindau, the old man without a hand, an iconic part of the body, standing for power, agency, but also for innocence and unity, lacks all agency, and cannot even effectively protect himself. Conrad, who wants to help him, cannot move his tongue, and is thus unable to articulate the truth. The police on the opposing side are part of the institutional infrastructure that is supposed to guarantee order, and also protection for the citizens, but as presented in this scene, it is just the tool of "irresponsible and involuntary authority." Such authority is, by definition, not trustworthy. Applying Tilly's and Hosking's categories here, we can again identify the rise of the relevance, and, in this case, the tragic failure, of strong, thin trust in modern, especially urban (anonymous, coordinated) environments (Hosking 2016, Tilly 2009).

The death of Lindau and Conrad is the climax of the novel, followed by a long denouement in which the individual responsibilities of the characters are reflected. In a striking omission, the role of the police as the "mere image of irresponsible and involuntary authority" is not addressed at all. There is no room to follow up on this here, but the lacuna is all the more surprising given Howells's involvement in trying to save the so-called Haymarket anarchists, who, as Howells wrote: "were put to death in the prime of the freest Republic the world has ever known, for their opinions' sake" (Unpublished letter to the *New York Tribune*, November 11, 1877, quoted in Goodman/Dawson 2005: 284).

About the Picturesque "Poseuse": How Can She Be Trusted?

The third thought-experiment I look at in *A Hazard of New Fortunes* is concerned with the changing role of women in American society, and, more specifically, with the question why women were generally not trusted to be able to take on public functions. The last decades of the nineteenth century were characterized by industrialization, urbanization, the closing of the frontier, and immigration—but also by the rapidly growing public activities of female reform activists (Buenker 1971; Matthews 1992; McCammon et al. 2001; Perry 2002; Schüler 2004). The most important manifestation of these was the struggle for the vote, but women advocated many other causes beside suffrage. The often-charitable projects in urban settings were carried forward by some well-known icons, but also by countless middle-class women who are forgotten today. The main arguments against female public activity followed a pattern based on the notion that women were incapable of taking over public roles because of their essential "femininity": women could not be trusted in public tasks and offices, no matter how well prepared they were, because they were women. This idea was directly tied to what was seen as their most important function in society: their reproductive role, or, as the rhetoric of the time put it, the holy role of motherhood, which included also the potentiality of becoming a mother, or the missed opportunity to have become one. Thus, it was imperative that women remained in their "separate spheres."[21]

Nevertheless, by the end of the nineteenth century, women, especially in urban environments, had become active in public roles: as reformers, journalists, and organizers. In her article, "Men Are from the Gilded Age, and Women are from the Progressive Era," Elizabeth Perry focuses on the careers of those female activists whose contributions to this era are often overlooked—simply because they were not always explicit about their motives, out of fear to appear "unsexed" (Perry 2002:3). This strategy acknowledged society's general suspicion of women with public agency, or those wielding any form of power. The

---

21   The first ideological cornerstones in the construction of the "separate spheres" ideology in US history were laid during the foundation of the Republic. When Abigail Adams admonished her husband John Adams to "Remember the Ladies" in 1776, with little success. The "ladies" were instead offered the task of bringing up men for public office. Later, this cult of "republican motherhood" merged with the Victorian "angel of the house" or "true woman" paradigm, emphasizing even more that women would lose their femininity if they pursued professional or political careers (Klaiber 2005: 476–77; Kelley 1984).

degree of distrust that activist women had to contend with becomes immediately apparent in anti-suffrage caricatures. Beside the predominant motifs showing women activists as negligent mothers and frigid shrews, their appearance was also a popular way of suggesting that women were not trustworthy:

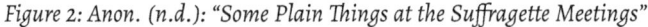

Figure 2: Anon. (n.d.): "Some Plain Things at the Suffragette Meetings"

University of Northern Iowa, Palczewski Suffrage Postcard Archive.

It seems paradoxical that it was possible to question women's motives and thus the extent to which they could be trusted to seriously participate in public life on the seemingly contradictory (not to mention irrelevant) grounds that they were thought to be either too ugly, *or* too pretty. But these two caricatures display their true meaning exactly in this juxtaposition: as an expression of the same kind of distrust stretched across the spectrum of possible perceptions of women as "vain" creatures, who could not be trusted to have truly political motives. The aspect of "spectacle" in the male (and conservative female) view of women is part of an argument that rendered them untrustworthy—something which can also be observed in *A Hazard of New Fortunes*.

Historians of the female reform movements have demonstrated in detail how political and institutional factors led to the weakening of the "sepa-

Figure 3: James Montgomery Flagg: "We Don't Want A Thing—We Are Just Showing Off"

THE AMERICAN SUFFRAGETTES

Flagg 1907

rate sphere" ideology (Buechler 2013; Langley 1998; Schüler 2018; Dubois et al 2019). Although trust in women outside the home did not appear overnight, there are only a few cursory discussions of the dynamic of trust relationships in the historiography of the women's movement, and none at all, as far as I can find, in theoretical discussions of scholars writing about trust.[22] In spite of the fact that the changing perception of women is related to various established trust-related analytical categories (for example, to the role of social

---

22   In her comparative study on women's movement and social reform, Anja Schüler refers to the conviction of early German reformers such as Alice Salomon and other, less known activists, that social reform is not conceivable without trust in the helping hand, which is even more effective if it is offered by a female to a female (Schüler 2004: 197, 202). But this relationship concerns charity, not the public perception of women in general. In other recent studies by Denney (2018), and Rosenblatt (1999) the role of trust is of course implicit, but not explicitly discussed. Other influential studies on trust have been silent on the subject (Hardin 2002; Frevert 2013; Hosking 2016; Hartmann 2020).

capital, to institutional trust, or to the definition of trust relationships as encapsulated interest, etc.) it seems that neither philosophers, nor historians, nor sociologists have undertaken a study of trust with respect to gender, or for short, "gender trust."[23] The existing research on trust and gender is currently centered on empirical surveys or on case studies comparing female to male behavior when it comes to well-defined, mostly institutional, political, sociological, psychological, and economic interactions (Jeanquart-Barone/Sekaran 1994).[24]

The historical study of changing dimensions and limits of gender trust faces two major methodological problems: First, it is not possible to conduct surveys in the past, a popular—although often problematic—way to collect data about trust. Second, since "trust" is not an established analytical category in historical gender studies, it is also not possible to gather systematically scholarly observations from previous work. Here, it is again literature that we can turn to, and, in particular, returning to Howells's novels of manners, we can see that the question of trust and trustworthiness was indeed of relevance when the most momentous changes in gender relations first began to manifest themselves in public contexts.

Howells wrote a fair amount about the changing role of women in the cultural sphere of the late nineteenth century. The "feminization" of the realist artist has been discussed elsewhere (Miller 1990), and there are also several studies about the female figures in his works. Some of these results and conclusions are, however, distorted by what we now recognize as an underlying and unresolved category error: the definitions of the "essence" of femininity (historical view), as opposed to the implicit denial that such an "essence" exists in the first place (the contemporary, performative view of gender) are often not sufficiently acknowledged. It is easy to find statements in Howells's

---

23   For example, a recent publication on the "Invisible Power of Trust," by philosopher Martin Hartmann (2020), discusses a great number of interpretations of trust relationships, but there is no reference to the significant historical change in gender trust, i.e. how the perception of women's trustworthiness in public and professional life has changed. Or on how it perhaps has not changed: As a commentary on this point see Devorah Blachor's satirical "I Don't Hate Women Candidates—I Just Hated Hillary and Coincidentally I'm Starting to Hate Elizabeth Warren" (2019).

24   Peters's 2018 monograph *Trust Women* carries the term "trust" in the title, but it discusses current debates on reproductive justice. A similarly promising paper with the title "A Feminist Re-Reading of Theories of Late Modernity: Beck, Giddens, and the Location of Gender" by Mulinari and Sandell does not discuss trust at all.

work which, from today's perspective, sound antiquated and are dominated by stereotypes of how women supposedly "are."[25] But the representations of polyphonic opinions in his novels automatically provide views on both con-servative and progressive developments side by side. Additionally, his liminal status as observer of social change accounts for his insights into details of the *processes* of societal transformation.

Margaret Vance's rite of passage from a young and beautiful socialite to her involvement in the social gospel movement helping the poor presupposes an urban environment and takes place before the backdrop of the countless reform and charitable organizations existing in New York at the time (Boyer 1978; Boehm/Corey 2017:141–182). Her "case" as a thought-experiment with respect to trust and trustworthiness in the perception of women is low-key at the beginning, but towards the end of the book she steps into the foreground, and her controversial role in the plot becomes apparent.

Miss Vance's function in the final section of the novel is tied to the strike of the streetcar workers discussed above. She is sympathetic to the strike and the plight of the workers (even calling them even "true heroes"), and is concerned about their fate in the violent conflicts with the police. She thinks somebody should try to act as an intermediary and considers going herself to the scene of the fighting, but decides against it, as she explains to her friend Conrad: "I have wanted to go and try; but I am a woman, and I mustn't! I shouldn't be afraid of the strikers, but *I'm afraid of what people would say!*" (468, my empha-sis). Thus, her conflict is caused by the rules of expected gender behavior: she wants to go, and has no reason to be afraid of the strikers, but she is too wor-ried about public perception. Conrad, as a conventional male, is not capable of distinguishing "fear of conflict" from "fear of public censure." Overcome by infatuation and the "trust she had shown him" Conrad approaches the scene of the fighting (ibid. 469). Following public gender expectations, Conrad should be there, yet as a meek and rather passive individual, he should not. Before he can say or do anything, he is killed, without affecting the outcome of the fight.

In the aftermath of Conrad's death, Miss Vance has the vague and unde-fined worry that she was somehow responsible for it. Since the readers have been granted insight into Conrad's thought, they know that yes, indeed, she

---

25   In her essay "The Feminization of American Realist Theory," Elise Miller has done just that and gathered many of his statements about women in general, and female writers in particular (Miller 1990).

was responsible—but not in the way she thinks. Conrad went to the demonstration out of the wish to impress *her*, to honor her "trust" in him, but therein lies a fatal misunderstanding on his part. Miss Vance expressed just general "gender trust" in his masculine role, while Conrad carried it into the realm of individual, interpersonal trust, hoping to impress her: "Was not that what she meant when she bewailed her woman's helplessness? She must have wished him to try if he, being a man could not do something ... thinking of her pleasure in what he was going to do, *he forgot almost what it was*" (469, my emphasis).

The differences are crucial: Miss Vance did not think she was not capable, but she worried about how breaking the conventions of expected gender performance would look. The momentous role of a *visible* performance is expressed again after Conrad's funeral and a meeting with the March couple. Especially Isabel March is perplexed and unsure about her: "She is a strange being; such a mixture of the society girl and the saint" (482). The "riddle" continues when, in a later encounter, the Marches see Miss Vance again, this time at the deathbed of the anarchist Lindau:

> They both stopped. Lindau's grand, patriarchal head, foreshortened to their view, lay white upon the pillow, and his broad, white beard flowed upon the sheet, which heaved with those long last breaths. Beside his bed Margaret Vance was kneeling; her veil was thrown back and her face was lifted; she had clasped between her hands the hand of the dying man she moved her lips inaudibly (493).

This scene, which remains uncommented upon, is like a tableau vivant, i.e. a live recreation of a painting. The description is also painterly, talking about foreshortening, describing the visible surfaces of expression; it is a "word-picture" that emphasizes Miss Vance's appearance. And, indeed, a couple of pages later, Isabel March returns to the question of "how did she look" (503), because: "[Isabel March] had her feminine misgivings; she was not sure but the girl was something of a *poseuse, and enjoyed the picturesqueness*, as well as the pain" (503, my emphasis). Her husband indicates he does not agree, but it seems that he does not want to get into an argument with his conservative wife, who worries that too much female public reform work would be "rather dismal for the homes" (504).[26]

---

26   Howells references here the well-known phenomenon of conservative female anti-suffrage attitudes (Perry 2002:37).

The final scene of the novel, when the Marches meet a joyful Miss Vance in the uniform of a charitable "sisterhood" on the street, provides closure to the thought experiment whether women can be trusted to take on roles outside their "womanly" and domestic circles; for example, as social reformers. As in the caricatures mentioned earlier in this chapter, or in the scenes in which Isabel March accuses Miss Vance of being a vain "poseuse," it is again the interpretation of a visible social performance which is at stake. In this final case, however, there is an added extra complexity, because ‚this time, Miss Vance looks back at the Marches, who "felt that the peace that passeth understanding had looked at them from her eyes"[27] implying that she no longer feels guilty about Conrad's death. Still, Isabel March is not entirely convinced, but this time her husband has the final word: "Well, we must trust that look of hers" (552). "Look" can mean two things here: Miss Vance's own active gaze, but also "how she looks"—in other words, her appearance as a woman that had previously invited so much negative, distrustful commentary from Isabel March's conservative perspective. The phrasing of the sentence, especially the use of the modal "must," implies, moreover, a general *imperative* to trust.[28] Trust theory suggests that cultural trust-networks stabilize situations of uncertainty (Hartmann 2020: 145), yet Mr. March's statement returns to a moment of self-authorization, a crucial component in dynamic situations where epistemological questions ("how can we know whom or what to trust") also play a role.

Conclusion

Trust is often said to be in a crisis today,[29] but, in fact, there is nothing new about crises of trust. Indeed, not only are such crises a recurring feature in the history of the developed democracies, but they are invariably accompanied (in fact documented) by contemporary analytic commentary—that commentary being a valuable resource for social history. In his novels, Howells was not just a prolific chronicler of his milieu; he was one of the most sociopolitically aware authors of his time, and, in particular, a careful analyst of

---

27   The phrase refers to a biblical quotation, Philippians 4:7, but the context distances it
      from a religious interpretation.
28   For a discussion of trust as something we can always rightfully demand from others,
      see Hertzberg (1988).
29   See the most recent results of the Edelman Trust Barometer project (Edelman, 2019).

the ways particular social disruptions challenged "incorporated" America. In *A Hazard of New Fortunes*, he applies his realist poetics to the problem of describing—and analyzing—the phenomena of trust and trustworthiness in the first American metropolis, New York. Although Howells never presents an explicit analytical framework (there is no reason why, as a novelist, he should), we can clearly discern a theory of trust that is remarkably congruent with later theoretical frameworks (such as the "thick/thin," "weak/strong" classification of Hosking), and that can be viewed as a sophisticated attempt to investigate both the dynamics and the limits of "strong, thin," trust relationships and their importance for an understanding of 19th century American urban society.

Works Cited

Anon. (n.d.): "Some Plain Things at the Suffragette Meeting," in: University of Northern Iowa, Palczewski Suffrage Postcard Archive. https://scholarwor ks.uni.edu/suffrage_images/733/ (accessed April 22, 2020).

Arms, George Warren (1939): "Further Inquiry into Howells's Socialism," in: *Science & Society* 3.2, 245–248.

Baier, Annette (1986): "Trust and Antitrust," in: *Ethics* 96, 231–260.

Blachor, Devorah (2019). "I Don't Hate Women Candidates—I Just Hated Hillary and Coincidentally I'm Starting to Hate Elizabeth Warren," *McSweeney's*, December 30, 2019, https://www.mcsweeneys.net/articles/ i-dont-hate-women-candidates-i-just-hated-hillary-and-coincidentally-im-starting-to-hate-elizabeth-warren. Accessed March 25, 2020.

Blackburn, Simon (2005): *Truth: A Guide for the Perplexed*, London: Allen Lane.

Boehm, Lisa Krissoff / Corey, Steven H. (2017): *America's Urban History*, New York and London: Routledge.

Boyer, Paul (1978): *Urban Masses and Moral Order in America, 1820–1920*, Cambridge: Harvard University Press.

Bramen, Carrie Tirado (2000): "William Dean Howells and the Failure of the Urban Picturesque," in: *New England Quarterly* 73.1, 82–99.

Buechler, Steven M. (1990): *Women's Movements in the United States: Woman Suffrage, Equal Rights, and Beyond*, New Brunswick: Rutgers University Press.

Buenker, John D. (1971): "The Urban Political Machine and Woman Suffrage: A Study in Political Adaptability," in: *The Historian*, 33.2, 264–279.

Cady, Edwin H. / Cady, Norma W. (1983): *Critical Essays on W. D. Howells, 1866–1920*, Boston, MA: G. K. Hall & Co.

Cheape, Charles W. (1980): *Moving the Masses: Urban Public Transit in New York, Boston, and Philadelphia*, Cambridge, MA: Harvard University Press.

Conn, Steven (2014): *Americans Against the City*, Oxford: Oxford University Press.

Cudahy, Brian J. (2002): *How We Got to Coney Island: The Development of Mass Transportation in Brooklyn and Kings County*, New York: Fordham University Press.

Davies, David (2016): "Fictional Truth and Truth through Fiction," in: Noel Carroll / John Gibson (eds.), *The Routledge Companion to Philosophy of Literature*, London, New York: Routledge, 372–381.

Denney, Colleen (2018): *The Visual Culture of Women's Activism in London, Paris and Beyond: An Analytical Art History, 1860 to the Present*. Jefferson NC: McFarland & Company, 2018.

Dwight, Theodore W. (1888): "The Legality of Trusts," *Political Science Quarterly* 3.4, 592–632, https://jstor.org. /stable/2139114 (accessed March 23, 2020).

Elgin, Catherine Z. (2007): "The Laboratory of the Mind," in: John Gibson/Wolfgang Huemer/Luca Pocci (eds.) *A Sense of the World: Essays on Fiction, Narrative, and Knowledge*, London: Routledge. 43–54.

Ernst, Jutta / Matter-Seibel, Martina / Schmidt, Klaus H. (2018): *Revisionist Approaches to American Realism and Naturalism*. Heidelberg: Universitätsverlag Winter, 2018.

Flagg, James M. (1907): "We Don't Want a Thing – We Are Just Showing Off," *Harper's Weekly*, August 10, 1907, Virginia Humanities and Library of Virginia. https://edu.lva.virginia.gov/suffragetttes/wedontwantathing/ (accessed April 23, 2020).

Fluck, Winfried (2018): "Misrecognition, Symptomatic Realism, Multicultural Realism, Cultural Capital Realism: Revisionist Narratives about the American Realist Tradition," in: Jutta Ernst / Martina Matter-Seibel / Klaus H. Schmidt (eds.), *Revisionist Approaches to American Realism and Naturalism*, Heidelberg: Universitätsverlag Winter, 1–34.

Frevert, Ute (2013): *Vertrauensfragen: Eine Obsession der Moderne*, München: C.H. Beck.

Goodman, Susan / Dawson, Carl (2005): *William Dean Howells: A Writer's Life*; Berkeley: University of California Press.

Gronlund, Laurence (1984/1965): *The Cooperative Commonwealth*, Cambridge, MA: Belknap Press of Harvard University Press.

Hardin, Russell (2002): *Trust and Trustworthiness*, New York: Russell Sage Foundation.

Hartmann, Martin (2020): *Vertrauen: Die unsichtbare Macht*, Frankfurt: S. Fischer.

Hertzberg, Lars (1988): "On the Attitude of Trust," in: *Inquiry* 31, 307–22.

Hosking, Geoffrey (2016): *Trust: A History*, Oxford: Oxford University Press.

Howells, William Dean. (1887): "Editor's Study," in: *Harper's Magazine* 76, 154-155. https://archive.org/details/harpersnew76various/page/156/mode/2up . (accessed July 17, 2020).

Howells, William Dean (1890/1952): *A Hazard of New Fortunes*, New York: E.P. Dutton and Company.

Howells, William Dean (1891): *Criticism and Fiction*, New York: Harper and Brothers.

Jeanquart-barone/ Uma Sekaran (1994): "Effects of Supervisor's Gender on American Women's Trust," in: *The Journal of Social Psychology*, 134:2, 253-255. DOI: 10.1080/00224545.1994.9711391 (accessed July 18, 2020).

Jones, Karen (1996): "Trust as an Affective Attitude," in: *Ethics* 107, 4–25.

Kaplan, Amy (1986): "The Knowledge of the Line: Realism and the City in Howells's *A Hazard of New Fortunes*," in: *PMLA* 101.1, 69–81.

Kelley, Mary. (1984): *Private Women, Public Stage: Literary Domesticity in Nineteenth-Century America*, Oxford, New York: Oxford University Press.

Klaiber, Isabell (2005): "Women's Roles in American Society," in: Bernd Engler / Oliver Scheiding (eds.), *Key Concepts in American Cultural History: From the Colonial Period to the End of the 19th Century*, Trier: Wissenschaftlicher Verlag Trier, 475–477.

Konrad, Hans. W. (1986): *Die demokratischen Künste: Howells' Ansichten über die Wechselwirkung von Literatur und Gesellschaft*, Frankfurt: Peter Lang.

Langley, Winston E. (ed.) (1998): *Women's Rights in the United States: A Documentary History*, Westport CT: Praeger.

Matthews, Glenna (1992): *The Rise of Public Woman: Woman's Power and Woman's Place in the United States: 1630–1970*, New York: Oxford University Press.

McCammon, Holly J./ Campbell, Karen E. / Granberg, Ellen /Mowery, Christine (2001): "How Movements Win: Gendered Opportunity Structures and U.S. Women's Suffrage Movements, 1866 to 1919," in: *American Sociological Review* 66.1, 49–70. JStor. (accessed April 23, 2020).

McGrath, Brian S. (2012): "W. D. Howells and the Perplexity of Henry James," in: *American Literary Realism* 44.3, 230–248.

Melzer, Arthur M. (2003): "What Is an Intellectual?," in: Arthur M. Melzer / Jerry Weinberger / M. Richard Zinman (ed.), *The Public Intellectual: Between Philosophy and Politics*, Lanham et al.: Rowman and Littlefield Publishers, 3–14.

Miller, Elise. (1990): "The Feminization of American Realist Theory," in: *American Literary Realism* 23.1, 20-41.

Möllering, Guido (2001): "The Nature of Trust: From Georg Simmel to a Theory of Expectation, Interpretation, and Suspension," in: *Sociology* 35.2, 403–420.

Mulinari, Diana and Sandell, Kerstin (2009): "A Feminist Re-Reading of Theories of Late Modernity: Beck, Giddens and the Location of Gender," *Critical Sociology* 35.4, 493–507, https://journals-sagepub-com.ubproxy.ub.uni-he idelberg.de/toc/crsb/35/4. (accessed May 13, 2020).

Orbach, Barak / Rebling, Grace Campbell (2012): "The Antitrust Curse of Bigness," in: *Southern California Law Review* 85.605, 605–655.

Perry, Elizabeth (2002): "Men Are from the Gilded Age, Women Are from the Progressive Era," in: *The Journal of the Gilded Age and Progressive Era* 1.1, 25–48, JStor. (accessed March 25, 2020).

Peters, Rebecca Todd (2018): *Trust Women: A Progressive Christian Argument for Reproductive Justice*, Boston: Beacon Press.

Puskar, Jason (2018): "William Dean Howells, A Hazard of New Fortunes (1890)," in: *Handbook of the American Novel of the Nineteenth Century*, ed. Christine Gerhardt, Berlin: De Gruyter, 2018, 490–507.

Redling, Erik (2006): *"Speaking of Dialect,"* in: *Translating Charles W. Chesnutt's Conjure Tales into Postmodern Systems of Signification*, Würzburg: Könighausen & Neumann.

Riis, Jakob A. (1890): *How The Other Half Lives: Studies Among the Tenements of New York*, New York: Scribner's Sons.

Sabl, Andrew (2012): *Hume's Politics: Coordination and Crisis in* The History of England, Princeton University Press.

Schüler, Anja (2004): *Frauenbewegung und soziale Reform: Jane Addams and Alice Salomon im transatlantischen Dialog, 1889–1933*, Stuttgart: Steiner.

Schüler, Anja / Sklar, Kathryn Kish / Strasser, Susan, eds. (2018): *Social Justice Feminists in the United States and Germany: A Dialogue in Documents, 1885–1933*, Ithaca, NY: Cornell University Press.

Sedlmeier, Florian (2018): "On the Conditions of the Field Imagination: Realism and William Dean Howells," in: Frank Kelleter / Alexander Starre (eds.), *Projecting American Studies: Essays on Theory, Method, and Practice*, Heidelberg: Universitätsverlag Winter, 81–94.

Simmel, Georg. (1903/1995): "Die Großstädte und das Geistesleben," in: Rüdiger Kramme / Angela Rammstedt / Ottheim Rammstedt (eds.), *Aufsätze und Abhandlungen, 1901–1908*, Frankfurt: Suhrkamp, 116– 131.

Skyrms, Brian (2008): "Trust, Risk, and the Social Contract," in: *Synthese* 160, 21–25.

Strong, Josiah (1885): *Our Country: Its Possible Future and Its Present Crisis*, New York: The American Missionary Society.

Tilly, Charles (2009): *Trust and Rule*, Cambridge: Cambridge University Press.

Trachtenberg, Alan (1982): *The Incorporation of America: Culture and Society in the Gilded Age*, New York: Hill and Wang.

Warren, Mark E. (2017): "What Kinds of Trust Does a Democracy Need? Trust from the Perspective of Democratic Theory," in: Sonja Zmerli / Tom W. G. van der Meer (eds.), *Handbook on Political Trust*, Cheltenham: Edward Elgar Publishing, 33–52.

Wetzel-Sahm, Birgit (1995): *The Novel Ends Well That Ends Faithfully: Strategien der Konfliktlösung im Romanwerk von William Dean Howells*, Frankfurt: Peter Lang.

White, Morton and Lucia (1961): "The American Intellectual versus the American City," in: *Daedalus* 90. 1, 166–179.

Wills, Gary (2002): *A Necessary Evil: A History of American Distrust of Government*, New York, London: A Touchstone Book.

"We believe that we have a right to revelations, visions, and dreams from God"[1]
Joseph Smith, Ralph Waldo Emerson and the Transformation of Religious Authority in the Antebellum Period

Jan Stievermann and Claudia Jetter

Joseph Smith Jr. (1805–1844) and Ralph Waldo Emerson (1803–1882) are rarely viewed or discussed in connection with each other. And there are obvious reasons for this. Both men were separated by readily-apparent and deep-reaching differences, not just in terms of their ideas and teachings but also with regard to their social and cultural position. Raised in humble circumstances and amidst the turmoil of popular revivalism on the Western frontier, the poorly-educated Smith became the self-declared prophet and founder of what would turn into America's most successful new religious movement of the nineteenth century: the Church of Jesus Christ of Latter-day Saints, which, based on the revelations contained in the *Book of Mormon* (first published 1830), claimed to be the consummation of the Jewish and Christian religion. By contrast, Emerson was a rebellious scion of New England's liberal Protestant establishment, who—despite his radical forays into a post-Christian, decidedly un-churchly spirituality—remained deeply rooted in its culture of religious learning and gentility. The *spiritus rector* of the Transcendentalist movement, Emerson produced poems, lectures, and essays that are usually categorized as forms of Romantic literature rather than scripture. It is therefore not altogether surprising that few scholars have compared Smith and Emerson as religious figures. (Albanese 2008; Conkin 1997; Holland 2011; Park 2010) Those who did tended to note similarities in Smith and Emerson's postures as modern-day

---

1   Smith Jr. 2002c: 458–9.

prophets, but usually without a systematic look at deeper affinities as well as differences.

This chapter argues that Smith and Emerson can be understood as responding to the same general and profound crisis of religious authority in early nineteenth-century American Christianity, which will be examined in the first section. The Weberian tradition of sociology provides a useful analytical framework to think through this crisis of religious authority, especially if it is combined with current sociological research on trust as a complementary concept to authority. In this way the careers of Smith and Emerson—as sketched out in the two vignettes to follow—become legible as attempts to come to grips with a dramatic loss of trust in the institutional authority of existing churches as purveyors of salvation, but also the authority of biblical tradition as the fixed and sufficient foundation of a saving faith. The writings of both men then appear as different, but structurally related, attempts at restituting what Weber calls charismatic authority, grounded in an immediate experience of the divine. They did so by various performative practices and through distinct forms of prophetic communication. These prophetic communications are similarly informed by a "tendency to engage scripture through emendation and addition" (Maffly-Kipp 2010: vii; see also Stein 1995), even though they aimed at very different effects, just as they attempted to harness their charismatic authority for opposing ends. While Smith and Emerson each emphasized the possibility of continuing revelation in the modern age and promoted an open canon, they significantly diverged on how they understood revelatory communication and prophecy and, more profoundly, the very nature of religion. Beholden to an inherited Protestant notion of supernatural revelation, Smith claimed for himself the role of the chosen prophet in the long succession of Old and New Testament prophets called to perfect the Judeo-Christian religion and restore Christ's true church in which people should invest their ultimate trust. This new religion and church, however, he understood in fairly conventional terms. Emerson's performance of charismatic authority, by contrast, was rooted in a naturalized understanding of revelation and religion that was at once universalized and highly individualized. In contrast to Smith, Emerson actively worked against any (re-)institutionalization of the charismatic authority that people might ascribe to him and also against the quasi-religious canonization of his writings. Emerson's solution for the religious malaise of his age was a radically-individualized seeker spirituality.

The Post-Revolutionary Crisis and Transformations of Religious Authority

If genuine authority is to be understood, with Weber, as the capacity to elicit voluntary obedience, it is a quality that must be recognized as legitimate (Weber 1968/1992). It therefore has to rest, as Frank Furedi writes, "on a foundation that warrants its exercise." This foundation, according to Furedi, is constituted by basic norms that "provide the resources for narratives of validation" (Furedi 2013: 8–9), which, obviously, vary widely between different cultures, historical communities, and social sphere and are subject to constant change and contestations. While the Weberian tradition tends to conceive of the recognition of legitimate leadership primarily as a cognitive-rational act, research on trust helpfully highlights that the authority people ascribe to individuals or institutions has much to do with emotional attachments and investments in which societal norms are embodied.[2] People recognize authority because they trust it, and they trust it because it is perceived as part of an order that is believed and felt to represent a higher good. The foundational norms and aspirations of which Furedi speaks thus have much to do with a shared sense—embodied as much as cognitive, emotional before it becomes the object of rationalization—of the higher good. "Trust is a passion," Thomas Hobbes wrote in his *Elements of Law* (1640) at the eve of the English Civil War, "proceeding from belief of him from whom we expect or hope for good, so free from doubt that upon the same we pursue no other way" (Hobbes 1640/1889: 40).

The newly-founded United States faced a general crisis of authority and trust even more profound than that of Hobbes's England. The Age of Revolution that began in America, as Shmuel Eisenstadt and Anthony Giddens have pointed out, set into motion a de-ontologizing of traditional social orders, while introducing a new kind of self-reflexivity on all levels (Eisenstadt 2006: esp. 141–142; Giddens 1991: esp. 14–21). As people experienced the collapse of the ancient regime and saw their entire world subject to dramatic change and potential future alteration, trust in every kind of traditional institutional authority eroded. For, as Furedi writes about this period, the past itself "lost some of its authorizing role." In the wake of the Revolution, authority was increasingly perceived as conventional rather than natural, fostering "a climate where authority can be contested, either implicitly or explicitly.

---

2   See for example Frederiksen (2014) or Weber and Carter (2003).

The most important outcome of this process was the gradual dissolution of the authority of tradition—which is the authority of the past" (Furedi 2013: 3). With the crumbling of inherited norms that had long stabilized a hierarchical order based on birth and privilege, distrust pertained not only to traditional institutions as such, but also to the social elites that had customarily controlled them. For America's rising middle-class "traditional arguments about the sanctity of hierarchy and authority lost much of their capacity to motivate" (Furedi 2013: 246). The new form of government by consent invested ultimate sovereignty in the people. Thus, institutions and their representatives now had to actively garner and constantly sustain authority through effective performance of leadership for the perceived public good and by command of public opinion. Indeed, the fierce battles over public opinion and winning the trust of the people became one of the hallmarks of America's emerging partisan democracy. The project of government by consent and command of public opinion also raised much concern and created countertendencies based on new ideals of social order, leadership, and authority hailed as natural or divine, and thus as absolute, rather than conventional and negotiable.

These post-revolutionary changes also impacted the realm of religion in the US, which, at the time, was overwhelmingly Protestant but internally diversified into a great number of churches. In the Christian tradition, religious authority is ultimately situated in God alone. By way of mediation, it is recognized in the charisma of the patriarchs, prophets, apostles and, most fully, in Jesus Christ—all of whom are believed to be from God and lead to God. The institutional and traditional authority of the church and the offices of its representatives are an extension of this mediatory function. They rest on trust in its ability to provide access to and correctly administer the means of God's grace and secure for the believer the salvation and blessings won by the Son of God and redeemer of the world, Jesus Christ. Especially in the Protestant context, the trust in this ability was closely tied to the correct interpretation of the Holy Scriptures as the authoritative record of God's revelation to mankind. In the post-revolutionary United States, the full dynamic—first unleashed by the Reformation—of inner-Christian division into competing confessional churches based on opposing scriptural interpretations came to be felt. A pluralistic and highly dynamic denominationalism developed. With the constitutional guarantee of religious freedom as an inalienable natural right of every citizen and disestablishment on the federal and state level, the realm of religion became increasingly hived off and internally differentiated. Just as religious dissent had contributed to the American Revolution, the new democratic dispensation furthered the problematization of traditional forms of religious authority. Americans more and more refused to simply accept by force of custom the mediatory function of a given church or trust its scriptural warrant. As Emerson perceptively put it in his early lecture "The Present Age": "We have lost all reverence for the state. It is merely our boardinghouse. We have lost all reverence for the Church; it is also republican" (Emerson 1964b: 169). Under the republican dispensation, for a church to elicit recognition of its authority required voluntary consent and thus active trust-building.

From the beginning, the American tendency to distrust a strong centralized state was tied to similar distrust of European-style ecclesial hierarchies and clerical elites—a distrust that was now freely articulated in popular print and newspapers. This de-legitimization was pushed forward from different sides. It involved voices of Enlightenment skepticism, such as Thomas Paine (1737–1809), as much as representatives of popular Protestant "sects" seeking freedom from previous religious monopolies such as the famous Baptist leader Isaac Backus (1724–1806). By the 1830s, most Americans would have agreed that religion was a matter of choice based on the individual's freedom of conscience, and that churches should operate on principles of voluntarism.

The effects of this tendency were readily apparent in the crises of the formerly established churches, most prominently the Anglican Church, but they worked, more or less subtly, within every single denomination. Nathan Hatch described these effects in his classical study as *The Democratization of American Christianity* (1989), claiming that "the early republic was the most centrifugal epoch in American church history. It was a time when the momentum of events pushed toward the periphery and subverted centralized authority and professional expertise" (Hatch 1989: 15). The resulting populist turn in American Protestantism was most strongly felt on the Western frontier, where a lack of available clergy and a general vacuum of institutional structures exacerbated the erosion of traditional forms of religious authority as new waves of massive revivals hit the area. The West was also a hotspot in the rapid pluralization of the American religious landscape that resulted from disestablishment, increasing and more diversified immigration, as well as racial and ethnic divisions that led to the founding of many new denominations in the United States. These trends were compounded by the countless church schisms and new religious movements that arose in the context of revivalism. In such an environment, churches and religious groups more and more had to work and compete for the trust of people, if they wished to retain and recruit members.

Most historians of religion, including Hatch, have viewed this process as a liberation and successful individualization that made an important contribution to the growth of democratic culture more generally. Indeed, many Americans at the time hailed this emerging marketplace of religion as an expression of Protestant and republican liberty that gave power and choices to people also in matters of ultimate concern. For many others, however, it was a veritable Babel of confusion that induced insecurity and anxiety. Assuming that there was only one true religion, how was one to pick it out from amidst all the false options? If a church and its ministers were to lead people on the way to salvation, how could the authority of their rites and teachings be dependent on the assent of the people? A number of recent studies have foregrounded the widely felt confusion and spiritual frustration amidst America's denominational chaos and the upheavals of the Second Great Awakening (Bratt 2004; Porterfield 2012).

In his autobiographical "History, 1838" Joseph Smith remembers how, as a young man, he experienced the surrounding diversity and the absence of a generally recognized religious authority as deeply unsettling—as something that threw him back upon himself in the search for a saving truth:

> Presbyterians were most decided against the Baptists and Methodists, [...].
> On the other hand the Baptists and Methodists in their turn were equally
> Zealous in endeavoring to establish their own tenets and disprove all others.
>
> In the midst of this war of words, and tumult of opinions, I often said to
> myself, what is to [be] done? Who of all these parties are right? Or are they all
> wrong together? And if any one of them be right which is it? And how shall I
> know it? (Smith Jr. 2002a: 229)

Overzealous Baptist and Methodists might have made few inroads into Boston. Religious pluralization and the struggles attending it, however, were hardly any less intense in America's capital of liberal Protestantism and spiritual experimentation. With the old Congregationalist unity and ascendancy gone, countless options vied for the attention and trust of Boston's genteel class. Looking back over the New England scene in 1860, Emerson would write in "Worship": "The stern old faiths have all pulverized. 'Tis as whole population of gentlemen and ladies out in search of religion" (Emerson 2003: 108).

The pulverization of the stern old faiths, like the dynamics of religious experimentation and diversification, was connected to another dimension of the crisis of religious authority that went deeper than distrust in traditional clerical elites and forms of church government. At the very same time that traditional and institutional authority came under pressure, American Protestantism was thrown into further turmoil as the trust in its inherited *auctoritas auctoritatum* came to be shaken: the Bible. Deist attacks on Scripture as a deeply irrational and mythic text à la Paine's *Age of Reason* had gained considerable traction in the early nineteenth century; even among common folk (Porterfield 2012). In more elite circles, a revolutionary type of histori-cal-contextual criticism from Europe, notably Germany, did much to dispel orthodox Protestant beliefs in the unity and infallibility of the Bible as the inspired Word of God (Grusin 1991; Packer 2007).

While a full-blown de-supernaturalization and historicization of the Bible remained confined to the upper echelons of society, few Americans during the antebellum period would have escaped the sense that the authority of Scrip-ture was not what it used to be. For more than anything, the forces of religious freedom and democratization were—albeit wholly unintentionally—under-mining its foundations. Unshackled from the restraints of binding traditions, institutional control, and clerical oversight, scriptural interpretation in ante-bellum American Protestantism multiplied to an unprecedented degree. Every religious debate and church schism saw scriptural arguments tossed back and forth, contributing to this proliferation of opposing readings. Many religious reform movements aimed to restore the unity of the church on purely scrip-tural grounds and ended up adding another denomination to the American religious marketplace. The self-declared Restorationist movement of Barton Stone and Alexander Campbell that gave birth to the Disciples of Christ is only the most obvious example here. An overwhelming number of different Bible translations and commentaries flooded the print market (Gutjahr 2000). Self-taught individuals, in the spirit of the prevalent "common sense realist"-approach to the Bible, turned to their own private judgment as they attempted to decipher the mysteries of the Word, especially the Book of Revelation (Noll 2005). In the early 1840s, William Miller gained widespread attention and a large following with his predictions about the imminent coming of the return of Christ. He was not the only exegete-turned-prophet of this kind.

For those who put their trust in these inspired exegetes, these interpre-tations might have, at least temporarily, cured the crisis of biblical authority. For those who did not trust figures like Miller or Smith, this flood of com-peting interpretations was only further evidence for how malleable biblical texts were. Especially to intellectuals like the Transcendentalists, who already harbored radical doubts about the divine stature, coherence, exclusivity, and final truth of the Bible, the exegetical "civil wars" that swept the US during the antebellum period would have deepened their skepticism that this book alone provided a reliable and permanent basis for modern religion. But even to seminary theologians and ordinary "Bible Christians" with a firm faith in the divine stature of Scripture it became painfully apparent that the good book could not be simply referred to as an unquestionable, unified source of authority, from which an unambiguous message of salvation and precepts for modern life could be derived. As they watched with frustration how interpreters tried and failed to settle central questions of religious and political life (what was the nature of Jesus Christ and his relation to the Father? Was slavery biblically sanctioned or a sin?), they felt keenly the wide distance between nineteenth-century America, the biblical texts, and the historical realities behind them. Could this gap be bridged by better interpretations, be it in terms of method, be it in terms of piety? Or was further divine communication possible and indeed necessary to fill out the lacunae in Scripture, maybe even to fulfill its true meaning only incompletely revealed in the canonical Bible? As Seth Perry has recently argued, the canonical Protestant Bible was still widely regarded as the most important source of authority during this period, but in actual cultural practice it was an increasingly contested site of authority which created "authoritative relationships" that were constantly renegotiated within and among religious groups as well as the larger public (Perry 2018). Hence the problematization of biblical authority and the problematization of ecclesial and clerical authority kept feeding each other.

The outcome of this crisis, however, was not simply a diminishment of religious authority per se; certainly not in the sense that would neatly fit into older grand narratives of secularization. After all, religious life in America flourished, even though it took forms increasingly different from those of the Old World. Nineteenth-century American Christianity could not and did not dispense with need for religious authority—even in its most populist strands. Rather, the post-revolutionary crisis brought forth changing configurations of religious authority and trust that found embodiment in new types of leadership, communication, church structures, devotional practices, and approaches to Scripture, together with fresh conceptualizations of the divine and its relation to humanity and revelation. Two general trends are observable in these processes. One is that religious authority becomes increasingly and self-consciously performative. Under the conditions of denominationalism and voluntarism, the recognition of one's authority from God now has to be more actively pursued and negotiated; it can no longer be taken for granted, is highly instable, and in constant need of re-affirmation. The other trend is that the ultimate locus of recognition is the individual and its experience. Men and women have to personally experience a message or practice as convincing, meaningful, and, ultimately, potent with divine power, or else, in the long run, they will not keep attending to them. Heightened participation is crucial to this. But what changes most dramatically across the American religious landscape are the modes of communication, now geared toward actively eliciting trust from the respective target audiences, and constantly appealing to individual experience. Besides innovative oratory and literary styles, a uniquely American type of religious evidentialism is part of this development. In preaching and print, religious authority has to be asserted by recourse to persuasive evidence, whether textual, commonsensical, empirical, or even somatic. The pronounced supernaturalism of American popular religion, with its proclivity for signs and wonders, ecstasies and revelations, is very much part of this. The performativity of religious authority also involves new forms of recourse to, and legitimization of, scriptural authority that foreground experientialism. In this, the boundaries often become fluid between biblical exegesis and forms of "devotional creativity" (Maffly-Kipp 2010: vii), in which inspired or visionary readings of the Bible turned into prophetic productions of new quasi-scriptural texts.

The resulting configurations of authority and trust are very diverse, often contradictory, and inadequately described by the totalizing category of "democratization"—although that process is certainly part of the picture. This is not the place to go into a fuller discussion of the different paths that American denominations took in adjusting to the new circumstances. Suffice it to say here that all denominations, to some degree, felt the necessity to replenish ecclesial authority by transforming the structures of church government and worship to balance traditional forms of institutional, clerical, creedal, and scriptural authority with the principles of voluntarism, lay participation, and the empowerment of ordinary Christians. Moreover, they had to work hard for a more effective socio-cultural accommodation of their congregations in terms of class, race, ethnicity, education, and style. These accommodations led to a great deal of differentiation and the founding of more and more churches even within the same denominational family. A key factor in these adjustments were communication styles and practices well-attuned to the needs and sensibilities of a highly diverse and stratified population. Some of the new religious movements that emerged in response to the pervasive revivalism, including the Latter-day Saints, combined steeply hierarchical, even authoritarian, models of church polity with a strong emphasis on lay priest-hood, while others, like Transcendentalism or Spiritualism, were more con-ducive to a hyper-individualized seeker spirituality.

In the second half of this chapter we will focus on one specific re-configu-ration of authority and trust that was uniquely characteristic of the American religious scene especially, but not exclusively, during the antebellum period: the restitution of what Max Weber called charismatic authority. For Weber, *charisma* is the original form of all religious authority, before its, from his per-spective, inevitable routinization and institutionalization. It has its purest ex-pression in the figure of the prophet and thaumaturge who "is set apart from ordinary men and treated as endowed with supernatural, superhuman, or at least specifically exceptional powers or qualities." Because of their gifts of the spirit, or charisma, that "are regarded as of divine origin " (Weber 1968/1992: 48), people follow such figures and their teachings. In a situation where inher-ited institutions and ways of doing church failed to convince, and Scripture appeared doubtful, not a few Americans once again felt the pull of charismatic authority embodied in and performed by exceptional preachers, writers, or even self-declared prophets and miracle workers. The spectrum of such fig-ures in antebellum America was as wide as the religious landscape itself. It reached from spell-binding revivalist preachers, such as the fabled Lorenzo Dow (1777–1834), who used their gifts in the service of conveying the gospel and expanding an existing church, to American thaumaturges and messianic figures like Jacob Cochran (1782–1836) or Robert Matthews (1788–c. 1841), who healed, resurrected the dead, and proclaimed themselves divine. It also in-cluded a host of new prophets that produced a variety of American scriptures. Weber himself saw Joseph Smith with his *Book of Mormon* as a truly extraor-dinary new example of a charismatic prophet in the modern world (Weber et al. 2013, 491–492). There were many more, however, including, as we wish to argue, genteel "apostles of culture" (Robinson 1982) like Emerson, who mes-merized their audiences not by miracles or golden plates, but by the poetic expression of their revelatory spiritual insights drawn from a direct experi-ence of God in nature and history.

Joseph Smith Jr.—The "Ethical Prophet"

In 1842, Joseph Smith, founder and prophet of the Mormon church, had been asked by "Chicago Democrat" newspaper editor John Wentworth to write a sketch on the foundation and 12-year history of the Mormon church. Besides recounting the already familiar story of his "First Vision" and the founding of the church, Smith responded with a "Historical Sketch, 1 March 1842," in which he described the hardships and persecutions Mormons had endured, especially during their time in Missouri. In spite of these trying experiences, Smith boldly predicted that

> no unhallowed hand can stop the work from progressing, persecutions may rage, mobs may combine, armies may assemble, calumny may defame, but the truth of God will go forth boldly, nobly, and independent till it has penetrated every continent, visited every clime, swept every country, and sounded in every ear, till the purposes of God shall be accomplished and the great Jehovah shall say the work is done. (Smith Jr. 2002a: 247)

Needless to say, Smith believed God's truth to be exclusively incorporated within the restored sacred order of his church and would continue to be channeled through his person. While the "Sketch" was a refined version of the foundation of Mormonism than earlier accounts, it was more than just a reflection on Smith's life and the twelve-year history of the church. The "Sketch" presented a powerful religious leader who had successfully performed as a modern-day prophet and established a loyal and trusting followership that would thrive as a church within a competitive religious landscape. In several accounts of his life prior to his "First Vision," Smith reported to have witnessed a "great clash in religious sentiment; if I went to one society they referred me to one plan, and another to another; each one pointing to his own particular creed as the summum bonum of perfection." Believing in a consistent God, however, Smith decided to take matters into his own hands and "investigate the subject more fully, believing that if God had a church it would not be split up into factions" (Smith Jr. 2002a: 242). All existing churches therefore had to be wrong and new revelation, as would become apparent in the production of the *Book of Mormon*, was necessary to complement the Christian canon and correct false traditions in order to restore the one salvific Christian church.

In a powerful vision that came upon Smith after meditating on James 1:5, God warned Smith, "that I must join none of them [i.e. existing churches], for they were all wrong, and [...] all their creeds were an abomination in his sight" (Smith Jr. 2002b: 230–1). Substantiating this warning of existing apostate traditions even further, Smith received scorn and encountered skepticism for his revelatory experience by a Methodist minister and fellow citizens (Smith Jr. 2002b: 231). Yet, the hostile reaction would not prevent Smith from continuing to believe in his revelations. Although the production of the *Book of Mormon* and the foundation of the church would take another decade, the future path for Smith had already been made clear in this very first vision: direct divine guidance displaced ecclesiastical tradition and clerical authority. And in this, Smith believed he was following the traditional biblical prophets who similarly faced adversity and rejection. Sharing most Americans' common faith in biblical prophecy, Smith concluded from this experience that he had been chosen as the new mediator between God and the world, conveying divine orders he himself received through supernatural revelations, visions, and auditions. As historian and Smith biographer Richard Bushman has aptly put it, this self-declared modern prophethood created "a fear of the familiar gone awry. Joseph was hated for twisting the common faith in biblical prophets into the visage of the arrogant fanatic," as he had "turned something powerful and valued into something dangerous" (Bushman 2007: 553).

Unlike more spiritualized interpretations of revelation in the antebellum period, Smith believed in an actual, supernatural discourse between the believer and God or, as Terryl Givens has put it, "dialogic revelation" (Givens 2002: 218). And the *Book of Mormon* was a clear case in point of this continual revelation as a process of divine discourse, especially when considering how much divine communication was involved in the production process. Smith received divine instructions from the angel Moroni on how to obtain the plates with the original text. He then translated the plates, at times with the help of seer stones, at other times without. He would receive divine rebukes when breaching the covenant with God and handing out the proof sheets to Martin Harris who then lost them. All these aspects suggest a continuing divine interaction between God and man. The myth around the production testified to God's promise to communicate eternally.

The extent to which revelatory authority was available to other members of the Mormon church continues to be debated until today. Smith did not found a democratic church where all would be equal, but he nevertheless believed the reception of continuing revelation to be the natural right of every believer. Although he was the only one authorized to produce inspired translations and revisions and receive revelations effecting theology and church organization with comprehensive appeal for all believers, he did not think he was essentially different. Writing to a non-Mormon in 1839, Smith argued, that "We believe that we have a right to revelations, visions, and dreams from God, our heavenly Father; and light and intelligence, through the gift of the Holy Ghost, in the name of Jesus Christ, on all subjects pertaining to our spiritual welfare" (Smith Jr. 2002b: 458–9). In correction of Hatch's claim about Smith as a populist within a democratized church, historian Michael MacKay convincingly argued that Smith "established himself as a type of theological king, yet Mormonism succeeded because his concept of kingdom included the ability to distribute the power of governance to other leaders in a form of hierarchical democracy" (MacKay 2020: 2). Smith had been chosen by God in spite of his lack of education but he did not believe that God might elect competing new prophets who would simultaneously reveal new orders.[3] Instead, Smith embedded the "disruptive" element of revelation within a new ecclesial tradition that included additional rites and practices, and a clearly distinguished hierarchical order, and then legitimized it with new scripture. Religious authority thus became centralized, transferring the originally anti-hierarchical "pure charisma" in a routinized form to the highest offices in the church (Weber 1968/1992: 57–58). Smith efficiently created a new distinct tradition, tying elements of religious innovation to specific positions in church governance through new revelations. After all, he was a prophet, not a debater.

The day the church was officially founded on April 6, 1830, Smith received a revelation testifying to him being "a seer, a translator, a prophet, an apostle of Jesus Christ, an elder of the church through the will of God the Father" (Smith Jr. 2013a). Recorded as D&C 21 in the *Doctrine and Covenants*, a collection of authoritative commandments, the revelation established Smith as the central instrument to receive new divine commands from God in order to direct church governance, and directed all other members of the church to submit unto his orders. He was God's mouthpiece, as the "Comforter" had revealed unto him, thus his words would ultimately help bring about Zion (Smith Jr. 2013a). Smith's authority, however, did not remain unchallenged. Between the foundation of the church in April and September, Smith had been confronted with rivalling revelations by Hiram Smith, who professed to have received new divine knowledge with the help of seer stones. Shortly before a conference in September 1830, Joseph Smith received another revelation, now recorded as D&C 28, which responded to the confrontation and eventually dissolved the problem of rivalling revelation. While the "Comforter" may speak to all, only Joseph Smith had been given "the keys of the mysteries" as the head of the church and would therefore receive divine instructions and orders that would

---

3   The fact that he did not publish his "First Vision" until after the publication of *The Book of Mormon* and the foundation of the church, underlines this point. For a discussion on Smith as a visionary, see: Bushman (1997–98).

surpass individual edification. Only the chosen prophet could differentiate between Satan's words and God's and only he should preside over things relating to church governance. "For all things must be done in order, and by common consent in the church " (Smith Jr. 2013b).

Once Smith's position as sole prophet within the church had been cemented, theological innovation would continue to enter the church—but only through him. Revelation provided the mechanism to adjust a church and its tradition to present needs. God provided revelations so that truth could be "adapted to our situation and circumstances [...] to ameliorate the condition of every man under whatever circumstances it may find him" (Smith Jr. 2002b: 458–9). However, the centralized structure did not guarantee peace since new revelation would always pose the danger of upsetting even devout church members, as can be seen in Smith's unsuccessful proposal of plural marriage to the daughter of a leading Mormon. After Smith had introduced plural marriage as a part of the "new and everlasting covenant," many members of the church had been alienated. When Nancy Rigdon, daughter of one of Smith's closest associates, refused to become his plural wife, Smith, by then sole prophet of the church for over a decade, explained why the new doctrine was not unethical but instead part of a new covenant with God: "That which is wrong under one circumstance, may be and often is, right under another. [...] Whatever God requires is right, no matter what it is, although we may not see the reason thereof till long after the events transpire" (Smith Jr. 2002c: 538). That is to say that while plural marriage may seem disturbing at first, it would promote man's happiness in the long run because God had a plan and would make his will known to his people via his mediator Joseph—revelation by revelation.

Emerson—the Weberian "Exemplary Man"

Emerson, of course, would have had nothing but scorn for Smith's supernatural revelations, priestly offices and temple rites. He never dreamed of founding a new church. While there have always been self-declared Emersonians since the nineteenth century, this diverse and diffuse group never organized into a movement with a codified teaching tradition (Schmidt 2012). This has to do with the pronounced anti-institutionalism and anti-traditionalism of Emerson's own lectures and essays. "A religion," he would characteristically say in the eponymous lecture from the series *The Present Age* (1839/40), "that stands on authority, what degradation in the word! What a gulf between the supple soul and its well-being! Man [...] dares not say, I think; I am; but quotes some saint or sage" (Emerson 1972b: 282). Such a religion of authority was dead and no longer sustainable in democratic America. It was the root cause of the "decaying church and a wasting unbelief" (Emerson 1971: 88–9) that Emerson saw around him. Accordingly, Emerson did not wish to be a saint who would be quoted as a formal authority, but rather a sage whose charisma would inspire others to find its divine source inside themselves. In this, Emerson was much indebted to the Romantic discourse on the "religious genius," which, as sociologists of religion have pointed out,[4] also informed Weber's subcategory of charismatic authority: the "exemplary prophet." Such a prophet was one, as Weber writes, who "by his personal example, demonstrates to others the way to religious salvation," and whose preaching "directs itself to the self-interest of those who crave salvation" (Weber 1968/1992: 263). The Emersonian understanding of exemplary prophethood must be seen as part of his post-ministerial, Transcendentalist re-interpretation of religion, which was first fully articulated in several lectures and publications on the topic between 1836 and 1841, including his famous "Divinity School Address" (1838). In these, he radically challenged the exclusivity and finality of Christianity, while, at the same time, propounding a comparative, universalistic concept of religion.

Emerson's Romantic understanding of religion combined metaphysical, epistemological, and moral elements with a strongly experiential and expressivist twist: the divine is experienced primarily in the intuition of spiritual laws as emanations of a non-anthropomorphic divine, or "Over-Soul." These intuitions can also be reflected upon but make an immediate demand upon the individual to obey them by moral self-cultivation, virtuous action, and creative self-expression. In the "Divinity School Address," Emerson speaks of the "moral sentiment" that derives from an intuitive "insight of the perfection of the laws of the soul," and explicitly states that this sentiment is "the essence of all religion" (Emerson 1971: 77). This universalistic concept of religion allows Emerson to integrate a great variety of traditions across different periods and cultures, all of which now appear as historically and locally specific expressions of the religious nature of man without fundamental differences. Emerson thus imagines a religious history of mankind that neither

---

4   Several sociologists have pointed out the similarity between Weber's concept of charismatic leaders and the concept of the artistic or intellectual genius in Thomas Carlyle's *On Heroes*. Cf. Gerth and Mills (1958: 53).

started with nor culminated in the revelation of the canonical Bible and did not have its telos in Jesus Christ. Neither Son of God nor savior, Emerson's Jesus is no longer categorically different from Zoroaster, Muhammad, or Buddha, but appears as a *primus inter pares* among the moral teachers of humanity; one of the "primeval bards and prophets" who could be found among "each portion of mankind" (Emerson 1964a: 90). Provocatively, Emerson included in that group not only the founders and prophets of world religions, but also great philosophers along with more recent religious figures such as George Fox and Emmanuel Swedenborg, as well as major artists like Shakespeare or Milton.

Christianity's relative primacy of purity, for Emerson, was dramatically impaired because the churches had corrupted the historical Jesus's pure teaching through a mythologizing, cultic worship of his person and a false veneration of the Bible. This christocentrism and bibliolatry, which Emerson so forcefully denounced, pointed to a general problem of historical religions. As they, in Weberian terminology, routinized the charisma of their founders, they came to rely on traditional and institutional authority. But this "reliance on authority measures the decline of religion, the withdrawal of the Soul," Emerson asserted in the lecture "Religion" (Emerson 1972b: 282). What he called "historical Christianity" in his address to the Harvard divinity students, suffered from a detrimental "stationariness of religion; the assumption that the age of inspiration is past, that the Bible is closed"; just as much as from "the fear of degrading the character of Jesus by representing him as a man" (Emerson 1971: 89). Such a religion of mediation and tradition led people not to, but away from, the divine.

Emerson's critique of Christian bibliolatry reflected his conviction that revelation was not only progressive but also ought to be understood much more broadly. In contrast to Smith's more conventional views, revelation to Emerson was not a supernatural vision or auditory message sent only to elect men of God during a specific period of time. Like other Transcendentalists, Emerson basically viewed the entire developmental continuum of nature and history as a self-revelation of the divine, and, thus, as a medium through which every individual could have religious experiences. If all experience potentially revealed the divine, the "sacred writings" of all world religions, like great works of art or philosophy, or the teachings of modern prophets merely constituted revelatory media of a higher order: they condensed and interpreted the experiences of original religious geniuses in symbolic-poetic language. By necessity, these revelations took shape in historically conditioned, culture-bound forms, always affected by the limitations and errors of their own age and thus never wholly fitting for a later age. "But the Revelation and the church both labor under one perpetual disadvantage," Emerson announces in the lecture "Religion" from the series *The Philosophy of History* (1836/37). "They need always the presence of the same spirit that created them to make them thoroughly valid." For this reason, "[a]ll attempts to confine and transmit the religious feeling of one man or one sect to another age, by means of formulas the most accurate or rites the most punctual, have hitherto proved abortive" (Emerson 1964a: 93). In this regard, Emerson differed dramatically from Smith's belief in the possibility of a final revelation. There was always the possibility and felt need—if not institutionally suppressed—for new interpretation and expressions. For Emerson, revelation became a continuous, inherently pluralistic, process, co-extensive with humanity's historical development and its cultural achievements. Accordingly, he demanded that "We too must write Bibles, to unite again the heavenly and the earthly world" in a way fitting for the modern age, by revealing the deeper spiritual truth of "all that we know; [...] and first, last, midst, and without end, to honour every truth by use" (Emerson 1987:166).

However, this emphasis on the evolution of religion and the continuity of revelation did not imply a disdain for or a naïve rejection of tradition. No (religious) experience or utterance was made ex nihilo. Indeed, there was a right use of the rich heritage of the past, not as ultimate norm and limitation, but as inspiration and material for further creation. In a journal entry from July 21, 1836, Emerson noted: "Make your own Bible. Select & Collect all those words & sentences that in all your reading have been to you like the blast of trumpet out of Shakespear [sic], Seneca, Moses, John, & Paul" (Emerson 1965: 186). There is no room here to discuss the complex theory of creative reading and (re-)writing that Emerson developed in his lectures and essays, which themselves are woven from a dense fabric of intertextual references, including countless, often very idiosyncratic, readings of biblical citations, as well as passages from Asian scriptures. In very simplified terms, one can say, however, that the period's tendency to "devotional creativity" manifests itself in Emerson as a Romantic program of individualistic, free-wheeling appropriations of inherited canonical texts.

Emerson thus radically democratized religious authority as something theoretically available to all because it was rooted in a universal moral sense and individual spiritual experience. Yet, he also acknowledged massive differences in the degree to which this authority was realized in people. The religious genius was able to perceive more fully the divine in Nature and to effectively communicate this experience to others. The most gifted ones, Emerson described as "divine bards" (Emerson 1971: 83), who, like Jesus, could express their inspired insights in poetic-prophetic discourse that simultaneously harked back to and creatively transcended tradition. Their authoritative voice was enabled by perfect holiness or lack of egotism. Such a person, Emerson wrote in allusion to the Bible, "speaks with authority, and not as the Scribes, he becomes passive to the influence of God, and speaks his words." (Emerson 1991: 123) But this authority, in contrast to Smith, was not conceived of as commanding obedience. Instead, Emerson imagined the office of the "divine bards," past and present, as giving inspiration and "noble provocations," encouraging others "to emancipate [themselves]; to resist evil; to subdue the world; and to Be" (Emerson 1971: 83). Following in the footsteps of the poet-prophet, individuals were to learn to follow their own moral sense and inner genius, to achieve what Emerson calls self-reliance. Emersonian self-reliance must not be misunderstood as a crude notion of personal autonomy, but as a spiritual principle and aspiration of living in communion with the divine through the progressive cultivation of the moral sense—something for which he deemed the guidance of religious teachers indispensable, if only temporarily and in the right spirit. The oft-cited passage from "Self-Reliance," "Trust thyself: every heart vibrates to that iron string, ... [a] man should learn to detect and watch that gleam of light which flashes across his mind from within, more than the lustre of the firmament of bards and sages," does not translate into an imperative of solipsism. Instead, Emerson wants his audience to learn to instinctively recognize "[i]n every work of genius," which they read creatively and for a higher sense, "our own rejected thoughts" (Emerson 1972a: 77). But even the most inspired poet or prophet can only provide fragments—their particular angle—of the divine truth. Ultimately, every teacher was, by necessity, outlived.

Similarly, Emerson always underlined that revelation would not cease and thus new bards with new spiritual insights were always a-coming. Thus, he finished his "Divinity School Address" with a dramatic, John-the-Baptist-like gesture of messianic announcement, expressing his hope to see "the new Teacher, that shall follow so far those shining laws, that he shall see them come full circle" (Emerson 1971: 92). He never saw himself as that figure, however. And he did not expect this "new Teacher," this great religious poet of the modern age, when he would come, to have the final word. Indeed, in Emerson's mind, there never could be an ultimate revelation, a closed canon for all mankind and all ages. For different individuals would, based on their unique experiences, continue to find new and deeper meanings both in nature and in the religious and cultural traditions of the past. If no longer hindered by institutional authorities, people would pursue spiritual self-reliance and become religious geniuses in their own right. Mankind's religious development, in his view, would move forward through a progressive ethicization, de-institutionalization, and individualization of religion.

Emerson thus responded to his disaffection with "churchly" religion by an appeal to charismatic authority, ideally embodied in the religious genius or poet-prophet. His own writings are attempts to generate and convey that kind of charisma. At the same time, Emerson very self-consciously sought to decentralize and democratize charismatic authority by making its performance a vehicle for moral self-culture, the nurturing of spiritual experiences, religious experimentation, and, ultimately, the self-authorization of the democratic individual to which he appealed. Also, the charismatic authority of each prophet was marked as being only relative and temporary. No sacred text embodied the full truth, nor was to have a final, doctrinally fixed, meaning. In this spirit, he routinely undercut his own charismatic authority, always pointing out that he was "only an experimenter," "an endless seeker with no Past at my back" (Emerson 1979a: 188). With formulations like this one, Emerson can be seen as the pioneer of a post-Christian, thoroughly individualized and syncretistic seeker spirituality in the US.

Conclusion

Joseph Smith and Ralph Waldo Emerson were part of the deep-reaching, structural transformations of American Christianity during the first decades of the nineteenth century. Each in his own way exemplifies one specific form among many others that this transformation could take: a turning to what appeared to many a source of religious authority they could trust when established churches and their official Bible interpretations failed to convince - the charisma endowed by immediate relation with the divine. Smith and Emerson illustrate how this anti-traditional attitude required new forms of legitimization. Both no longer relied on ministerial office in an established church, or other kinds of institutional credentials. Instead, they spiritually empowered themselves by persuasive performances of their distinct prophetic personas. Smith, the "ethical prophet," was thus able to found a rapidly growing new church that promised his followers to lead them into latter-day Zion. Thousands of people were happy to trust him with "the authority of a prophet if he would connect them with heaven, and that was the key to his success" (Bushman 2007: 560). Thus, they submitted willingly unto him, as the "common man" Joseph Smith had finally restored the sacred order.

On the other hand, Emerson, the "religious seeker," rejected any institutionalized and centralized form of religious authority and actively worked against the routinization of his charisma. His oratory and literary performances created an enthusiastic but unorganized, highly individualistic circle of Emersonians, seeking to follow their teacher on the path to spiritual self-reliance until they could ultimately shed the need for any mediator. Instead of a new scripture in addition to the canonical Bible, he revealed a method of appropriating existing scriptures by creative higher readings in light of one's own spiritual experience. The teachings of the holy bards of the past were to serve as a means of self-revelation and realization for the modern individual that needed to trust their own "instinct to the end" (Emerson 1979b).

Works Cited

Albanese, Catherine L. (2008): A Republic of Mind and Spirit. A Cultural History of American Metaphysical Religion, New Haven, Conn., London: Yale University Press.

Bratt, James D. (2004): "Religious Anti-Revivalism in Antebellum America," in: Journal of the Early Republic 24/1, 65–106.

Bushman, Richard L. (1997–98): "The Visionary World of Joseph Smith," in: Brigham Young University Studies 37/1, 183–204.

—— (2007): Joseph Smith. Rough Stone Rolling, New York: Vintage Books.

Conkin, Paul K. (1997): American Originals. Homemade Varieties of Christianity, Chapel Hill: Univ. of North Carolina Press.

Eisenstadt, Shmuel N. (2006): Die großen Revolutionen und die Kulturen der Moderne, Wiesbaden: VS Verlag für Sozialwissenschaften.

Emerson, Ralph W. (1964a): "Religion," in: Stephen E. Whicher/Robert E. Spiller/Wallace E. Williams (Eds.), The Early Lectures of Ralph Waldo Emerson, Volume II, Cambridge, Mass.: Harvard University Press, 83–97.

—— (1964b): "The Present Age," in: Stephen E. Whicher/Robert E. Spiller/Wallace E. Williams (Eds.), The Early Lectures of Ralph Waldo Emerson. Volume II, Cambridge, Mass.: Harvard University Press, 157–171.

—— (1965): The Journals and Miscellaneous Notebooks of Ralph Waldo Emerson. Volume V: 1835–1838, Cambridge, Mass.: Belknap Press of Harvard University Press.

—— (1971): "An Address. Delivered Before the Senior Class in Divinity College, Cambridge, Sunday Evening, 15 July, 1838," in: Robert E. Spiller/Alfred R. Ferguson (Eds.), Nature, Addresses and Lectures, Cambridge, Mass.: Belknap Press of Harvard University Press, 71–94.

—— (1972a): "Genius (1839)" in: Robert E. Spiller/Stephen E. Whicher (Eds.), The Early Lectures of Ralph Waldo Emerson, Volume III, Cambridge, Mass.: Belknap Press of Harvard University Press, 68–84.

—— (1972b): "Religion (1840)" in: Robert E. Spiller/ Stephen E. Whicher (Eds.), The Early Lectures of Ralph Waldo Emerson, Volume III, Cambridge, Mass.: Belknap Press of Harvard University Press, 271–85.

—— (1979a): "Circles" in: Alfred R. Ferguson/Joseph Slater (Eds.), The Collected Works of Ralph Waldo Emerson II. Essays: First Series, Cambridge, Mass.: Belknap Press of Harvard University Press, 179–90.

—— (1979b): "Intellect" in: Alfred R. Ferguson/Joseph Slater (Eds.), The Collected Works of Ralph Waldo Emerson II. Essays. First Series, Cambridge, Mass.: Belknap Press of Harvard University Press, 191–206.

—— (1987): The Collected Works of Ralph Waldo Emerson: Volume IV: Representative Men: Seven Lectures. Joseph Slater (Ed.), Cambridge, Mass.: Belknap Press of Harvard University Press.

—— (1991): "CX. Every good and every perfect gift is from above and cometh down from the Father of lights, with whom is no variableness nor shadow of turning. James 1:17," in: Albert J. von Frank (Ed.), The Complete Sermons of Ralph Waldo Emerson. Volume 3, Columbia, Mo.: University of Missouri Press, 118–125.

—— (2003), "Worship" in: Barbara L. Packer/Joseph Slater (Eds.), The Collected Works of Ralph Waldo Emerson: Volume VI. The Conduct of Life, Cambridge, Mass.: Belknap Press of Harvard University Press, 106–28.

Frederiksen, Morton (2014): "Relational trust. Outline of a Bourdieusian Theory of Interpersonal Trust," in: Journal of Trust Research 4/2, 167–192.

Furedi, Frank (2013): Authority. A Sociological History, Cambridge: Cambridge University Press.

Gerth, Hans H., and Mills, Charles W. (1958): "Introduction," in: Hans H. Gerth/Charles W. Mills (Eds.), From Max Weber. Essays in Sociology, New York: Oxford University Press, 3–76.

Giddens, Anthony (1991): Modernity and Self-Identity: Self and Society in the Late Modern Age, Cambridge: Polity Press.

Givens, T. (2002): By the Hand of Mormon. The American Scripture that Launched a New World Religion, New York: Oxford University Press.

Grusin, Richard A. (1991): Transcendentalist Hermeneutics. Institutional Authority and the Higher Criticism of the Bible, Durham: Duke University Press.

Gutjahr, Paul C. (2000): An American Bible. A History of the Good Book in the United States, 1777 1880, Stanford, Calif.: Stanford University Press.

Hatch, Nathan O. (1989): The Democratization of American Christianity, New Haven, Conn.: Yale University Press.

Hobbes, Thomas (1640/1889): The Elements of Law, Natural and Politic. Edited with a Preface and Critical Notes by Ferdinand Tönnies, Reproduction of Original from Harvard Law School Library. London: Simpkin, Marshall.

Holland, David F. (2011): Sacred Borders. Continuing Revelation and Canonical Restraint in Early America, New York, Oxford: Oxford University Press.

MacKay, Michael H. (2020): Prophetic Authority. Democratic Hierarchy and the Mormon Priesthood, Urbana, Chicago, and Springfield: University of Illinois Press.

Maffly-Kipp, Laurie F. (2010): American Scriptures. An Anthology of Sacred Writings, New York: Penguin Books.

Noll, Mark A. (2005): America's God. From Jonathan Edwards to Abraham Lincoln, Oxford: Oxford University Press.

Packer, Barbara L. (2007): The Transcendentalists, Athens, Ga.: University of Georgia Press.

Park, Benjamin (2010): ""Build therefore, Your Own World". Ralph Waldo Emerson, Joseph Smith, and American Antebellum Thought," in: Journal of Mormon History 36/1, 41–72.

Perry, Seth (2018): Bible Culture and Authority in the Early United States, Princeton: Princeton University Press.

Porterfield, Amanda (2012): Conceived in Doubt, Chicago: University of Chicago Press.

Robinson, David (1982): Apostle of Culture. Emerson as Preacher and Lecturer, Philadelphia: University of Pennsylvania Press.

Schmidt, Leigh E. (2012): Restless Souls. The Making of American Spirituality, Berkeley, Calif.: University of California Press.

Smith Jr., Joseph (2002a): "History (1838)," in: Dean C. Jessee (Ed.), The Personal Writings of Joseph Smith, Salt Lake City, Utah, Provo, Utah: Deseret Book; Brigham Young University Press, 226–240.

—— (2002b): "To Isaac Galland. 22 March 1839," in: Dean C. Jessee (Ed.), The Personal Writings of Joseph Smith, Salt Lake City, Utah, Provo, Utah: Deseret Book; Brigham Young University Press, 454–62.

—— (2002c): "(To Nancy Rigdon) 1842," in: Dean C. Jessee (Ed.), The Personal Writings of Joseph Smith, Salt Lake City, Utah, Provo, Utah: Deseret Book; Brigham Young University Press, 537–40.

—— (2013a): "D&C 21," in: The Doctrine and Covenants of The Church of Jesus Christ of Latter-day Saints. Containing Revelations Given to Joseph Smith, the Prophet with Some Additions by His Successors in the Presidency of the Church, Salt Lake City, Utah: The Church of Jesus Christ of Latter-day Saints.

—— (2013b): "D&C 28," in: The Doctrine and Covenants of The Church of Jesus Christ of Latter-day Saints. Containing Revelations Given to Joseph Smith, the Prophet with Some Additions by His Successors in the Presidency of the Church, Salt Lake City, Utah: The Church of Jesus Christ of Latter-day Saints.

Stein, Stephen J. (1995): "America's Bibles. Canon, Commentary, and Community," in: Church History. Studies in Christianity 64/02, 169–184.

Weber, Linda R., and Carter, Alison I. (2003): The Social Construction of Trust, Boston, MA: Springer.

Weber, Max (1968/1992): in Shmuel N. Eisenstadt (Ed.), On Charisma and Institution Building: Selected Papers, Chicago: University of Chicago Press.

The Trust Debate in the Literature of the American Renaissance

Dietmar Schloss

Trust can be said to be an attitude which we adopt when we confront situations of uncertain outcome. The uncertainty relates to the fact that we do not have sufficient knowledge of—and/or sufficient control over—the elements involved in contributing to the outcome. Trust is thus a cognitive-emotional coping mechanism that facilitates action in insecure situations. The likelihood of encountering such insecure situations has increased in modern, diverse, fast-changing, and anonymous societies (Beck 1986; Giddens 1990). This might explain why trust has become such a central concern and issue in the fields of sociology, political science, and economy (Nuissl 2002; Hartmann 2001). While definitions and conceptual approaches differ greatly, there seems to be agreement that trust is a vital requirement for the functioning of modern societies. In fact, the more modern a society is (i.e., the more functionally differentiated and the more anonymous the relationships between its members), the more trust is needed for coordinated action. However, most researchers agree that trust is a scarce and precarious resource, demanding emotional energy and hard psychological "work" to be generated and maintained.

This essay intervenes in the contemporary academic trust debate from an unlikely quarter, namely the field of American Literature. I argue that central ideas of present-day trust theorizing can already be found in the literary discourse of the United States in the first half of the nineteenth century; in particular, in the works of the authors of the so-called American Renaissance. Trust, as well as such related terms as *confidence* and *reliance*, abound in these writings—Ralph Waldo Emerson's famous essay "Self-Reliance" (1841) and Herman Melville's novel *The Confidence-Man* (1857) being only the most visible expressions of these writers' profound interest in this issue. The period of the American Renaissance roughly coincides with the Age of Jackson, in which the more traditional, predominantly agrarian republic of the Founding

Fathers began to transform itself into an increasingly modern, urban, and industrial mass democracy. The literary writers of this period, I argue, had a profound sense of the social, moral, and emotional challenges of this process of modernization. Even though their works may not reveal it at first glance, they were deeply aware of the precariousness of trust under the conditions of modernity.

That the American Renaissance writers had a profound sense of the challenges of modernity is not new: F. O. Matthiessen, the period's first literary historiographer, associated them politically with a type of modern liberalism that was radically individualist and nonconformist—while welcoming equality, they harbored negative feelings towards modern political, social, and economic institutions. In aesthetic and philosophical respects, Matthiessen considered them forerunners of the literary modernists. Later generations of critics have largely taken over his assessments (for example, Fiedler 1960, Poirier 1966, Baym 1981, Tompkins 1985, Reynolds 1988), and, more recently, efforts have been made to associate these writers with postmodernism and deconstruction (for example, Rowe 1982, Jay 1990). I have no intention to challenge the view that American Renaissance writers were champions of modern individualism, subjectivism, and epistemological skepticism; however, I do take issue with the view that they advocated a retreat from society and social interaction. Approaching them from the perspective of trust, one clearly sees their desire to keep the individual enmeshed in the social process and to have him or her retain his or her capability for action in the world. Even their most radical gestures towards individualism—and Emerson's program of self-reliance is certainly one of these—must be seen as attempts to restore trust under the conditions of modernity.

In another aspect, too, this essay tries to somewhat reshuffle the weights in the established critical balance. The writers of the American Renaissance have generally been divided into two camps—Emerson and the other transcendentalists advancing an optimistic version of American modernity, and Nathaniel Hawthorne and Herman Melville reacting to it by providing a skeptical or even tragic view. Here, too, Matthiessen provided the cue: Emerson, he writes (using a phrase from Goethe), was "the cow from which the rest drew their milk" (1941, xii)—specifying that Thoreau and Whitman applied and extended Emerson's vision, while Hawthorne and Melville felt the need to complicate and react against it. In this essay, this sequence will be changed, and we will begin with Hawthorne and Melville first, and then consider Emerson. This will show that in respect to social trust in modernity, they were participating philosophically in a two-way conversation proceeding from similar epistemological foundations. Emerson's apparently uncomplicated forward-looking stance of self-reliance will reveal itself as being grounded in a skepticism similar to that of Hawthorne and Melville. In fact, one could say that Emerson provided an answer to a question originally posed by Hawthorne and Melville.

In order to describe the American Renaissance writers' positions in the trust debate, I will draw on the trust theory of the British sociologist Antony Giddens as laid out in his two books *The Consequences of Modernity* (1990) and *Modernity* and *Self-Identity: Self and Society in the Late Modern Age* (1991). Giddens identifies and elaborates a historical scheme that reveals the different conditions of trust in "pre-modern" and "modern" societies. This distinctive typology can provide a useful tool for the analysis of the trust thinking of the American Renaissance writers. In addition, the particular focus Giddens places on the experiential dimension of modernization, as well as the place he gives to self-reflexivity and temporality (see Wagner 1991), resonates with the trust thinking of these writers. All in all, the understanding that comes out of Giddens' trust theory—namely, that trust in the modern world can no longer be considered a given, but instead needs to be "worked at,"—is vitally present in the works of the American Renaissance writers, and thus pays witness to their innovative socio-psychological theorizing.

In the following, I will first introduce Giddens' concepts of modernization and trust, then move through a small number of trust scenarios in Hawthorne and Melville, and conclude with Emerson's trust philosophy.

Anthony Giddens' Concept of Trust and Its Place in His Theory of Modernity

At the core of Giddens' thinking about trust is the psychological concept of "ontological security," sometimes also referred to as "basic trust" (1990, 92). Ontological security describes "the confidence that most human beings have in the continuity of their self-identity and in the constancy of the surrounding social and material environments of action" (1990, 92). Representing the "normal" or non-pathological state of mind in which human beings experience themselves and the world as solid, it is a state in which they do not reflect upon themselves and the world, but take the integrity of self and world for granted. The experience of ontological security is the precondition that we feel at home in the world and can act in it. If basic trust is missing or overly compromised, we feel anxious and are debilitated in our actions.

Giddens argues that basic trust is the result of nurture, not nature, and that it derives from specific experiences in early childhood. Drawing on Sigmund Freud, D.W. Winnicott, and Eric Erikson, he maintains that the manner in which a child learns to cope with the absence of the primary caretaker determines his or her later trust capacity. He writes: "a fundamental feature of the early formation of trust is trust in the caretaker's return. A feeling of the reliability, yet independent experience, of others—central to a sense of continuity of self-identity—is predicated upon the recognition that the absence of the mother does not represent a withdrawal of love" (1990, 97). It is thus of utmost importance that the child learns to interpret the absence of the caretaker as a temporary measure and not as abandonment; otherwise, the dramatic loss of power it feels will produce a sense of non-recognition and unworthiness.

Trust is thus a psychological mechanism that allows the child to accept separation from the caretaker without falling prey to anxiety. It "brackets distance in time and space and so blocks off existential anxieties which, if they were allowed to concretise, might become a source of continuing emotional and behavioural anguish through life" (1990, 97). In other instances, Giddens refers to basic trust as an "emotional inoculation" (1991, 39) and as a "protective cocoon" (1991, 40).

The category of "absence" and the notion that trust is a psychological "bracketing mechanism" to counter and stem the fears arising from absence are central to Giddens' modern trust theory. They also play a central role in his conception of the modernization process. In his historical typology, he distinguishes between pre-modern and modern societies, attributing to each type of society a different "trust environment" (1990, 102). In pre-modern societies, life takes place within a fixed habitat with more or less the same people sharing experiences over long periods of time. The organizing structures are kinship ties and community relations that can be relied upon regardless of whether the individual is personally appreciated or not (1990, 101). In addition, pre-modern societies are equipped with religious cosmologies providing the individual with interpretations of the human and natural worlds (1990, 103) and with a body of traditions to secure the continuity of past, present, and future, thus supplying the individual with a set of routinised social practices (1990, 105). Like many of the classical sociologists such as Durkheim, Weber, and Elias, Giddens places the beginning of modern institutions and modern modes of behavior in post-feudal Europe (1991, 14–15) and associates them with the rise of industrialism, capitalism, and the nation state. However, unlike them, he does not conceptualize modernization in terms of a progressive process of differentiation and specialization, but rather in terms of severance and replacement (1990, 21–22). In fact, the central feature of the modernization process for Giddens is the separation of space and time—what he calls "time-space distanciation": "The advent of modernity increasingly tears space away from place by fostering relations between 'absent' others, locally distant from any given situation of face-to-face interaction. In conditions of modernity, place becomes increasingly *phantasmagoric*: that is to say, locales are thoroughly penetrated by and shaped in terms of social influences quite distant from them" (1990, 18–19).

According to Giddens, the invention of the mechanical clock was the precondition for this process. In what he calls the "emptying of time," time is depleted of (locally acquired) experiential content and transformed into a universal measure and conceptual unit applicable anywhere. The worldwide standardization of calendars and clocks leads to the "empty[ing] of space" in the course of which space is separated from place and turned into an abstract, universally applicable category (1990, 18). This severance of time from space "provides the very basis for their recombination in ways that coordinate social activities without necessary reference to the particularities of place." The "reintegration of separated time and space" allows modern organization to coordinate "the actions of many human beings physically absent from one another" (1991, 17).

New dynamic organizational structures—Giddens calls them "abstract systems"—emerge connecting the local and the global. These structures have been lifted out of one local context ("disembedding") and have undergone a process of rearticulation in order to do organizational work in other local contexts ("reembedding"). Giddens distinguishes between several types of abstract systems: bureaucratic institutions in the Weberian sense (1990, 20); symbolic token systems (e.g. money) (1990, 22–26); and expert systems such as science and technology (1990, 27). In some respects, these abstract systems take the place of family and kinship relations and make social activity under the conditions of time-space distanciation possible. They attain credibility and authority independently of the personal attributes of the human agents that represent them. Individuals place their trust in these organizational structures in the understanding that they are universally recognized and accepted; often their authority is vouched for by the state. The trust routines that are integrated with abstract systems are central to creating ontological security in conditions of modernity.

While abstract systems have made day-to-day life of modern societies safer and more predictable than it was in pre-modern societies, Giddens points out, they also create novel forms of vulnerability. Under the conditions of modernity, he thinks, trust changes its quality and becomes something else. For one, trust in abstract systems is experientially not as nourishing as trust in persons is (1990, 113). The trust bonds to family, kin, and community, developed over a long period of time, have an emotional reality ("presence") that the trust routines in abstract systems do not have. The former involve a mutuality of response and intimacy which is missing from the largely "faceless" commitments to abstract systems; the latter remain largely unconscious and are often "taken for granted" (1990, 113). Modern trust routines thus do not contribute to the ontological security in the same manner as pre-modern trust relationships were able to.

The second factor that makes trust in modernity problematic has to do with what Giddens calls the "reflexivity of modernity," which refers to the questioning and self-questioning principle inherent in modernity (1990, 36). The Enlightenment philosophers believed they were preparing the way for a securely-founded knowledge by making critical reason instrumental to all human pursuits. As Giddens points out, however, "the reflexivity of modernity actually undermines the certainty of knowledge" because "[s]cience depends, not on the inductive accumulation of proofs, but on the methodological principle of doubt." Thus: "No matter how cherished, and apparently well established a given scientific principle might be, it is open to revision" (1991, 21). Trust in modernity is thus laced with doubt, which is "not only disturbing to philosophers, but [also] *existentially troubling* for ordinary individuals" (1991, 21).

The third factor that makes trust in abstract systems prone to anxiety is related to new risks produced by the diversification and proliferation of expert cultures. The abstract systems that organize our lives are the product of a great number of expert cultures, each of which has little knowledge of—and even less control over—their combined effects. As these systems extend across the globe, any input at one point of the system can have an enormous impact at another (1990, 124–125). Giddens believes that the fear of catastrophes resulting from unintended effects is the subconscious keynote in modern existence. While human beings in pre-modern societies were exposed to dangers of various kinds (e.g. hazards of nature), they attributed them to fate or *for-*

tuna, that is, forces outside of the responsibility of the individual (1990, 130). Threats under the conditions of globalized modernity, however, are "risks" of a new kind—they are experienced as emerging from a man-made, institutionalized environment for which individuals carry a certain responsibility, yet over which they do not seem to have any control. The resulting experience of powerlessness leads to a feeling of numbness undermining the individual's trust and agency (1990, 127–128).

In light of these factors, to muster trust under the conditions of modernity is much more difficult than in pre-modern environments. The consciousness of risk is always present, and anxiety is built into the process. In fact, Giddens wants us to consider anxiety as a regular part of our "overall security system"; it can be a potential resource that makes us ready for action, but it can also be debilitating, when it is "free-floating" (1991, 43–44). He draws on Kierkegaard's existentialist philosophy considering existence as a "mode of being-in-the-world" (1991, 48). It is not enough for individuals to "just 'accept' reality," but they have "to do" reality. In a similar way, under the conditions of modernity, one has "to do" trust in a much more active way than in pre-modern conditions where kinship and community networks, religion, and tradition provided the script. The "leap to commitment" (1990, 95) requires more courage and moral effort in the modern than in the pre-modern risk environment. Furthermore, the experience of navigating life in modern settings feels much more—to quote another one of Giddens's favorite phrases—"like being aboard a careering juggernaut [...] than being in a carefully controlled and well-driven motor car" (1990, 53).

There is one further segment of Giddens' theorizing on trust that is relevant to the trust debate in the American Renaissance. It concerns the modifications modernization wrought upon the practices of private life. Giddens sees a direct connection between the globalizing tendencies of modernity and what he calls the "transformation of intimacy in contexts of day-to-day life" (1990, 114). The separation of time and space and the introduction of abstract systems as bridging mechanisms have made trust processes increasingly tenuous as they leave the individual bereft of firm reference points. To cope with the new insecurities, modern individuals look for new points of cognitive and emotional anchorage and find them in private life. For Giddens, the turn to private life is part and parcel of that self-reflexive movement in modernity that can be observed in other realms of life, too. It leads to new forms of cultivation of personal relationships and to a "turn inwards" towards human subjectivity. While in pre-modern society, as we have seen, the individual was immersed in a dense network of relationships, these relationships were not "personal" in the modern sense, but tied to relatively fixed social roles, which gave private life almost a semi-institutional character. As public life becomes increasingly institutionalized under the pressure of modernity, the private sphere becomes more "personal" and is turned into an arena of a new quest for personal meaning. The emergence of romantic love and a new, more intimate friendship culture represent the beginnings of that development. While the routines structured by abstract systems have an "empty, unmoralized character" (1990, 120), personal relationships are invested with self-conscious intentionality and carried out with great deliberateness: they become "projects" "to be 'worked at' by the parties involved" and require *"the opening out of the individual to the other"* (1990, 121). In this, they need to live up to the demands of a new ideal of "authenticity" (1990, 119).

Connected to the preoccupation with private relationships is the concern with the self. Under the conditions of modernity, self-identity is not a given, but has to be created through a process of self-inquiry. The individual needs to become engaged in a continuous process of "identity work." Drawing on Charles Taylor's idea of self-identity, Giddens argues that "we must continually integrate events which occur in the external world into our biography, and create a narrative and keep it going" (1991, 54).

Giddens distinguishes his way of accounting for the "transformations of intimacy" in modernity from the accounts of other modernization theorists (1990, 115–120). Most of the latter argue that modern institutions have taken over large areas of social life and drained them of meaningful content. The cultivation of relationships and the quest for self-identity are seen as a retreat from politics and society, signaling the individual's feeling of powerlessness that either leads to quietism or narcissistic hedonism (1990, 121–122). Although Giddens considers the transformations of intimacy as clearly related to the emergence of abstract systems, he does not see them in terms of diminishment and decline, but as a genuine and creative transformation of the nature of the personal in the modern trust environment (1990, 120). This transformation provides individuals with a new form of emotional anchorage that bolsters their ontological security and acts as a stabilizing force in the larger risk environment of modern society.

Hawthorne and Melville: The Dilemma of Trust in Modernity

Hawthorne's and Melville's narratives do not provide "realistic" depictions of the world with credible characters and plots that pass the test of probability; rather, they offer allegories employing character types, plot schemes, and symbols in order to conduct philosophical inquiries and deliver thought experiments. These authors, I claim, are psycho-sociologists who use fiction to theorize about trust and modernity. Although the worlds depicted in their fictions reveal few of the features identified by Giddens as modern, the trust experiences of their protagonists are decidedly so. The three narratives discussed here depict human beings placed at the threshold of modernity. With their emotional and cognitive apparatuses having been molded in a pre-modern trust environment, they are thrown into a modern situation and experience a radical crisis. Eventually they fail to perform Giddens' "leap to commitment" and remain caught in a debilitating limbo. In the following, I will briefly sketch the settings of the stories with Giddens' description of pre-modern and modern environments of trust and risk in mind. In the second step, I will highlight the protagonists' trust careers; and in the third, I will speculate on the reasons of their failure.

Nathaniel Hawthorne, "Young Goodman Brown": Self-Reflexivity as a Curse

Nathaniel Hawthorne's short story "Young Goodman Brown" (1835) takes us back to the earlier phase of the Puritan settlement of New England; references to the Salem witchcraft trials and to King William III suggest the 1690s as a time marker. The story is set in Salem Village and the adjacent forest. The protagonist is a young man by the name of Goodman Brown—"goodman" being a title used to address a man of humble, but respectable birth. We meet his pretty wife by the name of Faith—it seems that they have just gotten married. We also hear that he has a prominent line of ancestors, who played important roles in the colony's history. Later we encounter his catechism teacher, as well as the minister, and the deacon; and, finally, we get a glimpse of the whole village participating in a nightly congregation.

As these details show, Hawthorne situates the protagonist clearly in what Giddens calls a pre-modern trust environment. Goodman Brown still lives in a world shaped by kinship; although his immediate family has passed away, his father and grandfather are continuously on his mind and provide models for his conduct. His mother is mentioned only once, but he seems to harbor a deep sympathy and intense admiration for her. While we do not get much of a sense of Goodman Brown and Faith's married life—they still seem to be in their honeymoon stage—Faith is a constant presence in Goodman Brown's mind, and he considers their fates as immutably united. The church is the only building mentioned in the story apart from Goodman Brown's own house. While he does not seem particularly devout, the representatives of the church have a great significance for him—akin to the members of his family. In fact, he seems to consider family and church followership as identical concerns: "We have been a race of honest men and good Christians; since the days of martyrs" (YGB, 388). At the outset of the story, the pillars of the premodern trust environment—kinship, community, religion, and habit—seem still intact for Goodman Brown. Hawthorne gives us the sense that up to the point when the story begins, the protagonist has lived his life in a state of ontological security—not only does he have faith in his wife, but also in himself and the world.

This trust is profoundly shaken when he enters the forest at sunset, after having given a parting kiss to his wife. Hawthorne does not have him move very far away from the village world—the forest, in fact, borders on the village—and yet in the allegorical language of the story, this step marks the Giddensian time-space separation that comes with modernity: it distances and estranges him from his familiar world and catapults him into a new experiential time. Yet, although the forest is a far cry from Giddens' global, capitalist, urban modernity, Hawthorne has this modernity (or what exists of it in the late seventeenth century) enter the story through some interesting details: the person, with whom Goodman Brown has the appointment in the forest and who becomes his guide, is not a local; instead, he is described as one who "had an indescribable air of one who knew the world, and would not have felt abashed at the governor's dinner table, or in King William's Court" (YGB, 387). The stranger prides himself as having had intense commerce with many members of New England's religious and political elite, listing church deacons, municipal selectmen, members of the legislature, and even the governor as his close friends (YGB, 388–389). In this figure of radical mobility—he does not only move rapidly between places but also between times (he claims, for example, to have been an intimate acquaintance of Goodman Brown's father and grandfather)—Hawthorne brings modernity into the forest. In addition, the congregation that eventually assembles in the forest is not only made up of the residents of Salem village but also of those of "Falmouth and beyond"

(YGB, 391); there are also delegations from Connecticut and Rhode-Island as well as a group of "Indian powpows" (YGB, 391).

Wherein does the crisis of trust that Goodman Brown experiences in the forest consist? It comes down to his gradual realization that the persons that had guaranteed the stability of his self and his world are not what they seemed; the "caretakers" of the traditional world that provided him with a feeling of ontological security are suddenly experienced as unreliable and treacherous. His process of disillusion begins with the stranger with whom he has the appointment. The elderly man has a certain physical resemblance with him—the narrator even suggests that he could be his grandfather or grand uncle—and Goodman Brown wonders why a person like him would be in the forest. His somewhat immoral opinions and his cynical speech—the narrator gives him at times a satanic appearance—make Goodman Brown even more uneasy. When the stranger provides him with compromising details regarding the conduct of his revered grandfather and father, Goodman Brown's uneasiness turns into anxiety. As if that were not enough, when they encounter his catechism teacher, the minister, and the deacon of the village in the depths of the forest, his despair becomes complete. Finding the whole village assembled under the light of four blazing pines in a clearing, the riddle is finally solved: The congregation is celebrating a devil's sabbath with everybody waiting to welcome Goodman Brown and his wife Faith as the new "converts" in their midst (YGB, 393).

Hawthorne's allegorical narrative makes visible the high drama of Goodman Brown's psyche: it carefully records the steps of increasing anxiety when the old certainties are, piece by piece, put into question and crumble. It begins with doubts in the "elders," then moves to a questioning of the creator-God ("He looked up to the sky, doubting whether there really was a Heaven above him" [YGB, 391]), and ends with a questioning of the self, which, however, is aborted. Goodman Brown moves through a number of emotional states in this crisis—astonishment, anxiety, desperation, despair, and finally frustration and anger. In this final stage, Goodman Brown seems to want to give up his resistance, as he is turning into a fiend himself and moving through the forest in a destructive rampage. However, when he is finally facing Faith in front of the altar to partake in the satanic communion, he retracts urging his wife to "look up to Heaven and resist the Wicked One" (YGB, 395). The phantasmagoric action breaks off in this moment and Brown finds himself alone in the chilly and damp early morning forest.

The aftermath of this event, narrated in the brief last section, is important for Goodman Brown's trust career. The crisis of trust which he has gone through in the night in the forest leaves him traumatized for life. Though the narrator suggests that the wild witch meeting might have just been a dream (YGB, 395), Goodman Brown cannot forget it: "A stern, a sad, a darkly meditative, a distrustful if not a desperate man, did he become, from the night of that fearful dream" (YGB, 395). When he hears hymns sung at the meeting house, he thinks of the "anthem[s] of sin" in the forest (YGB, 395). When he listens to the minister give voice to the "sacred truths of our religion," he dreads that "the roof [of the meeting house] should thunder down upon the gray blasphemer and his hearers" (YGB, 395). Waking up at night at the bosom of his wife Faith, he shrinks back.

"Young Goodman Brown" is a story about a failed trust education. Looking at it from the perspective of Giddens' trust theory, one could say that the protagonist does not succeed emotionally in making the transition from a premodern localized trust to a more flexible modern trust. He has not learned—or is not prepared to learn—to negotiate ambiguity and doubt and perform that "leap to commitment" which is necessary to act in the world under the conditions of modernity. Brown suffers from "self-consciousness," which is part and parcel of "the reflexivity of modernity." After the night in the forest, Goodman Brown cannot accept appearances as reality anymore and is continuously plagued by suspicions and doubt: anxiety has become pathological.

Goodman Brown makes others—his ancestors, the church functionaries, the community, and even his wife—responsible for his loss of faith in mankind, perceiving himself as the only one who has remained pure. However, the story makes clear that the desire to leave the village at sunset and meet the stranger in the forest originated in his very own soul. Although Goodman Brown is already anxious and possessed by guilt when he gives the parting kiss to his wife, he never acknowledges his complicity in the depravity he detects in others. It is interesting that the narrator never officially confirms the reality of evil, but represents it as a dream that was perhaps inspired by Goodman Brown's own guilty conscience. Importantly, his abrupt withdrawal from the satanic confirmation ritual is not praised as a virtuous act, but marked as a kind of betrayal of the brother- and sisterhood of humankind. Hawthorne seems to be suggesting that it would have been much better for Goodman Brown's trust career if had he been pragmatic and joined the devil worshippers and thereby accepted his own sinfulness.

From the beautifully laconic description of his death and funeral, we learn that, in his scruples, he was a singular case, and that while he renounced cooperation with a sinful world, the other members of the community (including his wife) went on with their lives and performed their human duties: "And when he had lived long, and was borne to his grave, a hoary corpse, followed by Faith, an aged woman, and children and grandchildren, a goodly procession, besides neighbors, not a few, they carved no hopeful verse upon his tomb-stone; for his dying hour was gloom" (YGB, 395). Placing Goodman Brown's "hoary corpse" in the midst of an active community, which has assembled to fulfill their last duty to him, the narrator expresses a moral critique. The way Goodman Brown handled his crisis of trust had an element of self-indulgence, and his insistence on remaining pure appears selfish. It is the inflexibility of Goodman Brown's mind—his unwillingness to compromise and to accept a certain amount of ambiguity and risk regarding himself and others—that prevented him from transitioning into a modern, more robust trust attitude.

Nathaniel Hawthorne, "My Kinsman, Major Molineux": Democracy and the Demolishment of Pre-modern Trust

With "My Kinsman, Major Molineux" (1832), set in Boston a decade and a half before the American Revolution, Hawthorne moves closer to the modern age. Preceding the narrative is a long paragraph with historiographical reflections on the frequency of rebellions and crowd actions in the first half of the eighteenth century. Clearly Hawthorne wanted to see the story placed in the context of the American struggle for independence and the emergence of a new, more self-confident democratic mentality.

The protagonist, Robin, is again a young man, 18 and single. When the story starts, we see him on his way to Boston. He has grown up on the farm of his father, who is a clergyman; yet he has to pursue his fortune somewhere else, as he is not the first born and has several siblings. Robin has set his hopes on a kinsman by the name of Major Molineux, a crown officer who lives in "the little Metropolis" of the New England colony, since, on one of his visits, Molineux has promised to help Robin start a career (MK, 374). Religion is present in Robin's mind, yet does not determine his vision of the world as much as Goodman Brown's. We are told of "his father's custom to perform domestic worship" in the evening with neighbors and wayfaring men around the dinner table, the latter being treated like "brothers of the family" (MK, 381). Family, kinship, and community relations are thus powerful realities in Robin's life. The absolute confidence Robin invests in Major Molineux to provide for his future is, of course, the most significant indicator of how profoundly kinship relations shape his vision of life.

While Robin's frame of mind is thus still pre-modern like Goodman Brown's, his spirit is quite different. Goodman Brown was fearful of modernity. Although he was driven by an urge to leave the world of kinship and community, he felt guilty about it and consequently disowned it. Robin seems to be much more pragmatic about modernity. When he recounts the family's economic situation to a gentleman in the city, he describes his departure in quite a light-hearted way: "Well, Sir, being nearly eighteen years old, and well grown, [...] I thought it high time to begin the world. So my mother and sister put me in handsome trim, and my father gave me half the remnant of his last year's salary, and five days ago I started for this place, to pay the Major a visit" (MK, 383). Robin approaches the modern world in a seemingly relaxed, enlightened manner—somewhat in the spirit of a young Benjamin Franklin. His very name—Robin—indicates that he is Nature's creature, an "American Adam" who encounters the world with a fresh spirit, not burdened by the past. The protagonist of "My Kinsman" is thus cast in the new, "American," optimistic mold—one that promises an emotionally unproblematic entry into modernity and that is usually associated with Emerson's idea of self-reliance.

Despite Robin's new, seemingly modern spirit, he does not fare much better in the modern risk environment of Boston than Goodman Brown did in the forest of Salem. He, too, goes through a fundamental crisis of trust that leaves him in the end almost as devastated as it left Goodman Brown. Hawthorne represents Robin's encounter with modernity as a Gothic experience (just like Goodman Brown's). Robin enters the city at night—after having crossed the river by ferry—and is disoriented by the labyrinth of streets, the strange noises, and the irregular lights. In the course of the evening he encounters a wide array of people—they are from different classes (aristocrats, an innkeeper, craftsmen, country bumpkins, a watchman, a prostitute, the members of a mob) as well as from different parts of the world (punch-drinking sailors, British crown officials, a French Huguenot, "gay and gallant figures" from Europe, as well as their colonial imitators [MK, 377]), indicating that the little New England metropolis is well connected with the larger world. The multifaceted reality Robin encounters perplexes him, but for a while he accepts its riddles with a certain fascination and humor ("Strange things we travellers see!" [MK, 380]).

Robin's trust crisis ensues when he asks people for directions to the house of his famous kinsman and does not receive the response he expects. Assuming that Major Molineux is a well-known and well-respected resident, he imagines that people would feel honored to show his nephew the way. This is, however, not the case. When his interlocutors hear the name of Molineux, they behave in strange ways: some ignore him, some rebuff him, some try to detract his attention, some threaten him, some ridicule him, but no one answers to his request. Hawthorne's narrative in the main section of "My Kinsman"—as in "Young Goodman Brown"—makes visible the drama of Robin's inner psyche: Robin tries to find all sorts of excuses for the disrespectful treatment he is given, but with each rebuff, his anxiety moves up a notch—the amused astonishment turns into frustration then to anger and finally to violence. Carrying an oak cudgel with him, he feels the urge to hit back each time he is rebuffed.

Finally, an odd-looking stranger recommends that he wait in front of the church, promising the Major would pass by shortly. Soon, an uproar ensues, and a huge crown enters the scene—the atmosphere is as orgiastic as in the satanic congregation in the forest in "Young Goodman Brown." In their midst, Robin finds Major Molineux placed on a carriage "in tar-and-feathery dignity" (MK, 385). Robin becomes aware that he is in the midst of a revolution and that his patron is its first victim. Robin's eyes and those of his humiliated and powerless kinsman meet while the crowd roars with excitement and pleasure.

This is, of course, the turning point in Robin's trust career and also the moment of recognition. Despite his modern, seemingly self-reliant attitude, he had constructed his identity in the pre-modern mode, relying on family and kinship ties to provide him with a future. Realizing that his kinsman has been rendered powerless, the bottom falls out of his biography. His basic trust is shaken to the very roots. The narrator does not tell us exactly what is going on in Robin's mind at this point, but gives us a sense of profound agitation: "They stared at each other in silence, and Robin's knees shook, and his hair bristled, with a mixture of pity and terror" (MK, 385). Robin sees before his mind's eye all the people who "had made sport of him that night" and the riddle is easy to read (MK, 385). In what looks like a mixture of anger (the kinsman has failed him) and desperation (his future is in jeopardy), Robin joins the orgiastic crowd and sends forth "a shout of laughter" louder than anyone else (MK, 385).

Hawthorne goes to great lengths to portray Molineux as a good leader and an honorable individual—"an elderly man, of large and majestic person, and strong, square features, betokening a steady soul" (MK, 385)—and the mob as fickle and brutal. Hawthorne indicates clearly that by joining the crowd in shaming his kinsman, Robin commits an act of betrayal and becomes an opportunist. In terms of the iconography of the story, he "falls" and loses his Adamic innocence. At the same time, Hawthorne seems to consider this a "fortunate fall," an emotionally and morally necessary development for a human being. In fact, he dramatizes the recognition scene between Robin and Molineux and Robin's betrayal of his kinsman as an Aristotelian moment of catharsis (Robin stares at his kinsman with a "mixture of pity and terror" [MK, 385]). His joining with the crowd brings relief; the unbearable anxiety that had built up in him during the night disappears and an inner peace of sorts sets in.

As with Goodman Brown, Robin's trust career ends with his trust smashed. At the end, Robin asks a stranger to be shown the way to the Ferry—having grown, as he says, "weary" of town life (MK, 386). The reader knows—and Robin knows, too—that there is no home in the countryside anymore.

Will Robin end in the same impasse as Goodman Brown? The closing scene of "My Kinsman" suggests that Robin might perhaps overcome his trust crisis and not develop a trauma. In the last third of the story, Robin meets a gentleman—the only friendly encounter he has in town—who tries to comfort him and also gives him some advice. When Robin tells him that he wants to go back to the country, the gentleman encourages him to give town life a second chance: "as you are a shrewd youth, you may rise in the world, without the help of your kinsman" (MK, 386). Hawthorne has the story end at this point, and we do not know whether Robin will follow the advice of the gentleman or leave.

The gentleman indirectly suggests a way out of the pre-modern trust dilemma. Namely, that Robin abandon the whole pre-modern trust construct and transition to a more modern one. His reference to Robin's native shrewdness points to a Franklinian or Emersonian individualism, albeit one of a complex sort. Behind his suggestion that Robin give the city a second chance is a sense that Robin is emotionally robust and flexible enough to finally master the new trust environment in modernity. Critics have seen in the gentleman a guardian figure—a more modern stand-in for the kinsman that has failed. As a guardian figure, however, he is not very protective of the emotional welfare of his charge. While he is aware of the truth about Molineux and knows what a devastating effect this truth will have on Robin's psyche, he does nothing to mitigate this effect. He also witnesses Robin's "fall" (his joining the crowd and shaming his kinsman) and does not try to stop Robin or remonstrate with him afterwards. Although cast somewhat in the role of an eighteenth-century benevolent gentleman, he is a figure of enlightened, balanced, even scientific modernity. He observes Robin's development with genuine sympathy, but does not act as his protector; in fact, he seems to welcome Robin's "fall" as it represents an emotional preparation for an individual's ability to cope in a modern trust environment. In view of the complexity of the modern world, trust must become more flexible and robust: Individuals must be able to negotiate ambiguity and doubt—and above all recognize their own ambiguity. Only then will they be able to act in that world.

Melville, *The Confidence-Man: His Masquerade* (1857): Trust in a World of Strangers

Unlike Hawthorne's short stories, Melville's last novel, *The Confidence-Man* (1857), does not deal with the trust experience of a single individual, but with social trust processes in the American society at large. Melville, too, uses the allegorical method to analyze the epistemological and psychological underpinnings of trust activities. In contrast to Hawthorne's short stories, which were set in the colonial past, *The Confidence-Man* is situated in Melville's historical present: his choice of setting makes clear that he aspired to analyze American society in its most modern state. The action takes place on a Mississippi steamboat by the name of Fidèle. It starts its journey from St. Louis and is bound for New Orleans. The timeline takes up one day, from early dawn to midnight (on April 1 in the mid-1850s). The macro-setting is the American West, in particular the Mississippi River, running North to South, separating the more settled areas from the new territory, and crossing the boundaries between slave and free states. In the beginning of the novel, the narrator celebrates the West and the Mississippi as the space where the diverse elements of America come together like nowhere else and create a vibrant modernity: "Here reigned the dashing and all-fusing spirit of the West, whose type is the Mississippi itself, which, uniting the streams of the most distant and opposite zones, pours them along, helter-skelter, in one cosmopolitan and confident tide" (CM, 17).

America's radical diversity is also reflected by the passengers on board. The following list reminds one of Whitman's catalogues, except that Melville's satiric-sarcastic tone forecloses the possibility that an Emersonian Oversoul might bring harmony to this wild disarray:

> Natives of all sorts, and foreigners; men of business and men of pleasure; parlor men and backwoodsmen; farm-hunters and fame-hunters; heiress-hunters, gold-hunters, buffalo-hunters, bee-hunters, happiness-hunters, truth-hunters, and still keener hunters after all these hunters. Fine ladies in slippers, and moccasined squaws; Northern speculators and Eastern philosophers; English, Irish, German, Scotch, Danes; Santa Fé traders in striped blankets, and Broadway bucks in cravats of cloth of gold; fine-looking Kentucky boatmen, and Japanese-looking Mississippi cotton-planters; Quakers in full drab, and United States soldiers in full regimentals; slaves, black, mulatto, quadroon; modish young Spanish Creoles, and old-fashioned French Jews; Mormons and Papists; Dives and Lazarus; jesters and mourners, teetotalers and convivialists, deacons and blacklegs; hard-shell Baptists and clay-eaters; grinning negroes, and Sioux chiefs solemn as high-priests. In short, a piebald parliament, an Anacharsis Cloots congress of all kinds of that multiform pilgrim species, man. (CM, 16–17)

As regards the composition of society, the West as depicted in *The Confidence-Man* is fully-fledged modern—members of different nations, regions, classes, races, genders, professions and occupations, and religions come into contact. Here the time-space distanciation has clearly left its mark. Melville's choice of the steamboat as a micro-setting is also significant. On the shores of the Mississippi River life may be rural, but on board it is urban: strangers meet strangers, sizing each other up, often trying to do business with each other. The boat is in continuous transit, moving through different climate zones and connecting different cities. It loads and unloads passengers at every stop—the society on board is never composed of the same people:

> Though her voyage of twelve hundred miles extends from apple to orange, from clime to clime, yet, like any small ferry-boat, to right and left, at every landing, the huge Fidèle still receives additional passengers in exchange for those that disembark; so that, though always full of strangers, she continually, in some degree, adds to, or replaces them with strangers more strange; like Rio Janeiro fountain, fed from the Corcovado mountains, which is ever overflowing with strange waters, but never with the same strange particles in every part. (CM, 15)

In this world of anonymity and flux, Melville conducts his trust experiments. When he wrote the novel, the term *confidence man* was new. It was coined in 1849 by the *New York Herald* reporting on the case of a certain William Thompson who would approach people in the street and ask if they would place their trust in him. He would then try and borrow and never return a sum of money or a watch from them (Bergmann 1969). Melville must have been so fascinated by the figure and the term that he used the new phrase in his novel's title and made this figure the protagonist. Of course, "protagonist" is a misnomer as the novel does not have a single protagonist in the traditional sense. Instead, we get a series of different figures—eight of them to be precise—who come onto the scene out of nowhere (often after the ship has made a stop), approach one or more passengers, try to win their confidence and often their money and then disappear. The eight figures do not resemble each other; indeed, they differ greatly in appearance and behavior. If the reader conceptualizes them as one single character, it is mainly because of the title: *The Confidence-Man: His Masquerade*. Critics have puzzled over the true identity of this figure—Hershel Parker, Melville's biographer and one of the editors of the novel's Norton Critical Edition, wants to persuade us that he is the devil (Parker 2006; CM, 11, n.2); I would suggest he should be approached not as a real character but rather as a principle or tool devised by Melville to perform a particular function in his thought experiment on social trust in America.

If the confidence man is merely a tool, the reader's attention should focus on the passengers whose confidence he tries to win. Here, Melville gives us a fascinating cross-section of American mentalities—highlighting the diversity of trust attitudes as they are shaped by region, class, gender, religion, age, profession, political ideology, race consciousness, and moral temperament. Although the passenger figures (like the personae of the confidence man) are types rather than characters, we receive profound insights into their emotional processes during their conversations with the confidence man, as the narrator renders their utterances in direct speech and gives us Geertzian "thick descriptions" of their behavior. It is difficult to generalize about these conversations, as the objects the confidence man offers in return for the passenger's trust differ greatly: when he appears as a black handicapped beggar, he simply asks for money; in the guise of a man in a gray coat and white tie, he collects money for widows and orphans; as John Truman, he solicits investments on behalf of the Black Rapids Coal Company; and in the role of the herb doctor, he sells natural medicines to cure various ailments. Sometimes there is no object to be sold or exchanged and the confidence man just tries to convince his interlocutors—via a direct religious or moral appeal or lengthy philosophical argument—to adopt a trustful attitude towards the world. The trust solicitations also differ greatly in their outcome—sometimes the confidence man succeeds in his entreaties, but often he fails, or his gain is small. Trust negotiations in the comparatively secular, capitalistic, democratic modern society are tiresome and enervating—and often when trust is built up after a lengthy persuasive endeavor, it falters and comes to nothing. The anxiety level of many of the passengers is high. In these exchanges, little or nothing can be felt of "the dashing and all-fusing spirit of the West" and the "cosmopolitan and confident tide" of the Mississippi which is celebrated so emphatically by the narrator in the beginning of the novel (CM, 17). In the anonymous, shifty, and fluid atmosphere of the Fidèle's numerous decks, trust has become a scarce resource indeed.

It is not that the passengers of the Fidèle lack faith entirely. Melville shows us that many of them actually have a desire to trust (not infrequently, this desire is seconded by a hope for material gain), but somehow they do not have the stamina to make the "leap to commitment." In a world of strangers, the risks seem too high. Melville's modern world is not equipped with abstract systems or symbolic tokens that could reduce these risks. When asked for a travel document that could vouch for his identity, the confidence man is unable to produce one. The only means available to him to have his identity ascertained derives from the pre-modern world: he suggests another person who can vouch for him. While the mentioning of a third person known to both conversation partners usually gets the trust process started, it falters when the third person is not found. We are given to understand that the third person most likely left the steamboat at the previous stop. As there is no captain or any other official person on the ship who has the authority to ascertain identities, enforce rules, and penalize broken commitments, the passengers are caught in a dead-lock situation.

The passengers of the Fidèle are in a trust crisis similar to that of Goodman Brown. They cannot trust the surfaces anymore and are consumed by doubt, for they suffer from the self-reflexivity of modernity. Using the mask metaphor, Melville analyses this situation in an epistemological way: in one of the instances, when the confidence man is asked to supply the names of persons who can vouch for him, he lists other confidence-man figures who appear in the novel (CM, 21). Of course, none of them can be found onboard because they are his own impersonations. Melville casts social interaction in an anonymous modern society in a quasi-postmodernist way—as an encounter with masks where the person behind can no longer be found (Lindberg 1982, Wadlington 1975). The modern world is presented here as a surface without depth, or a sign without referent. The novel leaves us with the impression that Melville, like Hawthorne, wishes that the passengers could take their interactions with the confidence man as a game—a confidence game—and play along as if the masks were reality. It would keep the social process going and be healthier for their psychological well-being. However, Melville, like Hawthorne's Goodman Brown, is too much of a truth-seeker to be able to accept a life of surfaces. The novel thus ends at midnight in utter gloom.

Ralph Waldo Emerson, "Self-Reliance": A Modern Project of Self-Identity

In standard literary histories, Ralph Waldo Emerson is seen as the inventor of a concept of a "modern," democratic American identity that squared with the principles of Lockean Liberalism—for a long time considered to be the base of American political modernity. As individuals find their prime domain of self-realization in (a spiritualized) nature, they do not need other human beings, society, political institutions, or traditions to attain their identity. What for Hawthorne and Melville represents an unsurmountable obstacle—the attainment of a strong identity capable of acting in the world—seems entirely unproblematic for Emerson. Consequently, his concept of self-reliance or self-trust (he uses the terms interchangeably) has long been considered a forward-looking trust philosophy that easily embraces modernity rather than fears it.

Coming from Giddens' sociology of modernity, what are we to make of Emerson's trust philosophy? Of course, Emerson's notion that the self can validate itself goes squarely against Giddens' principal assumption of our sense of self and our experience of the external world depending crucially on the attention we receive from other humans. Giddens would thus probably not consider Emerson's theory of self-reliance as a scientifically sound description of the trust process in modernity; however, he might find it interesting as a phenomenon of modernity itself. In fact, Giddens' sociology can explain why Emerson developed a trust philosophy at the time he did. As shown earlier, Giddens makes the case that, in modernity, abstract systems increasingly take the place of human trust agents. This depersonalization of organizational processes in the public world brings forth changes in the private sphere such as the "transformation of intimacy" and a new concern with the self. Emerson's program of self-reliance can thus be seen as a Giddensian "project of self-identity" designed to provide a new pillar for the attainment of ontological security and, thereby, making amends for the "depersonalized" and "unmoralized" public trust structures. Emerson's trust philosophy is thus not so much an alternative to modern self-reflexivity, but a creative response to it. It does not side-step or eclipse the crisis of trust that is so troubling for Hawthorne and Melville, but tries to provide a remedy for it. In some of his writings, Emerson shows an awareness of this and gives a theoretical blueprint of Giddens' notion of "doing" trust in a modern risk environment.

If we look carefully at Emerson's essays, we find passages which express doubts similar to those articulated by Melville and Hawthorne. In "Self-Reliance" (1841), Emerson begins his argument by ascribing the state of ontological security to children and adolescents: "Their mind being whole, their eye is as yet unconquered" (SR, 270). Regarding "boys," he maintains that their "nonchalance", their "independent" and "irresponsible" behavior is the "healthy attitude of human nature," suggesting that grown-ups should take their cues from them (SR, 271). However, he next indicates that such a return to childhood confidence is not easy for adults. While "boys" judge the world in a "swift, summary way [...] as good, bad, interesting, silly," grown-ups are constantly preoccupied with second thoughts, considering what the consequences of their actions are, and how they may be judged by others (SR, 271). The adult, Emerson concludes, is "clapped into jail by his consciousness" (SR, 271). Emerson describes here a phenomenon highlighted in Hawthorne's short stories; namely, that in the process of becoming an adult, we develop a self-consciousness, which undermines our basic trust and prevents us from engaging in action. In his essay, "The American Scholar" (1837), Emerson connects this action-inhibiting self-consciousness explicitly with the modern age, rendering self-reflexivity in Giddensian terms:

> Our age is bewailed as the age of Introversion. [...] We are embarrassed with second thoughts. We cannot enjoy any thing for hankering to know whereof the pleasure consists. We are lined with eyes. We see with our feet. The time is infected with Hamlet's unhappiness,— "Sicklied o'er with the pale cast of thought." (AS, 254)

Emerson describes here the dialectics of Enlightenment in a beautiful series of metaphors. Reason, originally directed at the exploration and conquest of the natural and external world, turns back upon itself—with a vengeance. Hamlet's disease—Giddens' anxiety gone pathological—is holding the modern individual in its grip. Interestingly, however, Emerson does not let the matter rest here. He adds a third step to the dialectics when he asks: "Is that so bad then? Sight is the last thing to be pitied. Would we be blind? Do we fear lest we should outsee nature and God, and drink truth dry?" (AS, 254). Emerson demands that something new and creative must come out of this crippling self-reflexivity, thereby claiming that the age of "Introversion" must be followed by an age of "Self-Reliance." Emerson does not consider self-reliance as an alternative to self-reflexivity, but rather suggests that it has self-reflexivity at its experiential basis. Consequently, self-reliance cannot be achieved by returning to the spontaneity of childhood or youth, but it has to take the path of "consciousness"; in other words, it needs to become a Giddensian "project" pursued in a deliberate and conscious manner.

There is another strain in Emerson's conceptualizing of self-reliance that identifies it as Giddensian "project"; namely, when he indicates that this form of trust is a response to modern abstract systems. In the fictional worlds of Hawthorne and Melville, these abstract systems hardly figure at all. In Emerson's essays, however, they are constantly thematized, making it clear that, at the time he was writing, in the 1830s, American society had been modernized to a considerable extent. Emerson's critique of these abstract systems and how they shape the life processes in the United States is central to his trust philosophy. In "Self-Reliance" we read: "Society everywhere is in conspiracy against the manhood of every one of its members. Society is a joint-stock company in which the members agree for the better securing of his bread to each shareholder, to surrender the liberty and culture of the eater" (SR, 271). What is attacked here are such abstract systems as the shareholder principle, which was originally developed to organize private capitalist enterprise, but then turned into a universal method to structure the life process of the United States. Another example in "The American Scholar" occurs where Emerson criticizes the way in which the division-of-labor system reaches beyond the occupational sphere and organizes human identity as such: "Man is not a farmer, or a professor, or an engineer, but he is all. Man is priest, and scholar, and statesman, and producer, and soldier. In the *divided* or social state, these functions are parcelled out to individuals, each of whom aims to do his stint of the joint work, whilst each other performs his." As a consequence, human beings have lost their humanity and "strut about so many walking monsters" (AS, 244). Emerson not only promises that self-reliance will be able to heal the damages inflicted by modernization. He even claims that self-reliance can supply the central organizational structure for modern society, thus making abstract systems altogether dispensable.

Giddens would consider such a claim utopian. His sociology of modernity invites us to see Emerson's program of self-reliance from a historical perspective; namely, as a project of self-identity that acts as a complement to the abstract systems and compensates for their emotional deficiencies. While the abstract systems establish trust-processes under the condition of time-space-distanciation, however, they cannot provide the rich experiential textures of personal relationships. Thus, new forms of relationship and new types of identity work are needed to supply the modern individual with meaning in life. Emerson's transcendentalism, his program for self-discovery in Nature, is just such a new form of sense-making. In addition, by extending the identity work into the spiritual realm, Emerson provides an individualized substitute for the pre-modern cosmologies.

How is this identity work of self-reliance conducted? Emerson's essays offer theoretical guidance about the procedure. In a sense, there are no particular requirements—the individual does not need to have particular material or intellectual assets at his or her disposal. The identity work of self-reliance has somewhat the character of an aesthetic experience: it involves an act of will (one needs to pull oneself out of the reach of abstract systems) and has to become "deliberate" (one gives a particular kind of attention to nature and/or the inner self).

However, Emerson's essays do not only provide theoretical guidance for the attainment of self-trust: they want to bring it about by rhetorical persuasion. Emerson frequently addresses the reader directly—using imperatives and an incantatory style—turning his essays into an emotional trust generator, as can be seen in the following passage from "Self-Reliance":

> Trust thyself: every heart vibrates to that iron string. Accept the place the divine Providence has found for you; the society of your contemporaries, the connexion of events. Great men have always done so and confided themselves childlike to the genius of their age, betraying their perception that the Eternal was stirring at their heart, working through their hands, predominating in all their being. (SR, 270)

Such a rhetorical mode of trust building would not make sense in a traditional (pre-modern) trust scenario. We cannot be urged in the same way to have trust in other people because their actions are not in our hands. However, we can try and convince ourselves to get up in the morning, suppress our doubts, and keep our commitments. The tie that Emerson creates between self-trust and Nature is similarly self-reflexive. You can test the reliability of your spouse, your friends, your business partners, but can you put Nature to the test?

In a sense, Emerson's project of self-reliance can be considered as an invitation to autosuggestion, and that on a national scope. Although ostentatiously directed at the single individual, it addresses all individuals of the nation and thus has a collective effect. It works like a daily Sesame Street broadcast for adults, persuading them to feel good about themselves; that they can perform that "leap to commitment" which keeps the American social process going. The American Dream can be considered as such a program of self-reliance on a national scale—a type of modern civil religion invented by democratic modernity and promoted by the culture industry to keep the debilitating forces of modernity at bay and maintain the nation in the action mode.

Considering the Emersonian philosophy of self-reliance as a Giddensian project of identity helps us to see it as a program of social action. In the "American Scholar," Emerson argues that "action" is "essential" for the scholar (AS, 248). All of the figures Emerson wrote about in his book *Representative Men* were "men of action." Paradoxically, the individualistic, seemingly retreatist project of self-reliance serves as a national trust generator. In the insecure environment of modernity, it induces individuals to make a "leap to commitment" and keep the social process going.

Ralph Waldo Emerson, "Experience": "Doing" Trust

Hawthorne's "Young Goodman Brown" makes the point that nothing but certainty can satisfy the individual who has fallen into the state of self-reflexivity; however, it also makes clear that this certainty is difficult to attain under the conditions of modernity. While "My Kinsman, Mayor Molineux" suggests that it may be possible to acquire a more robust trust attitude and recover one's capacity for action, it does not show us how this new way of "doing trust" may work in practice. Here Emerson's essay "Experience" (1844) can offer guidance. It gives an interesting epistemological description of modern "trust work," thereby showing a way out of the trust dilemma as presented by Hawthorne and Melville.

Emerson wrote "Experience" under the influence of the death of his son. He begins the essay with the reflection that this event has left him in a state of numbness. Analyzing this feeling further, he comes to the conclusion that he is numb not because this tragic experience has drained him, but because he has failed to let it come close to him: "I grieve that grief can teach me nothing" (E, 312). The feeling of not being able to get into "touch" with the reality of his son's death leads to a series of generalizing reflections about the unbridgeable gap between mind and world and between one consciousness and another (Cameron 2006).

In the first third of the essay, the individual self is shown in a state of disorientation expressed by Emerson through the image of a staircase, where the individual neither sees the upper nor the lower end: "Where do we find ourselves? In a series of which we do not know the extremes, and believe that it has none. We wake and find ourselves on a stair; there are stairs below us, which we seem to have ascended; there are stairs above us, many a one, which go upward and out of sight" (E, 310). In a second series of images, he dramatizes this state of disorientation by metaphors of blurred vision: "All things swim and glitter" (E, 310). This "evanescence and lubricity of all objects, which lets them slip through our fingers [...] when we clutch hardest" appears to him "the most unhandsome part of our condition" (E, 312). Nature—the guidepost Emerson usually resorts to—seems to fail him here as it is experienced as having no substance. The self, too, is felt as being unreal: "Ghostlike we glide through nature, and should not know our place again" (E, 311). He comes to the conclusion that reality is a labyrinth of fictions: "Dream delivers us to dream, and there is no end to illusion" (E, 312).

Emerson's descriptions of the nature of experience evoke Hawthorne's world of appearance or that of Melville's masquerades: reality has lost its "solidity" and is perceived as a surface which can be manipulated independently of content. In "Experience," Emerson suspects that the manipulator is actually the experiencing individual self: what it perceives as reality may be the projection of its own subjectivity. The numbness that came over Emerson after the death of his son makes him realize how much of one's experience is colored by one's "moods," the latter regulating what and how one sees: "Life is a train of moods like a string of beads, and, as we pass through them, they prove to be many-colored lenses which paint the world in their own hue, and each shows only what lies in its focus" (E, 312).

These moods are not arbitrary and isolated experiential moments; but they are subject to a person's "temperament," which is presented by Emerson here as a quasi-deterministic force: It is an "iron wire on which the beads [namely our moods] are strung" (E, 312). Temperament determines our vision, e.g., the "system of illusions" that we take for reality (E, 313); it "shuts us in a prison of glass which we cannot see" (E, 313). This realization goes entirely against our every-day understanding that life is full of "inscrutable possibilities" and that every human being is a store of opportunities to which we hold the "key" (E, 314). If Emerson's mood and temperament epistemology is taken at face value, trust makes no sense. Every gesture in the direction of the other is a form of mirror fencing. Emerson faces here an impasse similar to the one confronted by Melville in *The Confidence-Man*.

In essays such as *Nature* or "Self-Reliance," Emerson had frequently created the impression that nature or reality is potentially transparent, allowing the individual to directly partake of the divine. In "Experience," Emerson seems to turn his back on this epistemological model and develop a new one on the basis of the temperament and mood imagery. This epistemology places a new emphasis on the temporality and situatedness of individual consciousness (Packer 2006). While earlier in his essay, temporality and situatedness were considered as "the most unhandsome part" of our existence, they now become facilitators of our freedom, however limited that may be (E, 312). The flow of time, which, to some extent, takes the control of our experience out of our hands, reveals itself as a blessing: "The secret of the illusoriness is in the necessity of a succession of moods or objects. Gladly we would anchor, but the anchorage is quicksand. This onward trick of nature is too strong for us: *Pero si muove*" (E, 314). Galileo's insistence (against the authorities of his time) that the earth moves around the sun (rather than the other way around) provides the cue for Emerson to accept the decentering of the human subject and to embrace historicity as the human predicament. While the constructed and temporary nature of experience earlier on almost led him to despair, he now rejoices over it. Rather than forever searching for the true essence "underneath" the surfaces, he now encourages us to develop a certain virtuosity in negotiating their flow: "We live amid surfaces and the true art of life is to skate well on them" (E, 316). Skating on surfaces is an "art"—the movements we perform must not be random, but should be guided by intuition and skill.

Emerson's new epistemology redefines the place of the divine. The conditions of temporality and situatedness preclude permanent access, yet if we "skate well" and with felicity, we will catch glimpses of the Oversoul: "Like a bird which alights nowhere, but hops perpetually from bough to bough, is the Power which abides in no man and no woman, but for a moment speaks from this one, and for another moment from that one" (E, 315). This insight brings the human other again within reach of the individual's subjectivity and opens a space for "the leap of commitment." Not vis-a-vis everybody and not always and forever, but ever so often the individual will encounter "this one" who for the time being will speak to his or her soul. For this felicitous encounter to happen, a new, robust self-reliance is required.

Emerson's image of the felicitous skater on surfaces captures a new trust attitude under the conditions of modernity. It symbolizes a type of trust that has gone through self-reflexivity and doubt and is able to accept contingency and a certain amount of risk. As for Giddens, modern trust is for Emerson an activity "in time" and a form of "doing day-to-day life." That said, Emerson's new trust concept is still conceptualized in terms of personal trust and not concerned with the dimensions of trust in abstract systems. In addition, it still has a metaphysical grounding. Although Emerson's image of the surface-skater seems remote from Giddens' simile of the individual being onboard a "careering juggernaut," Emerson still gives us a strong sense that we moderns are up for a rough ride and subjected to a process that is to a large extent out of our control.

Conclusion

As I hope to have shown, the major writers of American Renaissance were highly aware of the problem of trust in modern, diverse, and individualistic societies. They addressed the issue so extensively in their fictional and essayistic writings because they were deeply concerned about human agency under social conditions of anonymity and fluidity. Hawthorne's and Melville's protagonists find it difficult to give up pre-modern trust modes (based on kinship, community, religion, and tradition) and to fully engage in the complex "trust work" necessary to cope in an insecure, modern trust environment. Having already developed a considerable amount of "self-consciousness"—Giddens' "self-reflexivity of modernity,"—they continually doubt the reality of themselves and others and are debilitated in their capacity for action.

At first sight, Emerson seems to offer an easy fix for this problem. In "Self-Reliance," he presents a modern trust program—in tune with democratic liberalism—that promises to supply trust without taking recourse to the traditional trust sources and without plunging the individual into a sea of self-doubt. Self-reliance is presented as a trust-building mechanism through which the individual can authorize and validate him- or herself by an act of moral will. Later essays such as "Experience," however, show that Emerson had second thoughts regarding this "fix." Without renouncing the individualistic basis of his trust concept, he developed a more complex version of it—one that takes a more conscious account of self-reflexivity. In this manner, he was able to pioneer a notion of "doing trust" that anticipates the pragmatist or existentialist trust philosophies from which Giddens's trust sociology has copiously drawn. But even the earlier version of Emersonian self-reliance is interesting to a modern sociological trust analysis. The reformist "work" on the self by the self, proposed by him, can be interpreted as a Giddensian "project of self-identity" through which modern society tries to remedy the emotional and cognitive deficits of modern trust routines and thereby stabilize the social process.

However, there are also important omissions in the trust debate of the writers discussed here. While they are truly avantgarde in highlighting problems of modern trust on the emotional-cognitive level of the human individual, they largely ignore the trust routines connected with the emergence of abstract systems. According to Giddens, abstract systems are an important achievement of modernization; they are vital to stabilizing trust processes under the conditions of modernity. The literary writers, however, do not seem to be particularly interested in them. One party (Hawthorne and Melville) acts as if they did not exist and focuses entirely on the depiction of the existential despair of individuals who have been deprived of their traditional social anchors. The other party (Emerson), while being aware of abstract systems, denies that they are relevant for our existence and encourages us to put our energy into the cultivation of our private, personal selves. Why do these writers exclude abstract systems and institutions from their view? Is it because the development of abstract systems was not far enough advanced in the first half of the nineteenth century and their trust-building capacities were not yet apparent to contemporaries? Or is the omission a consequence of the profound aversion against institutions and abstract systems that has shaped Western culture—and also particularly that of the United States—since the Romantic period? Giddens claims that trust routines connected with abstract systems—unlike trust relations with persons—are largely pursued in an unconscious manner. Only in case of malfunction do they enter our consciousness; otherwise they are taken for granted and remain "unmoralized." This may offer a reason for why the literature of modernity, which is primarily invested in the exploration of private identity, largely disregards the institutional, organizational frame under which this identity operates. Or, if it considers this frame at all, it does so in negative terms, highlighting injustices but ignoring the structures that maintain regular processes. In ancient and Renaissance literature—the ancient epics or Shakespeare's tragedies and histories are good examples—the institutional and the private were seen as being deeply interconnected and were both considered worthy of literary and intellectual exploration. Despite the intellectual depth and sophistication of the American Renaissance writers' analysis of modern trust, the little regard they pay to abstract systems compromises the quality of their sociological analysis. At the risk of sounding like Georg Lukács—who censured the subjectivist, anti-society bias of modern literature—I think that in light of recent political developments in the Western world, it is dangerous if literature takes the institutions and the systems that organize our lives for granted. The ecstasies and anguishes of private life are surely worth exploring, but what maintains and structures our ordinary existence deserves cultural work, too.

Works Cited

Baym, Nina (1981): "Melodramas of Beset Manhood: How Theories of American Fiction Exclude Women," in: American Quarterly 33 (2), 123–139.

Baym, Nina/Robert S. Levine (Eds.) (2012): The Norton Anthology of American Literature. Volume B: 1820–1865. 8th edition, New York/London: Norton.

Beck, Ulrich (1986): Risikogesellschaft. Auf dem Weg in eine andere Moderne, Frankfurt: Suhrkamp.

Bergmann, Johannes Dietrich (1969): "The Original Confidence Man," in: American Quarterly 21 (3), 560–677.

Cameron, Sharon (2006): "Representing Grief: Emerson's 'Experience,'" in: Harold Bloom (Ed.), Emerson's Essays. Bloom's Modern Critical Interpretations, New York: Chelsea House, 125–154.

Emerson, Ralph Waldo (2012): "Experience," in: Nina Baym/Robert S. Levine (Eds.) The Norton Anthology of American Literature. Volume B: 1820–1865. 8th edition, New York/London: Norton, 310–326.

Emerson, Ralph Waldo (2012): "Self-Reliance," in: Nina Baym/Robert S. Levine (Eds.) The Norton Anthology of American Literature. Volume B: 1820–1865. 8th edition, New York/London: Norton, 269–286.

Emerson, Ralph Waldo (2012): "The American Scholar," in: Nina Baym/Robert S. Levine (Eds.) The Norton Anthology of American Literature. Volume B: 1820–1865. 8th edition, New York/London: Norton, 243–256.

Fiedler, Leslie (1960): Love and Death in the American Novel, New York: Criterion Books.

Giddens, Anthony (1990): Consequences of Modernity, Cambridge: Polity Press.

Giddens, Anthony (1991): Modernity and Self-Reflexivity. Self and Society in the Late Modern Stage, Stanford: Stanford University Press.

Hartmann, Martin (2001): "Einleitung," in: Martin Hartmann/Claus Offe (Eds.), Vertrauen. Die Grundlage des sozialen Zusammenhalts, Frankfurt/New York: Campus Verlag, 7–34.

Hawthorne, Nathaniel (2012): "My Kinsman, Major Molineux," in: Nina Baym/Robert S. Levine (Eds.) The Norton Anthology of American Literature. Volume B: 1820–1865. 8th edition, New York/London: Norton, 373–386.

Hawthorne, Nathaniel (2012): "Young Goodman Brown," in: Nina Baym/Robert S. Levine (Eds.) The Norton Anthology of American Literature. Volume B: 1820–1865. 8th edition, New York/London: Norton, 386–395.

Jay, Gregory S. (1990): America the Scrivener: Deconstruction and the Subject of American Literary History, Ithaca: Cornell University Press.

Lindberg, Gary (1982): "Melville's The Confidence-Man: Duplicity and Identity in a New Country," in: Gary Lindberg, The Confidence Man in American Literature, New York: Oxford University Press, 15-47.

Matthiessen, F. O. (1941): American Renaissance. Art and Expression in the Age of Emerson and Whitman, New York: Oxford University Press.

Melville, Herman (2006): The Confidence-Man. His Masquerade. A Norton Critical Edition, Hershel Parker (Ed.), New York: Norton.

Nuissl, Henning (2002): "Bausteine des Vertrauens – eine Begriffsanalyse," in: Berliner Journal für Soziologie 12, 87–108.

Packer, Barbara (2006): "'Experience,'" in: Harold Bloom (Ed.), Emerson's Essays. Bloom's Modern Critical Interpretations, New York: Chelsea House, 67–94.

Parker, Hershel (2006): "The Confidence Man's Masquerade," in: Melville, Herman, The Confidence-Man. His Masquerade. A Norton Critical Edition, Hershel Parker (Ed.), 293–303.

Poirier, Richard (1966): A World Elsewhere. The Place of Style in American Literature, New York: Oxford University Press.

Rowe, John Carlos (1982): Through the Custom-House: Nineteenth-Century American Fiction and Modern Theory, Baltimore: Johns Hopkins University Press.

Reynolds, David S. (1988): Beneath the American Renaissance: The Subversive Imagination in the Age of Emerson and Melville, New York: Knopf.

Tompkins, Jane (1985): Sensational Designs: The Cultural Work of American Fiction, 1790–1870, New York: Oxford University Press.

Wagner, Gerhard (1991): "Eine Bemerkung zum Problem sozialer Ordnung in der Gesellschaftstheorie Anthony Giddens'," in: ARSP: Archiv für Rechts- und Sozialphilosophie / Archives for Philosophy of Law and Social Philosophy 7 (2), 229–242.

Wadlington, Warwick (1975): The Confidence Game in American Literature, Princeton: Princeton University Press.

Authority, Genealogy, Infrastructure
Nineteenth-Century Discourses of
Transatlantic Relationality

Tim Sommer

When the first telegraph message was transmitted between Europe and North America in August 1858, the British satirical weekly *Punch* ran a poem that presented transatlantic contact in fraternal terms, turning technological rapprochement into corporeal connection. Imagining a transatlantic dialogue, the text has British and American citizens exclaim: "That wire will draw close you and me / As those famed twins of Siam" (Anon. 1858: 72). Entitled "The Anglo-Saxon Twins," the text illustrates a newly perceived Anglo-American proximity that was ushered in by the transatlantic telegraph not merely through an abstract reference to racial connections, but more immediately through linking race to family relationships. Reflecting "popular assessments of international telegraphy" as a technology "destined to promote diplomacy and sympathetic connection" (Hanlon 2010: 502),[1] the poem likens Britain and the United States to Siamese twins rather than just to siblings, a rhetorical choice that highlights the degree of intimacy between the two nations (with the transatlantic "wire" imagined as transforming them into a single social

---

1   Hanlon has written extensively on how antebellum debates about the transatlantic cable fed into discussions of Anglo-American relations as well as into relations between North and South (see Hanlon 2010 and Hanlon 2016). Paul Gilmore argues that telegraph technology furthered racialist ideology at the same time that it deconstructed its underlying logic: while "celebrated for extending the conquest of a disembodied white mind," the telegraph, through "rendering bodies unnecessary," "emphasized the disappearance of racial barriers defined in terms of bodily difference" (2002: 806). Brian Murray (2018) points to the discrepancy between Anglo-Saxonist celebrations of Anglo-American contact rendered possible by transatlantic telegraphy and the fact that the telegraph cable ran between Ireland and Newfoundland—Celtic (or, via emigration, Irish-dominated) peripheries of the British Empire.

and political body).[2] Yet "The Anglo-Saxon Twins" would not be a *Punch* piece if this image did not also simultaneously undercut its seemingly straightforward optimism about transoceanic contact. When ties become too close, the simile implies, they threaten to encroach upon the autonomy and physical integrity of the individual national organism. Combining a celebration of physical unity with an anxiety of excessive proximity, the text captures a prevalent mid-nineteenth-century dialectics of transatlantic relationality.

If the image of conjoined twins offers an extreme view of the nineteenth-century special relationship between the United States and the United Kingdom, it was certainly common enough at the time to conceptualize transatlantic links through the language of race and ancestry. As an ideology of origins and destiny, racial Anglo-Saxonism flourished on both sides of the Atlantic—in fields as diverse as comparative anatomy, philology, and cultural history (see Horsman 1981 and Hall 1997). The rhetoric of race offered an effective way of mobilizing sentiments, but its referents were by and large highly abstract. Complex fictions of blood or racial belonging were more palatable when they circulated in the form of a more tangible language of kinship relations that broke conceptual complexity down to the scale of the nuclear family. Using technological infrastructure as an occasion to speak about cultural contact, *Punch* specifically imagines two individuals becoming siblings rather than two peoples discovering their common lineage. Where the language of brotherhood implies equality and solidarity, the twin simile points to the potentially conflictual nature of genealogical connections. This aspect comes to the fore in another nineteenth-century metaphor of transatlantic relations, that of the relationship between parent and child—which frames international relations as a family affair at the same time that it raises questions of hierarchy and authority.

What follows explores such tensions through focusing on family and infrastructure, the two key dimensions of transatlantic connection referenced in the *Punch* poem and by countless nineteenth-century British and American writers. The first section of the chapter examines vocabularies of kinship, while the second looks at the technological developments that accompanied

---

2   Contemporary readers would have decoded the poem's allusion to "those famed twins of Siam" as a reference to Chang and Eng Bunker (1811–1874), Siamese-American conjoined twin brothers who had established a reputation touring the United States as freak show celebrities.

and informed them. Both family rhetoric and the celebration of infrastruc-tural transformations emerged against the background of political conflicts between Britain and the United States in the second third of the century. This period, Elisa Tamarkin reminds us, hardly constituted "good years for Anglo-American relations," despite talk of "collaborative enterprise and commercial alliance" (2008: 58). The disagreements were many: border conflicts between the United States and British Canada in the late 1830s and early 1840s; British meddling with the Texas annexation and the subsequent Mexican-American War in the mid-1840s; and British neutrality during the Civil War years (see ibid., 58–59 and Haynes 1997: 121–122). Genealogical and infrastructural dis-courses could mend such strained relations, but they could just as easily fuel existing conflicts—depending on whether fraternal solidarity or parental au-thority was emphasized or whether the bilaterally beneficial or unilaterally imperial effects of infrastructural advances were highlighted. These discursive frames provided the conceptual language through which nineteenth-century British and American commentators could imagine the special relationship between the United Kingdom and the United States as a constellation marked by shifting distributions of political and cultural authority that continuously redefined the character of transatlantic contact.

The Genealogical Rhetoric of Transatlantic Consanguinity

It requires an act of imagination to turn abstract disembodied concepts such as race or nationality into more intuitively accessible units like the family. The imagery of genealogical intimacy translates membership in a complex social organism into an interpersonal relationship. It collapses time and space into a continuum that condenses deep histories and territorial distances into a do-mestic frame of reference. Research on nationalism has accordingly explained the "special psychological dimension" of the nation as deriving from the "intu-itive sense of kindredness or extended family" that it subconsciously inspires in its members (Connor 1994: 74). In ethnically inflected varieties of nation-alism, Anthony Smith writes, "[t]he nation is seen as a fictive 'super-family,'" its individual members figuring as "brothers and sisters, or at least cousins, differentiated by family ties from outsiders" (1991: 12).[3] This imaginary also

---

3   What is important is obviously not so much the actual reality of kinship ties as it is the belief in them. As Max Weber pointed out, "it does not matter whether or not an

operates beyond the boundaries of individual political entities. In the Anglo-American case, it brought together two different nation-states under the umbrella of an extensive notion of ethnic community. Emphasizing bloodlines and common ancestry, genealogical language was thus also a racialized discourse, but as "an elaborate symbology of relatedness" (Tamarkin 2008: 69), it provided a more tangible version of racialist thought that revolved around individuals rather than large-scale collectives.

Two main forms of family imagery feature in nineteenth-century Anglo-American writing—one with a *vertical* emphasis (the parent-child relationship), the other with a *horizontal* one (the fraternal bond). Whereas vertical versions, with their double emphasis on parental authority and filial obedience, were the dominant form of the trope until the mid-eighteenth century, Jay Fliegelman has shown that the second half of the century witnessed a shift towards "a noncoercive rather than authoritarian model of the family," which, based on the pedagogical philosophies of John Locke and the Scottish Enlightenment, redefined the Anglo-American relationship through a new focus on parental responsibility (1982: 26).[4] Paradoxically enough, the call for colonial autonomy from British paternal control often came framed in a rhetoric of transatlantic racial inheritance that highlighted an Anglo-Saxon passion for liberty as among the colonists' chief family traits. Hypothetically conceding the idea of British parental authority but clearly emphasizing freedom over coercion, Thomas Paine, for example, stressed that wielding power also entailed a corresponding obligation to care. In *Common Sense* (1776), he accuses the British of emotional neglect at the same time that he argues that the nascent United States are in fact the offspring of a pan-European patchwork family:

> Britain is the parent country, say some. Then the more shame upon her conduct. Even brutes do not devour their young, nor savages make war upon their families; wherefore the assertion, if true, turns to her reproach; but it happens not to be true [...]. Europe, and not England, is the parent country

---

objective blood relationship exists" among the members of an ethnic community to make them subscribe to the idea of their relatedness (1978, 1: 389). What matters are "myths of common ancestry, not any fact of ancestry" (Smith 1991: 22).

4   By about 1750, Fliegelman argues, "[a]n older patriarchal family authority was giving way to a new parental ideal characterized by a more affectionate and egalitarian relationship with children"—a paradigm shift that amounts to a fundamental "revolution in the understanding of the nature of authority" (1982: 1, 5).

of America. This new World hath been the asylum for the persecuted lovers of civil and religious liberty from *every part* of Europe. Hither have they fled, not from the tender embraces of the mother, but from the cruelty of the monster; and it is so far true of England, that the same tyranny which drove the first emigrants from home, pursues their descendants still. (1995: 22–23; emphasis in original)

In Paine's analysis, Britain's call for filial obedience emerges as compromised by the country's poor parenting skills, with British "cruelty" framed as a form of domestic abuse. Rejecting the linguistic convention that describes relationships between established and emergent states in genealogical terms—Britain as the "mother" or "parent country" of the American colonies—allows Paine to call traditional power imbalances into question. Sociologist Richard Sennett in this context speaks of a "split between authority and legitimacy" that exists in situations where hierarchical relations continue to be in place while their self-evident rightfulness has become disputed (1993: 45). Since Paine's alternative to the American colonial configuration under British rule has not yet become an independent political entity, his main rhetorical effort is one of deconstructing the notion of maternal benevolence in order to make a case for what Sennett terms "disobedient dependence" (ibid., 28).

Analyzing English neglect half a century later, American author Washington Irving was following essentially the same reasoning as Paine but came to a more conciliatory conclusion. In his collection of essays and short fictions, *The Sketch-Book of Geoffrey Crayon, Gent.* (1819–1820), he asserts that Americans have continued to regard their "parent country" with "tenderness and veneration" despite political tensions during the Revolution and in the wake of the War of 1812:

There is a general impression in England, that the people of the United States are inimical to the parent country. It is one of the errors which have been diligently propagated by designing writers. There is, doubtless, considerable political hostility, and a general soreness at the illiberality of the English press; but, generally speaking, the prepossessions of the people are strongly in favor of England. Indeed, at one time, they amounted, in many parts of the Union, to an absurd degree of bigotry. The bare name of Englishman was a passport to the confidence and hospitality of every family, and too often gave a transient currency to the worthless and the ungrateful. Throughout the country there was something of enthusiasm connected with the idea of England. We looked to it with a hallowed feeling of tenderness and veneration, as the land of our forefathers—the august repository of the monuments and antiquities of our race—the birthplace and mausoleum of the sages and heroes of our paternal history. After our own country, there was none in whose glory we more delighted—none whose good opinion we were more anxious to possess—none toward which our hearts yearned with such throbbings of warm consanguinity. (1998: 54–55)

Irving describes genealogical sentiments as a phenomenon that generates social and individual trust. Even after political independence had been achieved following years of transatlantic family feud, the sense of an intimate connection between American and British citizens remained strong, encouraging "confidence and hospitality" among strangers and guaranteeing the collective welcoming of Englishmen into the sacred space of the American "family." To Irving, this amounts to "bigotry," however, because the kind of trust created by family feeling was being "ungrateful[ly]" exploited by the British. Prepared to pay their transatlantic respects, Irving's filio-pietistic compatriots are systematically snubbed by their "parent country." When he turns to "lament the waywardness of the parent that would repel the affections of the child," Irving—like Paine—reframes the charge of filial disobedience as one of emotional starvation due to neglect by the British (ibid., 55). His Americans proudly embrace their transatlantic parentage with "throbbings of warm consanguinity," but are profoundly troubled by the fact that the feeling seems not to be reciprocated. Irving's gesture of transatlantic sympathy illustrates well what Tamarkin has described as nineteenth-century American Anglophilia, a cultural disposition that "reinvests in patriarchal authority by understanding national ties through anterevolutionary metaphors of familial connections" (2008: 68). For Irving, unlike for Paine, English authority is not in itself problematic; what to him mars the picture of domestic bliss is British indifference.

If Irving was already more diplomatic than Paine, the last traces of transatlantic critique disappeared in a text like Edward Everett's 1824 oration commemorating the Puritan settlement—an address that wholeheartedly celebrates the idea of filial attachment. To Everett, Harvard professor and later U.S. ambassador in London, it was an unequivocal "matter of congratulation and joy, that our fathers were Englishmen" (1825: 42). On a more personal note appropriate to the affective intensity of invoking the bond between parent and child, Everett confessed that "after my native land, I feel a tenderness and a reverence for that of my fathers," speaking with awe of "this great consanguinity of nations" (ibid., 47). Far from being merely another country, Britain was to Everett "that other native land" which could become the emotional target of a transatlantically-extended patriotic admiration (ibid., 49). Everett's oration demonstrates that Anglo-American family rhetoric was not as neatly divided between an American renunciation of British parental authority and a British emphasis on "the older authoritarian model" as Robert Weisbuch has claimed (1986: 64). With British historian and man of letters Thomas Carlyle, for example, the use of the trope was considerably less straightforward than with either Paine or Everett. Although Carlyle often sounded a paternalistic note, he was also in command of the fraternal register. "What [...] is America but a *piece of England*," he asked John Stuart Mill in April 1833, adding that Americans were nothing less than "our Brothers" (1970–, 6: 373; emphasis in original). Writing to his American friend Ralph Waldo Emerson the following year, he expressed "the sentiment of all Englishmen, Cisoceanic and Transoceanic, that we and you are *not* two countries, and cannot for the life of us be; but only two *parishes* of one country" (Emerson/Carlyle 1964: 102; emphases in original). Where England to Everett was "that other native land," America to Carlyle similarly figured as merely "another part of my native country" (ibid., 118). If Carlyle, as Kenneth Marc Harris has noted, "was continually reminding Emerson of their consanguinity," in later years these reminders could also take on a more forceful character (1978: 138). Carlyle at times revelled in the idea of a globally expansive Anglo-Saxon population and attempted to sell this image to his American correspondents through referring to it as their shared "wide motherland" (Emerson/Carlyle 1964: 180). In a later letter, however, he reminded Emerson of the location of the true centre of this configuration. London "is properly *your* Mother City too," he wrote, urging Emerson "to come and look at it" at regular intervals to pay his filial respects (ibid., 423; emphasis in original).

Annoyed by such British exhortations, American writers less transatlantically minded than Everett or Irving went back to revolutionary rhetoric to highlight the emotional and genealogical distance between Britain and the United States. Like Paine, Young American journalist and editor John L. O'Sullivan, for instance, pointed out that Americans had "derived their origin from many other nations" in addition to the English and that their "patriotism" was hence not one "of ancestry" (1839: 426). Pluralist declarations like O'Sullivan's notwithstanding, many Americans at mid-century were interested in tracing their transatlantic heritage—and not just metaphorically, as in Everett's case. The 1840s and 1850s were boom times for the genealogy business on both sides of the Atlantic. More commonly employed in researching the history of the English peerage, British genealogist John Bernard Burke was overrun by American customers eager to trace their potentially august pedigrees. His recollections of their assignments from a decade's distance, at the peak of the Civil War, illustrate how closely the rhetoric of Anglo-American ancestry and contemporary political conflict were tied up with one another:

> Bitter has been of late the expression of animosity against England, and loud the denunciation of her in the United States; yet I cannot but hope and think that there is a deep-rooted affection in America for the "old country," and that when the angry passions, excited by the present most deplorable of wars, have subsided, better sentiments will resume their influence, and former kindly feelings be restored.
>
> For ten or twelve years before the civil conflict broke out, the most intelligent and zealous of my genealogical clients and correspondents were from the other side of the Atlantic, all yearning to carry back their ancestry to the fatherland, and to connect themselves in some way with its historic associations. Massachusetts was more genealogical than Yorkshire, and Boston sustained, what London never did, a Magazine devoted exclusively to genealogy. (1863: 288)

In 1845, a group of eminent Bostonians had founded the New England Historic Genealogical Society and began to issue the *New England Historical and Genealogical Register*. One of the Society's transatlantic correspondents, Burke's American colleague Horatio Gates Somerby, permanently relocated to England to study parish registers and family documents on behalf of his American clients (some of whose pedigrees he embellished or invented from scratch).[5]

Carlyle was not the only British author to seize upon such genealogical enthusiasm to make a case for English authority. Martin Farquhar Tupper, an English poet and moralist read widely on both sides of the Atlantic, tapped into a preexisting American desire for transatlantic attachment. Writing in *The Anglo-Saxon*, a short-lived magazine published in London in the late 1840s,

---

5   On Somerby and the history of genealogy in the United States more generally, see Weil 2013. Writing about Burke and the contemporary American mania for genealogy, Tamarkin speaks of "Anglophilia's genealogical romance of a historic homeland and source of self-fashioning to which all Americans—as members of a widely extended 'kinship'—could subscribe" (2008: 70). Hanlon, by contrast, reads the popularity of genealogy as evidencing not simply Anglophilia but also "a marked ambivalence in American attitudes toward England" (2007: 801).

he sought to capitalize on this sentiment to rally Americans under the banner of global Britishness. In a contribution entitled "A Word to the Yankees," Tupper, like Irving, asserted that the British and the Americans were "blood-relations, called by the same name, stirred by the same sympathies, sons or grandsons of the same stock" (1849: 26). But where the United States in Irving's account had figured as the deserted child, Tupper cast it as the prodigal son. Whenever he meets an American in England, Tupper writes, he treats him as

> a long-lost, long-loving, long-loved brother; an exile from home, whose grand object in life is then daily being realized (through the favour of Providence), in re-visiting the hearth of his ancestors, and in discovering how kindly and yearningly his kith and kin receive him; a son, once the wilful but generous-hearted youth who played truant from his father's house, (through the centrifugal force of unwise austerities,) but now travelling back once more, by land and by sea, over thousands of miles, in mature life, eager to be recognised again as a child, and reconciled to us, his brethren. (ibid., 28)

Although paternal and fraternal language is mixed here, the moral encoding of this parable of the American Revolution and its aftermath is itself straightforward. Whereas in Irving, Americans figure as the wrongfully disowned offspring, in Tupper, they have become "wilful" "exile[s] from home." When Tupper was addressing Americans more directly than in the medium of print, the hierarchical implications of his family rhetoric quickly backfired. He embarrassed himself when he extemporized a speech for a New York audience during an American tour in the spring of 1851, an incident the local press reported with glee:

> Mr. Tupper [...] said—My dear friends, I have not prepared a speech. All I have to say is, that I love you. I have come over the Atlantic ocean to say I love you—to tell you that England loves you. You have some faults, which I do not mean to flatter; but you deserve to be called Englishmen. (Cheers, mingled with suppressed murmurs.) I find no difference. I have crossed the ditch, and I find you are Englishmen at the other side. (Cheers and hisses.) Yankee Englishmen, I mean. (Cheers and laughter.) (*New York Herald*, 25 March 1851, qtd. in Coulombe 1996: 202)

Tupper's moment of failed identification demonstrates how volatile the language of transatlantic kinship could be where it was based on a sense of vertical distance and authority.

Emerson had argued against the condescending British paternalism of the type represented by Tupper in an essay entitled "The Young American" (1844), a text in which he described the danger of parental authority morphing into authoritarianism. Emerson here employs the image of the family to illustrate an argument about political organization. "The patriarchal form of government," he explains, "readily becomes despotic, as each person may see in his own family. Fathers wish to be the fathers of the minds of their children, as well as of their bodies, and behold with great impatience a new character and way of thinking presuming to show itself in their own son or daughter" (1971–2013, 1: 232). As a political strategy, paternalism is a form of exerting authority that, in Sennett's words, aims at "a legitimation of power outside the family by appeal to the roles within the family" (1993: 57). It thus constitutes "a bond of metaphor" that links authority and trust, but one in which both positive and negative connotations of the domestic roots of the image are evoked (ibid., 77). Emerson clearly emphasizes the authoritarian elements of paternalism (control, domination, despotism) more than its affective dimensions (care, protection, security). In *English Traits* (1856), some ten years later, he employs transatlantic family rhetoric in a more emphatic way. In the chapter on British "Manners," for example, he writes admiringly about an English penchant for domesticity: "An English family," he observes, "consists of a few persons, who, from youth to age, are found revolving within a few feet of each other" (1971–2013, 5: 60). The simile he chooses to describe this kind of intimate community is one with which we are already familiar: the "English family" seems to Emerson "as if tied by some invisible ligature, tense as that cartilage which we have seen attaching the two Siamese" (ibid.). Whereas in the *Punch* poem discussed above, the metaphor of the conjoined twins is essentially a negative image of excessive closeness, Emerson's image of the "ligature" binding together the members of the English household is an affirmative one. To him it was this kind of "[d]omesticity" that formed the secret of Britain's global success, "the taproot which enables the nation to branch wide and high" (ibid.).

Elsewhere in *English Traits*, family imagery is employed in a more specifically Anglo-American sense. Recounting a conversation with Carlyle during an excursion to Stonehenge, Emerson presents his response to Carlyle's charge that, for the time being, the Americans would have to receive their instruction from the English. England, Emerson replies, was "an old and exhausted island" and "must one day be contented, like other parents, to be strong only in her children" (ibid., 155). Like Paine, he transforms family rhetoric into a means of filial self-empowerment. His bid for an American pedigree is coupled to a topsy-turvy version of transatlantic authority that upends a vertical relationship of westward paternal dominance and replaces it with the idea of a generational succession that will see the youthful United States grow into becoming the guardian of a senescent British parent. An even more explicit sense of entitlement runs through the journals Emerson used for recording material destined for *English Traits* during his tour of the British Isles in 1847–1848. Reflecting on an English tendency for anti-American self-aggrandizement, in an 1852 entry he remodels American identity by erasing transatlantic difference:

> What is said of England,—every particular,—we Americans read with a secret interest, even when Americans are expressly &, it may seem, on good grounds, affronted & disparaged; for we know that we are the heir, that we & not he who is meant to be praised is the Englishman; but we, we are the Englishman, by gravitation, by destiny, & laws of the Universe. The good he praises is devolving to us, and our keen sympathy in every trait he draws, is the best certificate that we are the lawful son. (1977: 84)

Unlike Paine, Emerson openly endorses a transatlantic line of inheritance that casts the United States as unequivocally English. But instead of binding Americans to the onerous duties of filial piety, Emerson's family imagery formulates a claim to succession that entails a radical recalibration of the parent-child relationship and its underlying dynamics of authority.

Transatlantic Infrastructure: Distance and Rapprochement

As the *Punch* poem on the telegraph as a transatlantic lifeline indicates, the Anglo-American family metaphorics that surface in *English Traits* and countless other mid-century texts were proliferating in tandem with a widespread contemporary impression that Britain and the United States were technologically and infrastructurally growing ever more closely together. When Carlyle, for instance, noted that "America is not a country of strangers; it is a country of our Brothers," that statement was accompanied by the observation that "they are [...] building a Bridge over: there is little doubt but there will be

Steamboats ere long, and a passage of not many days" (1970–, 9: 97). Transatlantic brotherhood, Carlyle suggests, would be strengthened by revolutions in transportation infrastructure. It was the increased speed of transatlantic travel that led to a fundamental recalibration in the perception of genealogical and geographical distances. In 1843, Carlyle observed with surprise that, from a Scotsman's point of view, "America is in very fact *nearer* to us at present than London was fifty years ago" (1970–, 16: 187; emphasis in original). Within half a century, he suggests, the geographical reality of the transatlantic relationship had profoundly shifted. So, too, had the scale of the Anglo-American literary sphere in which writers of Carlyle's generation were moving—a space increasingly contracted through advances in communication, transport, and print technology.[6]

As in the case of racial rhetoric or genealogical imagery, reflections on transatlantic technological rapprochement could take various forms, ranging from cisatlantic isolation to transatlantic inclusion. Infrastructural progress, for example, often served not to highlight Anglo-American proximity but to underwrite cisatlantic difference. It was, after all, one of the argumentative stereotypes of mid-century American cultural nationalism that domestic literature had failed to manifest its cultural autonomy and potential excellence in the past simply because Americans had been preoccupied with building a nation rather than establishing a literary tradition. "We have had the primitive forests to clear away," Boston critic and editor Orestes Brownson declared,

> cities and villages to erect; roads, canals, and railways to construct; in a word, our whole material interests to provide for, and the field of our future glory to prepare. [...] While engaged in this work, we could not turn our attention to the cultivation of a national literature. Moreover, [...] while clearing away the forest, planting the rose in the wilderness, and erecting cities and villages

---

6   Transatlantic literary and cultural relations unfolded against the background of such a material history of Anglo-American exchange. Some recent research, especially in the field of Victorian studies, has begun to pay closer attention to infrastructure both as it shaped and as it was reflected in nineteenth-century writing. See, for example, Menke 2008 for an account of how information systems such as the penny post and the telegraph relate to Victorian realism, or Grossman 2012 on how "advances in public transport"—the stage-coach and railway systems, in particular—"were interconnecting" readers "by networking them together" (3). Both Menke and Grossman are writing about fiction, however, and they largely confine themselves to nation-sized infrastructures. My aim here is to think through the cultural repercussions of communication and transportation technologies on a larger transatlantic scale.

where lately prowled the beast of prey, or curled the smoke of the Wigwam, literature adequate to our wants was furnished by the mother country, of a better quality, and at a cheaper rate than we could furnish it for ourselves. Here is, after all, the chief cause of the deficiency of our literature, and the main reason why we have so long remained the literary vassals of England. (1840: 66)

Brownson frankly acknowledges the transatlantically-pervasive cultural authority of "the mother country," but turns it into an index of political dependence. Cultural identity to American writers like Brownson was intimately connected to questions of infrastructure. In contrast to celebrations of technology as bringing the two nations into closer contact, infrastructural efforts could also be used to shut down transatlantic dialogue through distancing national cultures that, thanks to "roads, canals, and railways," were growing internally more coherent but also transatlantically differentiated from one another. In "The Young American," Emerson, like Brownson, reflects on the kind of infrastructural revolutions that historian Daniel Walker Howe has described as the single most important factor in American history between 1815 and 1848 (see 2007: 203–242).[7] Emerson similarly celebrates infrastructural progress as a catalyst for national—rather than transatlantic—unification. "This rage for road building is beneficent for America," he explains: "Not only is distance annihilated, but when, as now, the locomotive and the steamboat, like enormous shuttles, shoot every day across the thousand various threads of national descent and employment, and bind them fast in one web, an hourly assimilation goes forward, and there is no danger that local peculiarities and hostilities should be preserved" (1971–2013, 1: 223–224). Emerson is not oblivious to the fact that the same logic of assimilation would need to apply to transatlantic distance as well. Yet rather than positing that national "peculiarities" will disappear just as "local" ones, he paradoxically argues that "now that steam has narrowed the Atlantic to a strait, the nervous, rocky West is intruding a new and continental element into the national mind, and we shall yet have an American genius" (ibid., 229). Instead of weaving the United States

---

7   Howe speaks of "twin revolutions" in communication and transportation (2007: 1). Among the first, he counts "[t]he invention of electric telegraphy," "improvements in printing and paper manufacturing; the multiplication of newspapers, magazines, and books; and the expansion of the postal system"; among the second range "the introduction of steamboats, canals, turnpikes, and railroads" (ibid., 1–2). Similar revolutions were of course transforming Britain during the same period.

and Europe more tightly together, transatlantic transportation in Emerson's view will create a distinctive American national identity genuinely independent of European influences.

Emerson's own bonds with Europe, however, were knit closer by the fact that "the Atlantic" had become a mere "strait." When transatlantic steamship travel took off from the late 1830s onwards, it significantly reduced distances between New York and Bristol or Boston and Liverpool. Emerson was among many of his contemporaries who benefitted from these improvements. On his first transatlantic voyage in 1832–1833, it took him thirty-nine days to get to Europe aboard a sailing vessel and another thirty-five to get back to Boston. Upon his return to England for his lecture tour in 1847, that time span had been reduced by more than half.[8] When in the 1830s and 1840s he tried to convince Carlyle to make a transatlantic visit, he noted that the two were in fact "getting to be neighbours," calculating that it would merely take "a day from London to Liverpool; twelve or eleven to Boston; and an hour to Concord," the Massachusetts village in which he resided (Emerson/Carlyle 1964: 355). Carlyle, too, celebrated the fact that steamships would eventually "bring us a thousand miles nearer, at one step" (ibid., 249). His vision of a "universal Saxondom" (ibid., 305) congregating in London at regular intervals—and the model of a centralized, globally expansive British empire that the image represented—relied on the existence of a transnational infrastructure that enabled such large-scale relocations. In developing this idea, Carlyle may have been thinking of Edmund Burke's famous March 1775 speech on "Conciliation with the Colonies," which framed the impending loss of the American territories as a result of transatlantic distance. "Three thousand miles of ocean" were "weakening" the power of British government abroad, Burke argued, regretting that distance was "the immutable condition; the eternal law, of extensive and detached Empire[s]" (1784: 32–33). Nineteenth-century steamships provided a way of rendering this problem "mutable," and Carlyle was quick to recognize the potential of infrastructure to tighten metropolitan control.

Many American writers tended to ascribe the same kind of power to transportation and communication, but some were troubled by what this transformation entailed for American national identity and literary culture. Remarking on the swiftness of the transatlantic passage and on the wide American availability of British periodicals which it had brought about, New York-based

---

8   Seventeen days from Boston to Liverpool and a mere twelve days for the return journey
     (for the exact itineraries of the trips, see von Frank 1994).

author and editor Nathaniel Parker Willis in 1839 worried about the dena-
tionalizing—and recolonizing—effects of an increasingly Anglocentric literary sphere:

> *In literature we are no longer a distinct nation.* The triumph of Atlantic steam
> navigation has driven the smaller drop into the larger, and London has be-
> come the centre. Farewell nationality! The English language now marks the
> limits of a new literary empire, and America is a suburb. Our themes, our
> resources, [...] the feeling of expanse, of unsubserviency, of distance from
> time-hallowed authority and prejudice—all the elements which were work-
> ing gradually but gloriously together to make us a nation by ourselves, have,
> in this approximation of shores, either perished for our using, or slipped
> within the clutch of England. (1839: 150; emphasis in original)

The "approximation of shores" brought about by transportation technology
here features not as a catalyst for cultural contact, but as a phenomenon that
clandestinely re-introduces Britain's "time-hallowed authority" over its former colonies. When Emerson reflected on the effect of innovations in transatlantic travel on a more abstract level than he did in "The Young American,"
he often lapsed into an anxiety of denationalization that matched Willis's
concerns. Like Willis, he tended to emphasize the drawbacks behind the extension of transatlantic network ties. As Laura Otis points out, "networks
both empower and disempower": they can be imagined as "a liberating de-
vice through which scattered individuals can form associations" (the United
States coming into its own regional and cultural identity, the "American genius" Emerson sees as emerging from such national unification), but they can
just as easily "represent the terrible efficiency of a power structure that commands its domain from a central point" (the infrastructurally reinvigorated
"clutch of England" that Willis dreads) (2001: 226, 49, 49).

Carlyle's rhetorical appropriation of transportation infrastructure to effectively recolonize Americans apparently hit a nerve. His private record of
transatlantic travel notwithstanding, Emerson's numerous critiques of "the
superstition of Travelling" take their point of departure from a desire for national autonomy similar to Willis's (1971–2013, 2: 46). If "the rage of travelling" was merely "a symptom of a deeper unsoundness," as Emerson writes
in the 1841 essay "Self-Reliance," the underlying illness was of a more deeply
ingrained cultural kind—imitation, the pathological tendency to "follow the
Past and the Distant" (ibid., 46–47). In as late a text as *The Conduct of Life*
(1860), Emerson still wonders when it would finally be possible to "extract

this tapeworm of Europe from the brain of our countrymen" (1971–2013, 6: 77). But rather than simply arresting the development of national identity, foreign travel is here also considered as a tool to strengthen it—providing "a point of comparison," it ultimately "recommend[s] the books and works of home" (ibid., 78). Emerson's fear of a loss of distinctive national qualities mainly surfaced when he was picturing Americans travelling to Britain. With the transatlantic passage in the opposite direction he argued more confidently—and implicitly against Carlyle—that steam travel would lead to a weakening rather than a consolidation of the British Empire and its political and cultural authority. In an 1853 journal entry, he writes: "The emigration to America of British [...] people is the eulogy of America by the most competent arbiters. In this age, steam has enabled men to choose their country & these men choose ours" (1977: 176). When he reworked the passage for publication in the later *English Traits*, Emerson transformed its American triumphalism first into a more general claim ("Great is the power of steam. Nations are given up" [ibid., 321]) and then into a fully fledged transnational vision from which any concrete reference to American nationality had been redacted: "Nations are getting obsolete, we go and live where we will. Steam has enabled men to choose what law they will live under" (1971–2013, 5: 91).

A similarly cosmopolitan vision of the global dissolution of national boundaries also surfaces in the poetry of Walt Whitman. In "Passage to India" (1870), for example, he celebrates the "technotopic cosmology" (Yandell 2019: 130) of transnational infrastructure and discovers a divine impulse behind the geographical and cultural approximation of the modern world:

> Lo, soul, seest thou not God's purpose from the first?
> The earth to be spann'd, connected by network,
> The races, neighbors, to marry and be given in marriage,
> The oceans to be cross'd, the distant brought near,
> The lands to be welded together. (1998: 316)

With Whitman, too, infrastructural rapprochement is linked to an image of racial amity, but it emerges more radically as an agent of genealogical amalgamation ("races [...] welded together") beyond the boundaries of individual groups—rather than simply imagining intra-racial proximity, as in the idea of British and American Anglo-Saxons connecting with one another but differentiating themselves from other identities. Whitman understands "network" technology as a development that engenders new kinds of family relationship—no longer only brotherhood or the parent-child relationship, but new connections created through the "marriage," the reciprocal espousal of op-posing forces. Whitman's world—unlike Emerson's, Willis's, and Carlyle's—is an egalitarian one in which the conflictual nature of family relationships has disappeared through the collapse of authority, through the dissolution of ge-ographical as much as of hierarchical distance.

Conclusion

Nineteenth-century transportation revolutions not only affected travel, but also resulted in the increased speed and improved reliability of international communication. As James McKusick notes, periodical publications, books, and letters "moved ever more rapidly across the Atlantic as the century progressed" (2017: 196). Steamships carried passengers as well as mail, and the correspondences of nineteenth-century British and American writers are full of reflections on the material preconditions that made transatlantic exchanges of letters possible in the first place. Marvelling at the increasing swiftness with which their missives arrived on each other's doorstep, Carlyle and Emerson, for example, immersed themselves in the minutiae of postage costs and the schedules of mail steamers. When Carlyle at one point com-plained about delayed letters, he was at the same instant prepared to grant that, "as the Atlantic is so broad and deep," one "ought [...] rather to esteem it a beneficent miracle that messages can arrive at all" (Emerson/Carlyle 1964: 112).[9] Anticipating twentieth-century media theories of globalization, he drew attention to the contracting power of an increasingly comprehensive movement of information in which "[s]team and iron are making all the Planet into one Village" (ibid., 209).[10] The kind of global convergence Carlyle here envisions depends on infrastructural networks that circulate people as well as objects across national boundaries. Plummeting costs for shipping manuscripts and books across the Atlantic created a unified transatlantic print sphere that allowed British and American writers of his generation to speak—and sell—to a readership larger than that of any single national

---

9   At other points, miscarried correspondence made the two painfully aware both of "their friendship's dependence on a material exchange" (Decker 1998: 45) and of the difficulties involved in "establishing intimate connections across oceanic separation" (Manning 2013: 164).

10   The most obvious parallel, of course, is that to Marshall McLuhan's classic notion of the influence of electronic media on the emergence of a "global village" (1964: 93).

book market. In addition, what made their professional careers transatlantic was the extensive distribution of the more peripheral print products—newspapers as well as periodicals—that spread their reputations abroad. If, as Joel Wiener has suggested, "the Anglo-American press was a product of a common culture and, as well, of a unified transatlantic sensibility," that very sensibility was also in turn the result of the emergence of such a shared culture of print (2017: 264).[11] Even though infrastructure and the networks that it created could alternatively be imagined as unifying or divisive, the nineteenth-century logistics of transatlantic communication and exchange created an Anglo-American literary and cultural sphere in which discourses of racial and genealogical identity were circulating ever more rapidly.

During his extended tour of the British Isles in the mid-1840s, Frederick Douglass relied on a similar sense of transatlantic contact and exchange to summon the powers of technology and convince his European audiences to stand up against American slavery. In a speech entitled "England Should Lead the Cause of Emancipation," delivered in Leeds on December 23, 1846, Douglass highlighted the connection between steam travel and transatlantic abolitionism:

> No geographical position can debar you from sympathising with the oppressed, denouncing the tyrant and oppressor, and pouring your execration on his head, no matter where he is placed, or to what nation he may belong [...]. [...] It is true you are a good way from America; but by the magic power of steam you are brought as it were within mooring distance of each other, and what is uttered this day in the Music Hall of Leeds, will, within fourteen days resound in Massachusetts [...]. (1979: 477)

Encouraging transatlantic sentiment, Douglass notes with a sense of empowerment the speed with which news of his address would travel across the

---

11   See Straub 2017 for a discussion of how the transatlantic circulation of print products shaped "transatlantic discourse" from the mid-eighteenth to the mid-nineteenth century. Caroline Levine, on the other hand, has drawn attention to the de-unifying dynamics of overlapping infrastructural networks: "One could certainly *imagine* the nation as a unity," she concedes, "but its multiple print, postal, economic, and regional networks, with their different organizing principles, broken links, and temporal delays, did more to hinder the nation from assuming a whole, unifying shape than to foster that reality" (2015: 121; emphasis in original).

ocean and circulate widely through getting reprinted in the United States.[12] Douglass does more than merely rely on print dissemination and "the magic power of steam," however. His appeal to British audiences to campaign against slavery would truly prove effective, he suggests, not simply through the force of quantity, but also—and more importantly—because of the kind of authority Britain began to exert over the United States upon abolishing slavery the previous decade. It was this reform image that gave the country the necessary moral leverage for Douglass to imagine a quasi-parental form of British intervention that would expose the wayward and inhumane American child to severe ethical reprimand. Yet if Douglass subscribes to the transatlantic family imagery Paine, Irving, Emerson, and others had employed before him, the rhetoric of genealogy here appears on another level as well. Whereas Douglass was advancing a case for transatlantic familiality on stage, the Leeds newspaper that reported his speech framed him as a "son of Africa" (ibid., 474) rather than as Anglo-American kin. Technological progress could be portrayed as facilitating cultural rapprochement and transatlantic social reform, but to the majority of nineteenth-century British and American commentators, differences of race and nationality were not "welded together" quite as easily as Whitman imagined. Like racial Anglo-Saxonism, family discourse dialectically relied on forms of exclusion to create the impression of inclusivist relationality. Like infrastructural rhetoric, it made neither difference nor authority disappear.

Works Cited

Anon. (1858). "The Anglo-Saxon Twins: Connected by the Atlantic Telegraph." *Punch* 35 (14 August): 72.

Bennett, Bridget (2011). "Frederick Douglass and Transatlantic Echoes of 'The Color Line.'" *Transatlantic Literary Exchanges, 1790–1870: Gender, Race, and Nation.* Ed. Kevin Hutchings and Julia M. Wright. Farnham: Ashgate. 101–113.

Brownson, Orestes A. (1840). "American Literature." *Boston Quarterly Review* 3.1 (January): 57–79.

---

12   On Douglass's transatlantic career (and on the ways in which his antislavery campaigning depended on transatlantic circuits of communication and print dissemination), see Bennett 2011, Eckel 2013: 71–98, and Wright 2017: 49–80.

Burke, John Bernard (1863). *Vicissitudes of Families: Third Series*. London: Longman, Green, Longman, and Roberts.

Burke, Edmund (1784 [1775]). *Speech of Edmund Burke, Esq. on Moving His Resolutions for Conciliation with the Colonies, March 22, 1775*. London: J. Dodsley.

Carlyle, Thomas, and Jane Welsh Carlyle (1970–). *The Collected Letters of Thomas and Jane Welsh Carlyle*. 46 vols. to date. Ed. Charles Richard Sanders et al. Durham, NC and London: Duke University Press.

Connor, Walker (1994). *Ethnonationalism: The Quest for Understanding*. Princeton: Princeton University Press.

Coulombe, Joseph L. (1996). "'To Destroy the Teacher': Whitman and Martin Farquhar Tupper's 1851 Trip to America." *Walt Whitman Quarterly Review* 13.4: 199–209.

Decker, William Merrill (1998). *Epistolary Practices: Letter Writing in America before Telecommunications*. Chapel Hill and London: University of North Carolina Press.

Douglass, Frederick (1979). "England Should Lead the Cause of Emancipation: An Address Delivered in Leeds, England, on 23 December 1846." *The Frederick Douglass Papers. Series One: Speeches, Debates, and Interviews*. Vol. 1: *1841–1846*. Ed. John W. Blassingame. New Haven: Yale University Press. 474–485.

Eckel, Leslie Elizabeth (2013). *Atlantic Citizens: Nineteenth-Century American Writers at Work in the World*. Edinburgh: Edinburgh University Press.

Emerson, Ralph Waldo (1971–2013). *The Collected Works of Ralph Waldo Emerson*. 10 vols. Ed. Alfred R. Ferguson et al. Cambridge, MA: Belknap Press of Harvard University Press.

—— (1977). *The Journals and Miscellaneous Notebooks of Ralph Waldo Emerson*. Vol. 13: *1852–1855*. Ed. Ralph H. Orth and Alfred R. Ferguson. Cambridge, MA: Harvard University Press.

——, and Thomas Carlyle (1964). *The Correspondence of Emerson and Carlyle*. Ed. Joseph Slater. New York: Columbia University Press.

Everett, Edward (1825). *An Oration Delivered at Plymouth, December 22, 1824*. Boston: Cummings, Hilliard & Co.

Fliegelman, Jay (1982). *Prodigals and Pilgrims: The American Revolution against Patriarchal Authority, 1750–1800*. New York: Cambridge University Press.

Gilmore, Paul (2002). "The Telegraph in Black and White." *English Literary History* 69.3 (Fall): 805–833.

Grossman, Jonathan H. (2012). *Charles Dickens's Networks: Public Transport and the Novel*. Oxford: Oxford University Press.

Hall, J. R. (1997). "Mid-Nineteenth-Century American Anglo-Saxonism: The Question of Language." *Anglo-Saxonism and the Construction of Social Identity*. Ed. Allen J. Frantzen and John D. Niles. Gainesville: University Press of Florida. 133–156.

Hanlon, Christopher (2007). "'The Old Race Are All Gone': Transatlantic Blood-lines and *English Traits*." *American Literary History* 19.4 (Winter): 800–823.

―――― (2010). "Embodied Eloquence, the Sumner Assault, and the Transatlantic Cable." *American Literature* 82.3 (September): 489–518.

―――― (2016). "On Transatlantic Simultaneity and Misunderstanding Telegraphy." *Traveling Traditions: Nineteenth-Century Cultural Concepts and Transatlantic Intellectual Networks*. Ed. Erik Redling. Berlin and Boston: de Gruyter. 213–229.

Harris, Kenneth Marc (1978). *Carlyle and Emerson: Their Long Debate*. Cambridge, MA: Harvard University Press.

Haynes, Sam W. (1997). "Anglophobia and the Annexation of Texas: The Quest for National Security." *Manifest Destiny and Empire: American Antebellum Expansionism*. Ed. Sam W. Haynes and Christopher Morris. College Station: Texas A&M University Press. 115–145.

Horsman, Reginald (1981). *Race and Manifest Destiny: The Origins of American Racial Anglo-Saxonism*. Cambridge, MA: Harvard University Press.

Howe, Daniel Walker (2007). *What Hath God Wrought: The Transformation of America, 1815–1848*. New York: Oxford University Press.

Irving, Washington (1998 [1819–1820]). *The Sketch-Book of Geoffrey Crayon, Gent.* Ed. Susan Manning. Oxford: Oxford University Press.

Levine, Caroline (2015). *Forms: Whole, Rhythm, Hierarchy, Network*. Princeton and Oxford: Princeton University Press.

Manning, Susan (2013). *Poetics of Character: Transatlantic Encounters, 1700–1900*. Cambridge: Cambridge University Press.

McKusick, James C. (2017). "Afterword." *Transatlantic Literary Ecologies: Nature and Culture in the Nineteenth-Century Anglophone Atlantic World*. Ed. Kevin Hutchings and John Miller. London and New York: Routledge. 196–198.

McLuhan, Marshall (1964). *Understanding Media: The Extensions of Man*. New York: McGraw-Hill.

Menke, Richard (2008). *Telegraphic Realism: Victorian Fiction and Other Information Systems*. Stanford: Stanford University Press.

Murray, Brian H. (2018). "Saxon Shore to Celtic Coast: Diasporic Telegraphy in the Atlantic World." *Coastal Cultures of the Long Nineteenth Century*. Ed.

Matthew Ingleby and Matthew P. M. Kerr. Edinburgh: Edinburgh University Press. 149–168.

O'Sullivan, John L. (1839). "The Great Nation of Futurity." *United States Magazine and Democratic Review* 6.23 (November): 426–430.

Otis, Laura (2001). *Networking: Communicating with Bodies and Machines in the Nineteenth Century*. Ann Arbor: University of Michigan Press.

Paine, Thomas (1995). *Rights of Man, Common Sense, and Other Political Writings*. Ed. Mark Philp. Oxford: Oxford University Press.

Sennett, Richard (1993 [1980]). *Authority*. New York and London: W. W. Norton.

Smith, Anthony D. (1991). *National Identity*. Harmondsworth: Penguin.

Straub, Julia (2017). *The Rise of New Media, 1750–1850: Transatlantic Discourse and American Memory*. New York: Palgrave Macmillan.

Tamarkin, Elisa (2008). *Anglophilia: Deference, Devotion, and Antebellum America*. Chicago and London: University of Chicago Press.

Tupper, Martin F. (1849). "A Word to the Yankees." *The Anglo-Saxon* 1.3 (July): 25–32.

von Frank, Albert J. (1994). *An Emerson Chronology*. New York: G. K. Hall.

Weber, Max (1978 [1921/1922]). *Economy and Society: An Outline of Interpretive Sociology*. 2 vols. Trans. Ephraim Fischoff et al. Ed. Guenther Roth and Claus Wittich. Berkeley: University of California Press.

Weil, François (2013). *Family Trees: A History of Genealogy in America*. Cambridge, MA: Harvard University Press.

Weisbuch, Robert (1986). *Atlantic Double-Cross: American Literature and British Influence in the Age of Emerson*. Chicago and London: University of Chicago Press.

Whitman, Walt (1998). *Leaves of Grass*. Ed. Jerome Loving. Oxford: Oxford University Press.

Wiener, Joel H. (2017). "British and American Newspaper Journalism in the Nineteenth Century." *Journalism and the Periodical Press in Nineteenth-Century Britain*. Ed. Joanne Shattock. Cambridge: Cambridge University Press. 263–280.

Willis, Nathaniel Parker (1839). *Al'abri, or The Tent Pitch'd*. New York: Samuel Colman.

Wright, Tom F. (2017). *Lecturing the Atlantic: Speech, Print and an Anglo-American Commons 1830–1870*. New York: Oxford University Press.

Yandell, Kay (2019). *Telegraphies: Indigeneity, Identity, and Nation in America's Nineteenth-Century Virtual Realm*. New York: Oxford University Press.

Shoppers, Worshippers, Culture Warriors
Reading and the Hermeneutics of Trust

Günter Leypoldt

Reading involves differing qualities of experience. As the American transcendentalist Ralph Waldo Emerson put it in 1841 (in "The Over-Soul"): "There is a difference between one and another hour of life in their authority and their subsequent effect." Some hours are merely "habitual," others have such a "depth" in them that we "ascribe more reality to them than to all other experiences" (1903, II: 267). A more recent term is "quality time," which, since the 1970s, has come to designate a more meaningful engagement with the world than the habitual regimes of "real time." If the "Age of Amazon" still thinks of literature as a site of "virtual quality time" (McGurl 2016, 466), how do readers distinguish between the various levels of quality they encounter in the vast "bookshop" of past and present literary culture? My claim, in this essay, is that people orient themselves in the literary field with the help of public and private selection regimes to which they extend various degrees of trust.

In what follows, I want to explore the different kinds of trust relations in the literary field by looking at the hermeneutics of reading. The first section will set up the perimeters of the discussion with a sketch of George Steiner's account of the "hermeneutic motion" as a four-fold process (involving trust, prejudgment, incorporation, and restoration). The subsequent section extends Steiner's account using Charles Taylor's theory of moral "frameworks." Whereas Steiner ties the donation of trust to a dialectics of submission and dominance that requires interpreters to find a restorative equilibrium (between reader and text or self and other), Taylor's distinction of strong and weak evaluative frameworks allows me to introduce three hermeneutic positions that ignore such an equilibrium by default: Readers as purpose-oriented consumers, as worshippers trusting a higher good, and as culture warriors revolted by a "toxic" kind of sacred. The section "Bad Reading" addresses how these positions jar with received ideals of "critical thinking" in a "procedural republic." The section "Atmospheres of Trust" takes the complex reception history of Henry Wadsworth Longfellow's *Evangeline* (1847) as a foil for discussing the difficult ontological status of more or less trustworthy artifacts. Using the phenomenological concept of aesthetic "atmospheres," I argue that a fuller understanding of hermeneutic positions requires scholarship that combines event-based descriptions of texts with an ethnography of strong and weak frames of reading. The final section, "Trusting the Canon," addresses how the nexus of trust and public authority shapes the cultural relevance and intrinsic value conflicts of canon-building.

Steiner's Concept of Hermeneutic Balance

Trust is key to Steiner's four-fold model of the hermeneutic process (see Felski 2015, 64). Before any kind of reading practice can begin, he argues, we need to "trust" that "there is 'something there'" worth our time. It can always transpire "that there is nothing there" (Steiner 1975, 296), but without an initial "donation of trust" (297) the act of reading will not take shape. "After trust comes aggression," Steiner continues. Once we have taken the "leap" (296) we encircle and invade the text in an "unavoidable mode of attack" (297). Since interpretation has to begin with what we already know, we "prejudge" the new, in Gadamer's terms (1990), by translating it into familiar categories, a process by definition invasive, appropriative, violent. Incorporating the new, however, might modify our sense of "being," as Heidegger might say. In Steiner's terms: "No language, no traditional symbolic set or cultural ensemble imports without risk of being transformed" (299). The outcome is far from clear: we might dislike our new sense of self or "horizon" of meaning. Hence the fourth move, Steiner explains, requires a politics of interpretation. We assess our losses and gains, and take restorative or protective measures, to ensure that the result of our self-transformation suits our purposes (see fig. 1).

In Steiner's account, the fourth move aims primarily at ensuring the "reciprocity" and "balance" of the exchange. "The a-prioristic movement of trust," he says, "puts us off balance." First we "'lean towards' the confronting text," then "encircle and invade cognitively," until we "come home laden, thus again off-balance, having caused disequilibrium throughout the system by taking away from 'the other' and by adding, though possibly with ambiguous consequence, to our own. The system is now off-tilt." Thus: "The hermeneutic act

Figure 1: Steiner's Four-Fold Hermeneutic Motion

Steiner's Four-Fold Hermeneutic Motion

1st Move	2nd Move	3rd Move	4th Move
Initiative Trust Something worth the effort	**Aggression** Violence of prejudgment	**Incorporation** Self-transformation through ingestion	**Restitution** Compensation, balance, parity of exchange

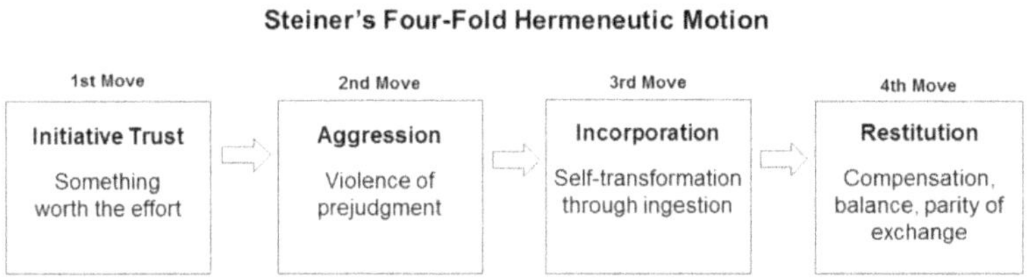

must compensate. If it is to be authentic, it must mediate into exchange and restored parity" (300).

Why this focus on "parity"? Steiner suggests that interpretive authenticity requires a neutral trade balance between the exchanging parties, that is, between the reader negotiating with an unfamiliar text, or the self with an "other." The image of trade balance suggests that the bargaining partners should have equal weight in their attempts at "fusion of horizons" (see Vessey 2009, 534). At the root of Steiner's emphasis on parity of exchange is a political analogy: Readers and texts, self and other, resemble participants in a democracy. Here, a balanced power relation ensures equal representation and reciprocal recognition, preventing structures of domination. In the case of democratic societies, the downsides of domination—social hierarchies and inequalities—are self-evident, but how do relations of dominance affect the hermeneutic process? Steiner thinks that a hermeneutic trade deficit undermines our expressive autonomy. As individuals, we might "be mastered and made lame by what we have imported," when a foreign "voice" will "choke" our own. As a group or a society, similarly, we "can be knocked off balance and made to lose belief in [our] own identity," like colonized minds who respond to the weight of cultural imperialism with self-alienating "mimicry" (299). Mimicry, in this case, indicates a deplorable loss of agency: dominated cultures, the story goes, struggle to express themselves on their own terms.[1]

---

1   The subaltern, so it is said, cannot speak, unless it manages to "write back" against the imperial center (Ashcroft et al. 1989). Literary theory developed a number of now classic modelings of this thesis. At the individual level, Harold Bloom (1973) invokes the figure of the "strong reader" who manages to overcome the "anxiety of influence" that inheres in the work of powerful predecessors. In accord with Bloom's psychoanalytic terminology, Homi Bhabha (1994, 86) uses Lacanian and Derridean concepts to refig-

Strong and Weak "Frameworks"

The democratic equality model of hermeneutics has its uses, but it obscures a range of self-other relationships for which the analogy to political auton-omy and democratic equality does not work. What if a literary text strikes me as embodying a "higher good" similar to the experience of moral or reli-gious meaning?[2] In Charles Taylor's broad definition of moral experience (one that cuts across moral-aesthetic and religious-secular divides), people orient themselves towards notions of higher good with the help of identity-defining "frameworks" of "strong evaluation" (1989, 19–20). Strong frameworks "involve discriminations of right or wrong, better or worse, higher or lower" whose validity does not follow from "our own desires, inclinations, or choices, but rather stand independent of these and offer standards by which these can be judged" (4). Thus: "To think, feel, judge within such a framework is to func-tion with the sense that some action, or mode of life, or mode of feeling is incomparably higher than the others which are more readily available to us" (19). Taylor uses the spatial qualifier "high/low" in generic terms that can be expressed with a range of different distinctions. "One form of life may be seen as fuller, another way of feeling and acting as purer, a mode of feeling or living as deeper, a style of life more admirable, a given demand as making an absolute claim against merely relative ones, and so on" (20). Of course, in theory, we can point to the deconstructability of absolute standpoints (always made rather than found) and, in the spirit of late-twentieth-century theo-retical skepticism, dismiss them as irrelevant. In *lived practice*, however, rele-vance is performative and hinges on the affective intensity with which we feel "placed" in relation to a perceived "higher good." Taylor's point is that in the performative sense all cultures have strong-valued frameworks, even though these can be hard to recognize, as they largely sit at the "background" (1989, 21) of actions, as tacit knowledge or a practical sense rather than a fully ar-ticulated account. While modern social imaginaries always pose a plurality of frameworks—we can be "moved" by many higher goods, and torn between incommensurable ones—they tend to come to us "ranked" (62) in an order of importance.[3] At the top of our hierarchical order of strong-value frameworks

---

ure cultural "mimicry" as a defense mechanism by which the colonized estrange and thus destabilize the colonizer's identity.

2   The following section draws from Leypoldt 2020.

3   "Thus, within certain religious traditions, 'contact' is understood as a relation to God and may be understood in sacramental terms or in those of prayer or devotion. For

lies the sphere of "hypergoods," that is, "higher-order goods" that strike us not only as "incomparably more important" than other goods of strong value, but also as providing "the standpoint from which these must be weighed, judged, decided about" (63).[4]

Not every evaluative activity, to be sure, is of identity-defining intensity. There is a large domain of practice—the domain of "weak valuation" (Taylor 1985, 16)—in which the ranking of frameworks seems less urgent. People can be passionate about their favorite ice-cream flavor, but they would hardly start a culture war about such issues. Weak valuation makes hierarchical scales feel less imperative, allowing us to be more tolerant of disagreement ("I like strawberry and you vanilla," *chacun à son goût* [Taylor, 2011, 297]). The further we move towards strong value issues that are more closely connected to our hypergoods—fair trade, abortion, Brexit, human rights violations, or the like—the harder it becomes to adopt a relativist tolerance of dissent. In practice, weak and strong values tend to be bundled together, as when your favorite food seems all the more enjoyable if it embodies the moral authority of "fair trade." The analytical distinction remains significant, however. Whereas weak frameworks concern our everyday desires, strong ones are linked to the hierarchical imaginaries with which we classify our desires into higher or lower kinds—"more and less fulfilling, more and less refined, profound and

---

those who espouse the honor ethic, the issue concerns their place in the space of fame and infamy. The aspiration is to glory, or at least to avoid shame and dishonour, which would make life unbearable and non-existence seem preferable. For those who define the good as self-mastery through reason, the aspiration is to be able to order their lives, and the unbearable threat is of being engulfed and degraded by the irresistible craving for lower things. For those moved by one of the modern forms of the affirmation of ordinary life, it is above all important to see oneself as moved by and furthering this life, in one's work for instance, and one's family. People for whom meaning is given to life by expression must see themselves as bringing their potential to expression, if not in one of the recognized artistic or intellectual media, then perhaps in the shape of their lives themselves. And so on" (1989, 44).

4   "For those with a strong commitment to such a [hyper]good, what it means is that this above all others provides the landmarks for what they judge to be the direction of their lives. While they recognize a whole range of qualitative distinctions, while all of these involve strong evaluation, so that they judge themselves and others by the degree they attain the goods concerned and admire or look down on people in function of this, nevertheless the one highest good has a special place. It is orientation to this which comes closest to defining my identity, and therefore my direction to this good is of unique importance to me" (62–3).

superficial, noble and base" (Taylor 1985, 16; Joas 2000, 129). Whereas weak values emerge in the situated rationalities of our personal lifeworld, strong ones seem to transcend our subjective moves. We experience them as appealing to us from the *outside* of our mundane purpose-rational selves (as in Max Weber's "Außeralltäglichkeit," something "outside [Außen]" "everdayness [Alltäglichkeit]" [1972, 140]).

If we move from moral to literary practice, Taylor's argument helps us to see that literary experience can involve two essentially different kinds of "trust devices" (Karpik 2010): one "calculative," the other "relational."[5] Consider how this distinction affects the meaning of the literary prize system. If we approach the system of literary prizes with "calculative trust" in the delivery of personal satisfaction, the Nobel, the Booker, or the World Fantasy Award become tools to reduce the opacity of the market, similar to Amazon's "people-who-bought-this-also-looked-at-that" algorithm. If, on the other hand, we become attuned to "relational" trust in how a text is "placed" in relation to cultural authority, award rankings do not just facilitate personal uses but sustain a hierarchical landscape that divides the "pleasure of reading" into higher and lower kinds ("serious" vs. "guilty pleasure") and puts the prize system itself in vertical tension, suggesting that some prizes outrank the others.

Calculative Trust: Readers as Consumers

Whether we attune ourselves to weaker or stronger frameworks matters to the balance of hermeneutic exchange. As weak evaluators, we tend to conduct the hermeneutic attack with a degree of self-centered carelessness. Subordinating the other to our situated concerns, we become Bloomian "strong readers" who (in Richard Rorty's apt phrase) "beat the text into a shape which will serve [their] own purpose" (1982, 151). Theorists of interpretation like to point to the integrity of the text or authorial intention to dismiss strong reading as a mere "playing" with texts (Fish 1994, 185). Others rejoin that rigid distinctions between interpreting and playing never hold up to deconstructive scrutiny.[6] Both positions in this longstanding quarrel tend to overlook the relevance of evaluative frameworks. Weak evaluation *welcomes* readerly

---

5   For a fuller discussion of this distinction, see Leypoldt 2017.
6   For this older debate about interpretation, see the dispute between Umberto Eco and Richard Rorty in Stefan Collini's *Interpretation and Overinterpretation* (1992).

play. Unlike professional interpreters, who are bound to peer-review-based notions of higher good, leisure readers focused on pragmatic outcomes resemble shoppers browsing in a supermarket aisle: they are perfectly entitled to carry home whatever they desire, and would be astonished if they were expected to worry about the integrity of the wares or the shop owner's intentions. Coming home "laden" with their spoils, moreover, need not put them "off-balance," as Steiner's image of equal trade balance assumes. For it is not clear how weak-valued goods affect our sense of being. If we read for no other reason than the enjoyment of instantly forgettable pleasures, the "risk" of "being transformed" by what we "import" seems minimal. In the sphere of weak valuation, our fourth hermeneutic move—a "politics" that weighs our losses and gains—boils down to measuring pragmatic outcomes: Did I enjoy the experience? Did I make the most of the material at hand? Was it good for my mental and bodily well-being? Did I choose well among conflicting pragmatic goods, or has my consumption practice perhaps prevented other desirable activities (see fig. 2)?

Figure 2: Reader as Consumer (Weak-Valued Hermeneutic Motion)

Reader as Consumer (Weak-Valued Hermeneutic Motion)

1st Move	2nd Move	3rd Move	4th Move
Initiative Trust (Calculative) Something worth the effort within the everyday	**Aggression** Beating the text into the shape that suits our purpose	**Incorporation** Consumption without self-transformation	**Calculation** Weighing of outcomes (did the experience suit my purposes?)

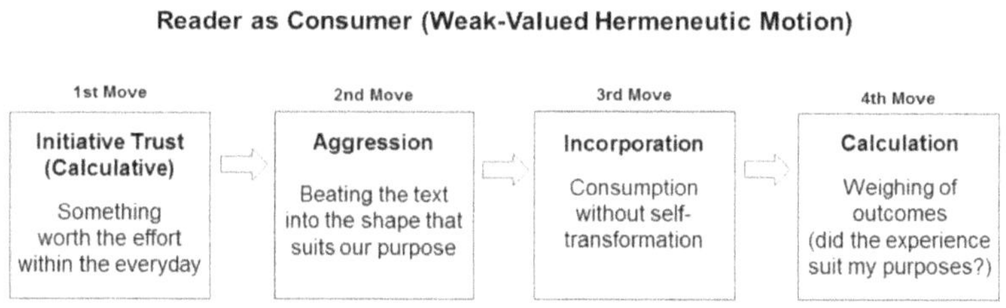

Vertical Resonance, Relational Trust: Readers as Worshippers

Once a text is perceived as embodying a higher good, it acquires a "vertical resonance" (Rosa 2019, 284) that unbalances the exchange between self and other in the opposite direction. Strong-valued works have a way of looking down upon us as if from a higher position. "You have to change your life," Rilke hears a Greek sculpture calling down to him in the Paris Louvre, suggesting he should make a greater effort to lift himself up to the elevated region within the cultural landscape.[7] This sense of "being spoken to from above" (Sloterdijk 2013, 22–3) tilts the hermeneutic relationship towards deference, even worship. If comprehension is always violent, because we force the foreign text into familiar categories, the felt presence of higher goods disarms our prejudgment at least by a degree. Our trust in something larger can turn the unfamiliar text into a "strong" agent (to adapt Bloom's image) that imposes *its* purpose upon *us*. In Paul Valéry's phrase, an artifact with overwhelming presence can make us feel "that we are in some profound sense transforming ourselves, in order to become the person whose sensitivity is capable of such fullness of delight and immediate apprehension" (1937, 965; see Rosa 2019, 284). Vertical resonance, then, turns us into reverent readers: we tread with care, anxious not to presume, with patience and a willing suspension of skeptical questioning, embarrassed if the text provides no everyday use for us, ready to attribute our inability to find "something there" to our own rather than the text's inadequacy. Worshipping interpreters are not entirely different from mystics "speaking in tongues": they power down their individual voice to make room for a higher language, which they want to transmit as truly as possible, engaging in voluntary "mimicry" that feels perfectly empowering. Here, being "knocked off balance" seems uplifting rather than oppressive, since the pull of being called upon from above justifies the imbalance of the exchange. Max Weber explains this voluntary self-surrender by distinguishing "power" from "authority." Where power *tout court* concerns a person's ability to impose their "will" upon us despite our "resistance," authority represents power that strikes us as "legitimate" because it accords with our sense of higher good (Weber 1972, 28, 122). The difference between authority and power decides whether we experience our self-surrender as a welcome connection to something larger or as the result of illegitimate domination (see fig. 3).

---

7   In his 1908 poem "Archaic Torso of Apollo" (1995, 66–7), which possibly refers to the Louvre's torso of a standing nude youth, *Kouros from Miletus*, ca. 490–480 BC (Louvre MND, 2792).

Figure 3: Reader as Worshipper (Strong-Valued Hermeneutic Motion)

Reader as Worshipper (Strong-Valued Hermeneutic Motion)

1st Move	2nd Move	3rd Move	4th Move
Initiative Trust (Relational) Something there, relational to a higher good	**Attraction** Proceeding with care, suspension of critical questioning	**Surrender** Self-renunciation, voluntary mimicry, self-colonization	**Vertical Resonance** Willing subordination to higher good

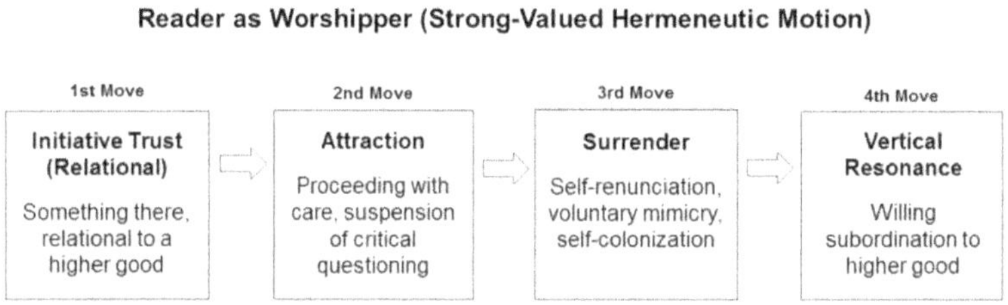

Mundane Trash, Toxic Presence: Indifferent Readers vs. Culture Warriors

Strong valuation has two negative slopes. The first concerns a process of trivialization or "de-singularization" (Kopytoff 1986), when the loss of authority renders a formerly consecrated artifact mundane. The circulation and visibility of mundane things depends on whether people trust that they have a quotidian use for them. Think of Henry Wadsworth Longfellow, the most prestigious mid- to late-nineteenth-century US poet, who, after 1940, dropped out of the transatlantic literary canon. No longer capable of "breaking the envelope of the mundane" (Alexander et al. 2013, 10), his poems became ordinary commodities that, after a brief life on the coffee tables of an aging generation, sank into the oblivion of minor heritage archives (the sphere of "uninhabited" cultural memory, in Aleida Assmann's terms [1999, 133]). Commodities without use or authority recall the phenomenology of trash: we see them only when they get in our way. This aspect of no-longer-consecrated artifacts encourages the misconception that museums or canons are mere "mausoleums" or "sepulchers" of once living things (see Marinetti 1909, Valéry 1923, Adorno 1953, Negrin 1993). However, while shutting things up in "priceless" or "inalienable" collections may sever them from their "living" uses, their real death occurs only when their disconnection from authority results in a loss of "presence" (Gumbrecht 2003), "charisma" (Shils 1982), "iconic aura" (Alexander/Bartmański 2012), "enrichment" (Boltanski/Esquerre 2020), or "singularity" (Kopytoff 1986, Leypoldt 2014, Reckwitz 2020).

A second negative slope of strong valuation concerns the "darkening" or "polluting" of artifacts that in the course of their de-authorization become powerfully offensive as opposed to merely mundane.[8] Darkened or polluted artifacts retain the visibility of sacred things, yet with a stigmatized presence that inspires negative affects: revulsion, disgust, hatred. Such "toxic" sacrality typically emerges when an artifact begins to embody mutually exclusive strong values, prompting a conflict between negative and positive perceptions that divides audiences and/or consecrating authorities. Such a conflict can emerge as a stain in a thing's sacred fabric, as when the stigma of racism entered the civil-religious iconicity of Thomas Jefferson in the recent flare-up of the Sally Hemings affair (after a widely publicized DNA analysis in 1998 proved an old rumor that he fathered several children with one of his slaves). The darker symbolism—a powerful white plantation owner abuses his teenage slave—is now part of the official "authorized heritage discourse,"[9] but it arguably has not polluted the site of memory as a whole: Jefferson's bright founding-father presence has—so far, at least—kept the implications of the Hemings affair at a level of minor blemish.[10] Compare this to how the recent #RhodesMustFall initiative finalized an already latent symbolic "narrowing" of Cecil Rhodes to an embodiment of exploitative "colonial heritage" that contemporary Britain struggles to commemorate with pride. Another, more divisive example is the "Confederate Monuments" debate: The narrowing of the Confederacy's icons to symbols of racism and oppression has been salient in civil-sphere discourse on US democracy for quite some time. But a national consensus is blocked by a polarized political scene that overdetermines disagreements about statues with the "hot-button-issues" of the US culture war. Whether people are sickened by a "toxic" statue of Robert E. Lee, or by the "toxic" attempt to tear this statue down, depends on their affiliation with increasingly separate social networks, lifeforms, party politics, regions, and group identities.[11]

---

8   On the idea of "dark heritage," see Thomas et al. 2019, on symbolic pollution, see Douglas 1966.

9   See, for example, "Thomas Jefferson and Sally Hemings: A Brief Account" on the website of the Jefferson museum at Monticello (2020). On the concept of "authorized heritage discourse," see Smith 2006.

10   This may change in the near future: see Truscott 2020.

11   To understand the conflicts around consecrated heritage, it is useful to consider Philip Smith's (2012, 172) distinction between *two kinds* of iconicity. Type 1 concerns the transformation of ordinary events, persons, or things into widely recognizable visual images, when pictorial representations of Thomas Jefferson, Cecil Rhodes, or Robert E. Lee acquire presence and visibility in the culture's visual field. This is the domain of Peirce-inspired iconography and the so-called "visual" or "pictorial turn" (Boehm 1994,

In literary or intellectual culture, conflicts about incommensurate hyper-goods are often restricted to field-specific quarrels, as when the consecrating authorities within a literary establishment are divided over whether a new paradigm is artistic excellence or barbarism parading as art (think of how even pre-modernist convention-breakers such as Whitman's *Leaves of Grass* [1855] revolted large parts of the literary establishments before becoming canonical). Longfellow, too, went through a brief phase of literary-field-specific darken-ing, when, between 1900 and 1940, he struck a younger generation of writers as a poster boy for what, in 1911, George Santayana called the "genteel tradi-tion" (1968, 86) —a cultural elite that was accused of furthering a dissociation of sensibility that threatened the nation's cultural fiber.[12]

Toxicity circulates more widely when struggles over symbolic meanings spill over into the larger public sphere. The classic scenario is a standoff

---

Mitchell 1986). Type 2 iconicity, in contrast, has more to do with Roland Barthes' anal-ysis of symbolic "mythologies," when icons are charged with a moral depth that their material surface puts—performatively—in sensuous manifestation. Type 2 iconicity concerns the strong values that the public iconographies of Jefferson, Rhodes, or Lee can embody for specific audiences. Smith suggests that dissent about type 2 iconic-ity—"emotive disputes" over whether an icon represents "the triumph or the degra-dation of the social" —heightens an icon's "charismatic energy." I would think the op-posite is also true: to produce a sense of toxicity, an icon needs to have already been charged with charismatic energy. A polluted *mundane* thing is more likely to strike us with a contempt we typically feel about objects that "are noticed only sufficiently so as to know that they are not noteworthy" (Miller 1997, 215). To the degree that polluted things have charismatic energy, they provoke the more powerful "agonistic emotion" of "disgust" (Ngai 2005, 335).

12   As Van Wyck Brooks complained in 1915, writers like Longfellow had helped America to break into "two publics," an effete "cultured public" that "reads Maeterlinck," and a "largely masculine" "business public" that "accumulates money" (1934, 78–9). The claim that Longfellow's work was detrimental to the growth of the American Mind emerged relatively early (see Willis 2006), with a number of hostile reviews (by Edgar Allan Poe and Margaret Fuller, among others), though the critical success of *Evange-line* (1847) and *Hiawatha* (1855) kept this at the level of a minor stigma in Longfellow's iconicity, until about 1900, when the weight of the Whitmanian paradigm made this stigma grow, and his work was narrowed to an embodiment of the "genteel" that crys-talized the disgust of modernist avant-gardes. Once the modernist aesthetics came to dominate the literary establishment in the 1930s and 1940s, Longfellow's work sank to the level of mundane harmlessness ("grandmotherly" poetry of the "schoolroom" and the "fireside"), and ceased to elicit strong negative responses (in later editions, Brooks even apologized for having been too "harsh" at a time "[w]hen we were tired of hearing Longfellow called 'The Just'" [1934, 10–11]).

between curational judgments about strong-valued artistry and civil-sphere perceptions of strong-valued democratic virtue or human decency (see Alexander 2006). Does Woody Allen embody a distinguished arthouse-film career or an offensive culture of misogyny and abuse? Should Lord Byron be "cancelled" because his private sexual transgression rendered his poetry dangerous (as Harriet Beecher Stowe claimed in 1869)? Is the high-canonical materiality of Richard Wagner's music ruined by his anti-Semitic beliefs? Should Heidegger's work be seen in the light of his ground-breaking philosophical idiom or his Nazi collaboration? And how should Peter Handke's stances on the Yugoslavian Civil War relate to his high-canonical literary status? Traditional philosophies of art like to attribute these conflicts to an intrinsic tension between artistic and moral-political "logics," "genres," or "intellectual spheres" (as Kant's influential separation of disinterested beauty from conceptual and moral truth-claims suggests). I would prefer to speak of tensions between social fields disagreeing on *which* genres and formal logics can constitute a higher good. Toxicity is an aesthetic quality (in the sense of *aisthesis*, perception), but one that can happen to all kinds of materialities, artistic or not. There is only a difference of degree, I think, between the felt disgust with polluted art objects—when Whitman's poetry feels like "hexameters [...] trying to bubble through sewage" (Wendell 1900, 473)—and polluted civil-sacred heritage sites—when Woodrow Wilson's legacy became so tarnished within the Black Lives Matter context that Princeton University felt compelled to remove his name from its public policy school and residential college (see Pietsch, 2020).

   With regard to the hermeneutic motion, the presence of darkened sacrality turns interpreters into culture warriors with a deep distrust of the other. Repelled by toxic presence, we become "suspicious minds" (Felski 2015), entering the text with the force of a police raid, eager to disarm and expose, confident that forced confessions will justify a higher good. The need to purge the self of an identity-polluting influence renders our prejudgment as relentless as a 1930s show trial: We shut down all "imports," silencing the other with the zeal of former colonials wishing to "write back against" an exploitative center so as to "decolonize" their "minds." Since true disgust perceives the object as harmful and infectious, it makes us draw others into the effort of radical expulsion, furthering the aggressive conviviality of "cancel culture" (Bromwich 2018, Asmelash 2019).[13] (See fig. 4)

Figure 4: Reader as Culture Warrior (Strong-Valued Hermeneutic Motion)

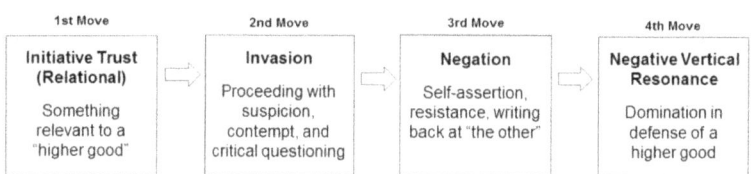

Bad Reading

Needless to say, my portrait of the reader as a mistrustful culture warrior, reverent worshipper, or self-involved consumer, jars with received notions of what it takes to be a good reader. A common objection draws from a cognitive model of the "open mind" as one that allows us to assess the text separately from strong-valued commitments (see Fish 1999, 247), in contrast to the "closed minds" of prejudiced or emotionally involved ("sentimental") readers. Traditional philosophies of art have connected the cognitive model of the "open mind" to a notion of literary-artistic "free play" that emancipates readers from political, moral, economic, and religious biases.[14] This "demo-

---

13   As Miller points out, disgust typically makes us not only want to "exclude" the polluted thing but also seek the "concurrence" of others in its exclusion. Disgust has "powerful communalizing capacities and is especially useful and necessary as a builder of moral and social community. It performs this function obviously by helping define and locate the boundary separating our group from their group, purity from pollution, the violable from the inviolable" (1997, 194–5).

14   The connection of art to mental "free play" derives from romantic theories of aesthetic *bildung* that in the Anglophone world became current through Matthew Arnold's *Culture and Anarchy* (1869). We can become "disinterested," Arnold said, if we habitualize "the free spontaneous play of consciousness" that helps "to float our stock habits of thinking and acting" (1993, 178). The objections against Arnold are too well known to require rehearsing here, but it is worth recalling the afterlife of the notion of "free

cratic emancipation" model of literature and art continues to shape the idea of "independent critical thinking" as an asset of the humanities or liberal-arts education (see Nussbaum 2016). Cultural historiographers like to frame the democratic free-play concept with a *bildungsroman* narrative of progressive autonomy: literature and the arts march through the periods in a series of incremental breakthroughs culminating in a postmodernist "incredulity towards metanarratives" (Lyotard 1984, xxiv). The view that skepticism liberates us from bias draws from a tacit secularization narrative that "exoticizes" the experience of religious higher goods as categorically different from secular ones (Joas 2019). Though simple secularization models have not aged well in the social sciences (Connolly 2000, Berger 2014), in literary scholarship they still flourish at the background of an influential "rise of modern literature" framework that explains modernity's supposed "loss of aura" (Benjamin 1968) as a fortunate fall: Since the modern condition stripped things of their sacred "halo," the story goes, artists and audiences have had to learn to see the real in the "cold light of day" (Levine 1981, 165, see Berman 1982, 116), graduating on to the tougher but also more authentic reality beyond pseudo-sacred fantasies.

The factuality/fantasy distinction helps to join the idea of open minds in free play to classic liberalism's procedural notions of democratic tolerance. The ideal of a "procedural republic" (Sandel 1998) suggests that one can combine justice with tolerance with the help of content-blind mechanisms of elimination that exclude from the "public square" what is merely private or lacks reasonable common sense (religion, affects, and other forms of irrationality). More recently, this view underlies a public misconception that open societies can defend themselves against illiberal threats by rejecting "populists" or "racists" on the grounds of their flawed or irrational "logic" rather than their political claims.[15] The "procedural" view allows Steiner to define the politics of interpretation as *internal* to the hermeneutic motion, as if we could ensure

---

play" (see Young 1995, 55–7), a phrase that appears in English translations of the deconstructive "play" ("le jeu") that Jacques Derrida first proposed in his "La structure, le signe et le jeu dans le discours des sciences humaines" (1966), his contribution to the Johns Hopkins symposium that produced the "structuralist controversy" (the proceedings translate "jeu" as "freeplay" [Derrida 1970]).

15   See, for example, Jan-Werner Müller's claim that populism has an "inner logic" based on a deceptive "illusion" (2016, 10–1), in contrast to Mudde/Kaltwasser (2017), who argue that a populist logic can have good or bad political effects, and Mouffe (2018), who in the spirit of Laclau (2005) interprets populism as a specific form of democratic dissent.

a good outcome to the potentially violent dialectics of prejudgment and in-corporation by adding a fourth stage of restored balance. Steiner's suggestion that a successful hermeneutic motion rests on parity of exchange is logically similar to the humanist claim that society's democratic health rests on peo-ple's ability to engage in "independent critical thinking." Balance is offered as a content-blind criterion that allows us to dismiss hermeneutic culture war-riors, worshippers, or consumers as "bad readers" (Emre 2017) regardless of their moral frames.

Let us pause for a moment to look at how the question of bad reading sits with present literary theories. Event-centered approaches would solve the problem of readerly bias by grounding the hermeneutic motion in objective text-context structures, often with a scientistic sense that an artifact's on-tology precedes its "social lives." Scholarship in this vein requests proof that the perception of sacred, mundane, or toxic qualities are rooted in the liter-ary event itself, rather than being mere reception phenomena that tell us less about "the text" than the history of its appropriations (or "fetishizations"). The ambition is, for example, to excavate the real Longfellow from his avatars by trying to separate the meaning of *Evangeline* from the social materialities that are "thrust upon" *Evangeline* after it has been propelled into social space. The misconception is that markets and institutions "transformed" *Evangeline*'s originary structure into a social construct by turning it into a bestselling com-modity, a canonical work, a polluted symbol of the genteel, or a mundane piece of minor heritage.

The attempt to find the real *Evangeline* behind the social fetishes is obvi-ous in "formalist" methodologies that reduce the literary event to its analyz-able "architecture." But it also shapes the now more common "anti-formalist" enterprise of ideology critique that reads texts "symptomatically" (Best/Mar-cus 2009), as expressive speech acts which reveal a society's "political uncon-scious" (Jameson 1981) or "the way a culture thinks about itself" (Tompkins 1985, xi). Treating the work as a window on social causes extends the status of "bad readers" virtually to all lay audiences. For to excavate a text's "political un-conscious" requires the penetrating eye of professional analysts who can ex-pose the hidden "investments" behind their patients' muddled tales and con-flicting emotions. Psychoanalytic criticism has become unfashionable, but the legacy of psychosocial concepts of readerly "desire" or the "pleasures" of am-bivalent attraction still widely pass as implicit explanations of why lay readers would want to bother consuming symptomatic texts. We find a work attrac-tive, the argument goes, if it provides *literary-artistic displacements* of political issues we are not yet able to work through on our own, either because we do not dare to face them in the cold light of day or because we have not yet acquired a language to bring them to terms. While the hermeneutic penetration of the real falls to the expert-analyst, the reader's felt sense of trust—the question whether *Evangeline* strikes us as sacred, toxic, or mundane—is relegated to the level of "mere" affective response (the ugly feelings a patient experiences on the therapeutic couch).

Atmospheres of Trust (Longfellow's *Evangeline*)

Wanting to separate structure from affect, however, ignores the relevance of an artifact's "atmosphere," as it is being theorized by recent phenomenology and affect studies (Böhme 2017, Zhang 2018, Bille et al. 2015, Griffero/Tedescini 2019). An atmosphere might be said to be a spatially extended quality of feeling that readers absorb into their "bodily state of being" during the process of perception (Böhme 2017, 15). Reducible neither to reader-independent structure or structure-independent interiority, aesthetic atmospheres emerge in the contact between people and things, in lived moments of *resonance* between a work's sensible features and the subjective sensitivity of the person immersed in these features. Due to their relational nature, atmospheres are hard to grasp with the toolkits of event-based criticism. They seem independent of our inner selves, a bit like weather systems, in Böhme's metaphor, that impose their "spatially extended quality of feeling" (2017, 15) on us as if from the outside (we can "happen upon" an atmosphere, feel "assailed," "enveloped," or "caught up" in it as something "quasi-objective," the existence of which we can "communicate with others" [11; 25]). Yet since such "attuned spaces [gestimmte Räume]" only exist in moments of experiential immersion, their materiality is performative, a structure of feeling that cannot be deduced from abstract text-context structures.[16]

---

16   Viewing atmospheres as "attuned spaces [gestimmte Räume]" recalls Heidegger's concept of "Stimmung" (German for "attunement" and "mood") that fundamentally shapes a person's "Da-sein [being-there]" (in his 1929 *Fundamental Concepts of Metaphysics*, Heidegger argues that *Stimmungen* "are *not side effects*" but something that "in advance determine[s] our being with one another." A *Stimmung* precedes "cognition and volition" because it is "already there, so to speak, like an atmosphere" in which we would "immerse ourselves" and which would then "attun[e] us through and through [von der wir dann durchstimmt würden]" [1995, 66–7, 2004, 100]). Some critics distinguish at-

Whether our contact with a thing leads to a sacred, mundane, or toxic atmosphere arguably hinges on the dialectics of acquired perceptive "schemes" and "conceptual models" that differ in time and place. Scholars wishing to determine the meaning of a work therefore need to combine the analysis of text-context structures with an ethnographic inquiry into the *affective quality* with which text-context structures are experienced by empirical reader collectives. How did it feel to be immersed in *Evangeline*, in 1847, 1900, or 1950, within differing spaces of practice? If we wish to take atmospheric experience seriously, knowing about the poem's abstract affordances (an epic, in unrhymed dactylic hexameters, on the expulsion of French Acadians, with a tragic love plot, involving heroic renunciation and moral fortitude, with picturesque descriptions of American wilderness, etc.) is a first step, but one that needs to be followed up with evidence about what sort of trust relations these affordances sustain, and how they are placed in the shifting high-low differentials of strong-valued cultural space. Does Longfellow's revival of Latin hexameters in English feel dignified or banal? Have readers found his embrace of a Walter Scott-inspired national-historical epic trite or ennobling? Does his use of simile come across as "natural" or "contrived"? Do his nature descriptions strike people as worthy or demeaning of the "American Sublime"?

Nineteenth-century reviewers liked to answer such questions with musical images that invoke the elusive quality—the *je ne sais quoi*—of aesthetic atmospheres. In *Evangeline*, Longfellow describes his heroine's "ethereal beauty"

---

mospheres and moods (Fuchs [2000, 215] defines *Stimmung* as closer to interiority than atmosphere: "we feel an atmosphere in a space and participate with it but are ourselves attuned [gestimmt]"; thus with atmospheres "the induction" runs "from the outside inwards", while with *Stimmungen* rather from the inside outwards"). But often these terms are used interchangeably (as are "affects," "feelings, and "emotions" [see Zhang 2018, 124–5]). Jonathan Flatley distinguishes Heidegger's *Stimmung* (which he calls "affective atmosphere," "mood," or "attunement") from Raymond Williams' notion of "structures of feeling": "Where *Stimmung* as a concept focuses attention on what kinds of affect and actions are possible within an overall environment, structures of feeling are more discrete, less total, and they orient one toward a specific social class or context. For example, depression is a mood, not a structure of feeling; however, we might describe the particular depression of the Russian peasant in the steppe in the 1920s as a structure of feeling, or the depression of the residents of a decimated New Orleans after Katrina as a structure of feeling, or [...] we might talk about the structure of feeling created by the civil rights movements and the Black Panthers, structures of feeling that were mobilized within the *Stimmung* that allowed the 1967 rebellion against the police in Detroit to happen" (2008, 26–7).

(1853, 5) in terms of sound in motion—"When she had passed, it seemed like the ceasing of exquisite music" (6). One rave reviewer quipped that this "elevating and hallowing" effect also pertains to reading Longfellow's poem: "When the perusal is finished, it seems, indeed, 'like the ceasing of exquisite music'" (anon. 1848, 108). Another reviewer, by contrast, thought that Longfellow ruined his poem's intended musicality by his stylistic choices ("the measure jars upon us; it is as though we were reading intense prose before a slowly nodding China mandarin" [Peck 1948, 7]). Of course, such statements require a propositional rationalization of atmospheric perception. Whether *Evangeline*'s "music" strikes us with positive or negative atmospheric feelings (or the absence of feeling, when it "leaves us cold") hinges on our perceptional schemes. But to experience this music as higher or lower (ennobling or base) requires a musical "program" that allows us to make sense of our atmospheric feelings. A "program" provides the conceptual model that crystalizes vague aesthetic atmospheres into communicable meaning.[17]

---

17   We need a conceptual model to determine, for example, whether or not the Italianate-Beethovenesque compositions of the "log cabin" composer Anthony Heinrich (1781–1861) strike us as expressing an American atmosphere (as the programmatic title of his 1823 Opus 3 suggests: *The Sylviad, Or Minstrelsy of Nature in the Wilds of North America*). Or, in a metaphorical sense: our musical "program" decides whether we think the "lawless music" of Whitmanian free-verse accords with the lifeforms of American democracy or rather with the anarchic traditions of Europe (as Barrett Wendell thought [1900, 467]) or even the archaic world of primal societies (as Edmund Stedman believed [1885, 371], referring to Whitman's parallels with Biblical rhetoric). This dialectics of perceptive schemes and conceptual models concerns all kinds of atmospheric sense-making. Take, for example, the shifting discourse of mental wellbeing. A person's embodied sensibility might determine whether they experience recurring atmospheres of anxiety or sadness. How to explain and live with such atmospheres, depends on a limited number of conceptual models of shifting cultural centrality and authority. One popular "program" is the "burnout" metaphor (you have worked too hard, depleted you batteries, but the problem can be solved if you take some time out to recharge, or develop more mindful forms of life); another one is the image of trauma (you repressed a hurt that happened to you some time ago, and to heal it you must learn to bring it to terms, "working through" rather than "acting out" the trauma, to reach "closure" and "move on"); a third one is the idea of physiological imbalance (you tend towards a minor neurological dysfunction, around serotonin or similar neurotransmitters, which can be helped with specific medications). We might say with William James (1981, 92) that "truth *happens*" to a causal explanation of atmospheres if it is good to believe (if it helps people to "cope"). But while perceptive schemes depend on people's acquired habitus, "what is good to believe" is regulated by public authorities.

The point of distinguishing between perceptive and conceptual levels of atmospheric experience is to pay attention to their shifting relations to a higher good. To feel enveloped in positive or negative atmospheres hinges largely on schemes we acquire in the everyday, during our social "trajectory" in which we pick up the more personalized habits of our "sensibility." Yet to feel that a positive or negative atmosphere brings us closer or further away from something larger—as the relational terms "sacred," "mundane," and "toxic" suggest—concerns a more public level of our habitus; one that involves truth-claims and causal narratives (a "creed" or "doctrine") subject to public authorization. Taylor's distinction between strong and weak frameworks helps us to understand how the public and personal levels of experience interact with one another. The contact between people and things can produce a variety of atmospheres, and in the mode of weak valuation, we are more willing to embrace the full plurality of human experience. Like ice-cream connoisseurs contemplating the multiplicity of tastes in the world, weak evaluators can live with the claim that *Evangeline*'s music has whatever atmospheric quality my personal sensibility produces, and that this atmospheric quality means—*to me*—whatever my preferred conceptual program defines. Once we switch to strong-valued frames, however, our perception of *Evangeline* becomes more closely tied to hypergoods, which is to say, the atmosphere that results from our contact with the poem will likely produce more powerful affective intensities, ranging from disgust with the toxic to love of the sacred. As we have seen, such affective intensities are more likely to make us take a public stand and seek community-building concurrence (Miller 1997, 194–5). While in theory individualized hypergoods would be thinkable, in lived practice clashing hypergoods make relativist compromises unsustainable, and so the plurality of possible conceptual programs is limited to a smaller number that inscribe themselves into the public sphere. Within the professionalizing nineteenth-century literary establishment, the increasing symbolic inequality between "experts" and "lay readers" led to a disconnect between people's atmospheric perceptions and the conceptual programs with which they feel obliged to make sense of their perceptions.[18] *Evangeline* became a classic after the 1850s

---

18   The symbolic inequality between lay and expert readers has little purchase for weak-valued literary experience. But in more strong-valued domains (traditionally associated with "serious reading"), the control over literary standards never rested with a general reading public, since the rise of popular literary markets coincided with the simultaneous rise of market-sheltered gate-keeping structures similar to those of the "liberal" or "learned professions" (the ministry, law, medicine)—credentialing systems

not because of its popularity but because it resonated with the best authorized "experts" in the literary field—critics who were in a numerical minority
position but due to their institutional weight could make their embodied experience and conceptual program dominate the public accounts about what
Evangeline is.

We can simplify a complex reception history (McFarland 2010) by saying that in 1847 *Evangeline* produced at least three relevant aesthetic atmospheres. In the first, some of the most prestigious experts in the literary field
were convinced that *Evangeline* was on a par with the best poetry of the age
("greater" than some of Tennyson's epics [Devey 1873, 363]). This charismatic
atmosphere connected Longfellow's writing to a literary-artistic higher good,
turning readers into hermeneutic worshipper who prejudge with care. Relational trust in *Evangeline*'s connection to the higher poetic life encouraged
readers to suspend their critical questioning, to embrace the poem's affordances with maximal good will, and to dismiss subjectively jarring aspects as
minor blemishes irrelevant to the larger whole (an attitude taken by multiple
reviewers who quibbled with some of the poem's formal micro-levels while
praising its higher "radiance").[19] This atmosphere convinced readers of *Evangeline*'s relevance as a "higher pleasure" that transcends mundane and merely
personal uses.

A second atmosphere shaped the verdict of a smaller group of experts who
experienced Longfellow's "music" as second-rate and programmatically inter-

---

that restrict the right to define what counts as higher good by peer review. The literary field may lack the high levels of "institutional certainty" (Chong 2020, 147) that
pertain to more "scientific" spheres of professional gatekeeping, but it does shape a
public economy of prestige. Moreover, Longfellow's rise and fall coincided with an increase in institutional certainty in the literary field: Whereas in the 1850s and 1860s his
authority rested on a culture of experts dominated by well-educated gentlemen who
read in their free time, the thickening literary-artistic networks of literary modernism
entrusted the literary peer review process to academic scholar-connoisseurs. By the
time modernism was institutionalized in post-1945 mass higher education, *Evangeline*
had become too simple to be taken seriously ("Who, except wretched schoolchildren,
now reads Longfellow?," Ludwig Lewisohn asked in 1932 [65]).

19   As Edmund C. Stedman put it 1885: "There are flaws and petty fancies and homely passages in 'Evangeline'; but this one poem, thus far the flower of American idyls, known
in all lands, I will not approach in a critical spirit. There are rooms in every house where
one treads with softened footfall. Accept it as the poet left it, the mark of our advance
at that time in the art of song—his own favorite, of which he justly might be fond, since
his people loved it with him, and him always for its sake" (201).

preted this deficiency as a result of its derivative relation to European conventions (Edward Dowden portrayed *Evangeline* as a "European idyl of American life, [Goethe's] Hermann and Dorothea having emigrated to Acadie" [1871, 34]). This atmosphere kept *Evangeline* on the level of mundane artifacts whose merits hinged on specific uses. Reviewers in this vein argued that while the poem was not in the upper league, it provided pretty enough scenes and an uplifting story, with beauties accessible to uninitiated readers. Such accounts often excused Longfellow's *literary* mundanity by pointing to a sense of the "civil sacred" (Alexander 2019, 108), the moral-political strong value he embodied as a writer who improved the American scene (as someone who could "laugh the philistine to scorn," according to Stedman, and bring Arnoldian "sweetness and light" to a pervading "atmosphere" of "rudeness, ignorance, and asceticism" [1885, 51]).

The third atmosphere concerned the large segment of lay readers for whom *Evangeline* served as pleasurable entertainment. The poem's binge-readable combination of love story and romantic wilderness scenery (including a picturesque boat ride down the Mississippi) attracted audiences that normally preferred novel reading to epic poetry—a fact that explains *Evangeline*'s unusual commercial success (which enabled Longfellow to resign his Harvard professorship in 1854 [Charvat 1968, 117]).

These three atmospheres (call them "high-artistic," "civil-sacred," and "pleasure-bingeing") differed widely in their cultural authority. Since the high-artistic program dominated the public square, it motivated binge-readers to redescribe their use as a higher pleasure, and urged audiences who had not yet found a use for *Evangeline*'s specific musicality to work on their musical sense. If *Evangeline* did not strike you as a pleasurable read, your relational trust in its authority could urge you to "change your life" in Rilke's sense, to become an aspirational reader willing to invest in the hard work of acquiring an ear for the poem's as yet unusable sounds. Of course, the aspirational desire to "get" a high-artistic atmosphere can be motivated by calculative trust in tangible assets (good grades, Bourdeusian "social distinction"), but consecrated atmospheres also promise a purpose-transcending connection to the "higher life of the culture."

Trusting the Canon

The "higher life of the culture" can sound odd in our pluralist age, and critics routinely question the reality of canons produced by "the so-called authorities." The idea that institutionalized canons are oppressive because they disenfranchise part of the demos continues to attract Foucauldian vocabularies about how "discourse/power" excludes the "unsayable" or (in Jacques Rancière's more recent formulation) "polices" the "distribution of the sensible" (2004, 3–4).[20] Such imagery suggests that democratic societies had better abolish their canons to help "redistribute" the "sensible" on equal terms.

A Weberian response would be to stress that people submit willingly to a dominant order if it fills them with relational trust. The relevance of trust is obvious for aspirational schoolroom readers, who learn to recognize the authority of atmospheres for which they have not yet acquired a taste by following the gaze of trustworthy authorities: teachers selecting a literary canon, curation cultures structuring the museum's white cubes or sites of civil-sacred memory. Relational trust in this case can mean to accept the authority view of Longfellow's greatness even though one is as yet unable to feel his greatness or make a coherent argumentative case for it. The ethos of "independent critical thinking" suggests, of course, that people should learn to form a more "self-reliant" verdict (trust "thyself" rather than a consecrated canon). But it is hard to see how strong evaluators can ever "grow out" of authorized trust relations, since the sheer size of literary heritage condemns the most erudite experts to fall back on trustworthy evaluation regimes. The nineteenth-century critics who thought *Evangeline* was better than *Enoch Arden* (1864) and on a par with *Hermann and Dorothea* (1797) already knew that Tennyson and Goethe stood in the upper regions of laureate space. They acquired this knowledge in the virtual schoolroom of legitimized "tradition;" that is, by following the gaze of preceding authorities whose verdicts they happened to trust. If canonization involves constant reevaluation (forging a "living tradition" from the totality of inherited tradition), this process can only begin after a preliminary donation of trust in previous foundations.[21]

---

20   By "distribution of the sensible" Rancière means an aesthetic-political order imposed upon the demos by an organizational system that he significantly labels "the police" (2004, 3–4), while "politics" is defined as an emancipatory counter-power.

21   Alexis de Tocqueville already makes this case in the second volume of *Democracy in America* (1840), in relation to the authority of knowledge foundations: "If a man were forced to prove all the truths he makes use of every day, he would never finish; he

The contentious nature of canonization has therefore less to do with the undemocratic nature of peer-oriented hierarchies than with a conflict between two incommensurable hypergoods. Our relational trust seems torn between a strong-valued desire to rank better over worse lifeforms and the equally strong-valued desire to exempt all human lifeforms from the indignity of hierarchical ranking. A traditional attempt to solve this tension is to relativize the act of ranking by framing competing artifacts as "different-but-of-equal-dignity." This move first emerged in the romantic period, when Johann Gottfried Herder defended the literature of Germany against the dominance of French writers by emphasizing their incommensurable expressive sources (a German vs. a French national spirit). The relativist culture model initiated by Herder (and further developed by twentieth-century anthropologists like Ruth Benedict [see Kuper, 1999, 66] and cultural pluralists like Horace Kallen [see Sollors, 1986, 97]) helped to unsettle rigid universalisms, but it also explains away the uncompromising force of strong evaluation. The "Herder effect" (Casanova 2004, 77) that continues to shape proliferating notions of literary identity (national, cultural, ethnic, racial, etc.) treats the varied cultures in the world like independent nations under the UN: different-but-equal political collectives that should be cosmopolitan (willing to engage with other collectives, open to a mutually benefiting exchange), but own a right to protect their autonomy and integrity against more dominant players (cultural imperialists who, in Steiner's terms, cause smaller nations to "be knocked off balance and made to lose belief in their own identity" [1975, 299]). But this model of the world as a patchwork of autonomous cultures ignores rather than solves the intrinsic tension between the higher good of equal recognition and the necessity to rank *some* moral goods *higher* than others (equal dignity itself being part of a strong hierarchy with which democratic discourse distinguishes "civil" from "uncivil" lifeforms [Alexander 2006, 57–9], thus withholding the status of "equal dignity" from those whom society considers to pollute its moral core).

---

would exhaust himself in preliminary demonstrations without advancing; as he does not have the time because of the short span of life, nor the ability because of the limits of his mind, to act that way, he is reduced to accepting as given a host of facts and opinions that he has neither the leisure nor the power to examine and verify by himself, but that the more able have found or the crowd adopts. It is on this first foundation that he himself builds the edifice of his own thoughts [...]. There is no philosopher in the world so great that he does not believe a million things on faith in others or does not suppose many more truths than he establishes" (2000, 407-8).

In the literary field, moreover, the trouble with the "different-but-equal" figure is that it requires an expressivist concept of literary production: it only makes sense if we treat literary artifacts as speech acts by which cultural identities represent themselves. Of course, if texts are first and foremost representations of autonomous cultures, canon-building looks like a dubious attempt at ranking identities into better or worse kinds. But literary texts are also often seen as strong-valued acts of "world-disclosure" that we can experience as higher achievements rather than as representations of specific groups. The models we choose will affect how we judge the problem of canon-building: If we apply the expressivist concept of literature as a representative speech act, the "canon wars" in US literature departments since the 1970s look like an emancipatory politics of recognition by which underrepresented identities (sexual, ethnic, racial, or social minorities) struggle for democratic parity. If we view literary practice as the realization of higher goods, by contrast, the ranking of texts with no regard to their representativeness seems not only legitimate but indispensable.

How to solve this dilemma? Debates about prize winners (another white-male Nobel laureate from Europe!) can sound as if hierarchical ranking were unproblematic so long as each section of the demos received proportional representation. But it is hard to see how such a proceduralism could work (should Nobel committees devise a system of rotating recognition in which each identity in the world could enjoy Warhol's fifteen minutes of fame?). In practice, rotating recognition proceduralisms only work when the stakes are low (when each ice-cream flavor, say, gets a turn on the national menu). Since no-one expects a prize committee to rotate sacred and toxic moral positions ("This year's award will have to go to the proponents of fascism"), strong-valued notions of literary excellence remain hard to square with democratic demands that "the next laureate should be an X" or "the canon needs more Ys." This clash between hypergoods can easily be overlooked whenever the prize system happens to settle on laureates that are lucky enough to satisfy both demands. A Nobel Prize winner like Toni Morrison, for example, seems at once a transcultural literary heavyweight and a representative of a specifically African-American kind of literariness. Morrison's particular iconicity can also make us overlook another crucial tension that plagues the battles around heritage: between our trust in the peer-oriented (professionalized) credentialing networks of strictly literary-artistic institutions, and the more generalist court of opinion that Morrison accessed a few years after her Nobel through the televised mediation of Oprah Winfrey. The public atmospheres of Morrison as author's author, Oprah Winfrey-enhanced bestseller, and icon of diversity and African-American liberation, harmonize literary prestige and democratic virtue so well that one can forget how rarely literature's curation cultures attune with a larger public consensus. But Morrison's ability to balance out all demands strikes me as sheer "moral luck" (Williams 1981, Rorty 2007); a happy alignment of incommensurable goods that detracts from the normality of conflict. For less lucky seekers of strong value—ordinary readers and writers in various states of worship, culture-warriordom, or indifference—the often smug conviction that virtue and literary excellence naturally follow from open-minded human decency should not be an option. The restorative act of balance that Steiner locates as the fourth "piston-stroke" is better described as a political move that comes *after* the hermeneutic motion is complete, a weighing of the *consequences* of our trust relations that we perform as citizens rather than hermeneuts.

Works Cited

Adorno, Theodor W. (1953). "Valéry, Proust, Museum." *Kulturkritik und Gesellschaft* (Frankfurt: Suhrkamp, 2003) 181-94.

Alexander, Jeffrey C. (2006). *The Civil Sphere* (Oxford: Oxford UP).

Alexander, Jeffrey C., and Dominik Bartmański (2012). "Introduction: Materiality and Meaning in Social Life: Toward an Iconic Turn in Cultural Sociology." *Iconic Power: Materiality and Meaning in Social Life*. Ed. Jeffrey Alexander et al. (London: Palgrave) 1–12.

Alexander, Jeffrey C., Gordon Lynch, and Ruth Sheldon (2013). "The sociology of the sacred: A conversation with Jeffrey Alexander." *Culture and Religion: An Interdisciplinary Journal*. 1–15.

Alexander, Jeffrey C. (2019). *What Makes a Social Crisis? The Societalization of Social Problems* (Cambridge: Polity).

Anon. (1848). "Evangeline." *Universalist Quarterly and General Review* 5 (Jan.): 104–109.

Arnold, Matthew (1993). *Culture and Anarchy and Other Writings*. Ed. Stefan Collini (Cambridge: Cambridge UP).

Ashcroft, Bill, et al. (1989). *The Empire Writes Back: Theory and Practice in Post-Colonial Literatures* (London: Routledge).

Asmelash, Leah (2019). "Why 'Cancel Culture' Doesn't Always Work." *CNN*, September 21. https://edition.cnn.com/2019/09/21/entertainment/cancel-culture-explainer-trnd/index.html. Last accessed June 17, 2020.

Assmann, Aleida (1999). *Erinnerungsräume: Formen und Wandlungen des kulturellen Gedächtnisses* (München: Beck).

Benjamin, Walter (1968). *Illuminations: Essays and Reflections* (NY: Harcourt Brace).

Berger, Peter L. (2014). *The Many Altars of Modernity: Toward a Paradigm for Religion in a Pluralist Age* (Boston: de Gruyter).

Berman, Marshall (1982). *All That's Solid Melts Into Air: The Experience of Modernity* (NY: Simon & Schuster).

Best, Stephen, and Sharon Marcus (2009). "Surface Reading: An Introduction." *Representations* 108.1 (Fall 2009): 1–21.

Bhabha, Homi (1994). *The Location of Culture* (London: Routledge).

Bloom, Harold (1973). *Anxiety of Influence: A Theory of Poetry* (Oxford: Oxford UP).

Bille, Mikkel, Peter Bjerregaard, and Tim Flohr Sørensen (2015). Special Issue: "Staging Atmospheres: Materiality, Culture, and the Texture of the In-Between." *Emotion, Space and Society* 15: 1–90.

Boehm, Gottfried, ed. (1994). *Was ist ein Bild?* (München: Fink).

Böhme, Gernot (2017). *The Aesthetics of Atmospheres* (London: Routledge).

Boltanski, Luc, and Arnaud Esquerre (2020). *Enrichment: A Critique of Commodities* (Cambridge: Polity).

Brooks, Van Wyck (1934). "America's Coming of Age." [1915] *Three Essays on America* (NY: Dutton) 13–112.

Bromwich, Jonah Engel (2018). "Everyone Is Canceled." *New York Times*, June 28. https://www.nytimes.com/2018/06/28/style/is-it-canceled.html. Last accessed June 17, 2020.

Casanova, Pascale (2004). *The World Republic of Letters* [1999] (Cambridge, MA: Harvard UP).

Charvat, William (1968). *The Profession of Authorship in America: 1800–1870* (Columbus: Ohio State UP).

Chong, Phillipa K. (2020). *Inside the Critics' Circle: Book Reviewing in Uncertain Times* (Princeton: Princeton UP).

Collini, Stefan, ed. (1992). *Interpretation and Overinterpretation* (Cambridge: Cambridge UP).

Connolly, William E. (2000). *Why I Am Not a Secularist* (Minneapolis: U of Minnesota P).

Derrida, Jacques (1970). "Structure, Sign, and Play in the Discourse of the Human Sciences." *The Structuralist Controversy: The Languages of Criticism and the Sciences of Man*. Ed. Richard Macksey and Eugenio Donato (Baltimore: Johns Hopkins UP) 247–65.

Devey, Joseph (1873). *A Comparative Estimate of Modern English Poets* (London: Moxon).

De Tocqueville, Alexis (2000). *Democracy in America*. Transl. and ed., Harvey Mansfield, and Delba Winthrop (Chicago: U of Chicago P).

Dowden, Edward (1871). "The Poetry of Democracy: Walt Whitman." *Westminster Review* XCVI: CLXXXIX (July): 33–68.

Douglas, Mary (1966). *Purity and Danger: An Analysis of Concepts of Pollution and Taboo* (London: Routledge).

Emerson, Ralph Waldo (1903). *Complete Works*. Centenary Edition (Boston: Houghton Mifflin).

Emre, Merve (2017). *Paraliterary: The Making of Bad Readers in Postwar America*. (Chicago: U Chicago P).

Felski, Rita (2015). *The Limits of Critique* (Chicago: U of Chicago P).

Fish, Stanley (1994). *There's No Such Thing as Free Speech…And it's A Good Thing, Too* (New York: Oxford UP).

Fish, Stanley (1999). *The Trouble with Principle* (Cambridge: Harvard UP).

Flatley, Jonathan (2008). *Affective Mapping: Melancholia and the Politics of Modernism* (Cambridge, MA: Harvard UP).

Fuchs, Thomas (2000). *Leib—Raum—Person: Entwurf einer philosophischen Anthropologie* (Stuttgart: Klett-Cotta).

Gadamer, Hans-Georg (1990). *Wahrheit und Methode. Gesammelte Werke 1* (Tübingen: Mohr-Siebeck).

Griffero, Tonino, and Marco Tedeschini, eds. (2019). *Atmosphere and Aesthetics: A Plural Perspective* (London: Palgrave).

Gumbrecht, Hans Ulrich (2003). *Production of Presence: What Meaning Cannot Convey* (Stanford: Stanford UP).

Heidegger, Martin (1995). *The Fundamental Concepts of Metaphysics: World, Finitude, Solitude*. Transl. William McNeill and Nicholas Walker (Bloomington: Indiana UP).

Heidegger, Martin (2004). *Die Grundbegriffe der Metaphysik: Welt—Endlichkeit—Einsamkeit* (Frankfurt: Klostermann).

James, William (1981). *Pragmatism*. Ed. Bruce Kuklick (Indianapolis: Hackett).

Jameson, Fredric (1981). *The Political Unconscious: Narrative as a Socially Symbolic Act* (Ithaca: Cornell UP).

Joas, Hans (2000). *The Genesis of Values* (Chicago: U of Chicago P).

Joas, Hans (2019). "Was weiß, wer glaubt?" *Süddeutsche Zeitung*, Nov. 15. https://www.sueddeutsche.de/kultur/juergen-habermas-opus-mag num-auch-eine-geschichte-der-philosophie-vernuenftige-freiheit-1. 4680022?reduced=true. Last accessed May 27, 2020.

Karpik, Lucien (2010). *Valuing the Unique: The Economics of Singularities* (Princeton: Princeton UP).

Kopytoff, Igor (1986). "The Cultural Biography of Things: Commoditization as Process." *The Social Life of Things*. Ed. Arjun Appadurai (Cambridge: Cambridge UP) 64-91.

Kuper, Adam (1999). *Culture: The Anthropologists' Account* (Cambridge, MA: Harvard UP).

Laclau, Ernesto (2005). *On Populist Reason* (London: Verso).

Levine, George (1981). *The Realistic Imagination: English Fiction from Frankenstein to Lady Chatterley* (Chicago: U of Chicago P).

Lewisohn, Ludwig (1932). *Expression in America* (NY: Harper & Brothers).

Leypoldt, Günter (2014). "Singularity and the Literary Market." *New Literary History* 45.1 (Winter): 71–88.

Leypoldt, Günter (2017). "Knausgaard in America: Literary Prestige and Charismatic Trust." *Critical Quarterly* 59.3 (October): 55–69.

Leypoldt, Günter (2020). "Spatial Reading: Evaluative Frameworks and the Making of Literary Authority." *American Journal of Cultural Sociology* 9. Special Issue of Reading, ed. Angelica Thumala. https://doi.org/10.1057/s4129 0-020-00107-w.

Longfellow, Henry Wadsworth (1853). *Evangeline: A Tale of Acadie*. Fourth Edition (London: Vizetelly).

Lyotard, Jean-François (1984). *The Postmodern Condition: A Report on Knowledge* (Manchester: Manchester UP).

McFarland, Ron (2010). *The Long Life of Evangeline* (NY: McFarland).

Marinetti, F.T. (1909). "The Foundation and Manifesto of Futurism." *Art in Theory: 1900–2000*. Ed. Charles Harrison, Paul Wood (London: Blackwell, 2003) 146–150.

McGurl, Mark (2016). "Everything and Less: Fiction in the Age of Amazon." *Modern Language Quarterly* 77.3 (September): 447–71.

Miller, William I. (1997). *The Anatomy of Disgust* (Cambridge, MA: Harvard UP).

Mitchell, W.J.T. (1986). *Iconology: Image, Text, Ideology* (Chicago: U of Chicago P).

Monticello.org (n.d.). "Thomas Jefferson and Sally Hemings: A Brief Account." https://www.monticello.org/thomas-jefferson/jefferson-slavery/thomas-jefferson-and-sally-hemings-a-brief-account/. Last accessed June 15, 2020.

Mouffe, Chantal (2018). *For a Left Populism* (London: Verso).

Mudde, Cas, and Cristóbal Rovira Kaltwasser (2017). *Populism: A Very Short Introduction* (Oxford: Oxford UP).

Müller, Jan-Werner (2016). *What is Populism?* (London: Penguin).

Negrin, Llewellyn (1993). "On the Museum's Ruins: A Critical Appraisal." *Theory, Culture, and Society* 10: 97–125.

Ngai, Sianne (2005). *Ugly Feelings* (Cambridge, MA: Harvard UP).

Nussbaum, Martha (2016). *Not for Profit: Why Democracy Needs the Humanities* (Princeton: Princeton UP).

Peck, George W. (1848). *A Review of Mr. Longfellow's* Evangeline: *From the American Review*, February 1948. (np., nd.)

Pietsch, Bryan (2020). "Princeton Will Remove Woodrow Wilson's Name From School." *New York Times*, June 27. https://www.nytimes.com/2020/06/27/nyregion/princeton-university-woodrow-wilson.html. Last accessed June 29, 2020.

Rancière, Jacques (2004). *The Politics of Aesthetics: The Distribution of the Sensible* (London: Bloomsbury).

Reckwitz, Andreas (2020). *The Society of Singularities* (Cambridge: Polity).

Rilke, Rainer Maria (1995). *Ahead of All Parting: Selected Poetry and Prose of Rainer Maria Rilke*. Ed. and transl. Stephen Mitchell (NY: Modern Library).

Rorty, Richard (1982). *Consequences of Pragmatism* (NY: Harvester).

Rorty, Richard (2007). "Honest Mistakes." *Philosophy as Cultural Politics: Philosophical Papers* 4 (Cambridge: CUP) 56-70.

Rosa, Hartmut (2019). *Resonance: A Sociology of Our Relationship to the World* (Cambridge: Polity).

Sandel, Michael (1998). *Democracy's Discontent: America in Search of a Public Philosophy* (Cambridge, MA: Harvard UP).

Santayana, George (1968). "The Genteel Tradition." [1911] *Selected Critical Writings of George Santayana*. Ed. Norman Henfrey (Cambridge: Cambridge UP) 85–107.

Shils, Edward (1982). *The Constitution of Society* (Chicago: U of Chicago P).

Sloterdijk, Peter (2013). *You Must Change Your Life* (Cambridge: Polity).

Smith, Philip (2012). "Becoming Iconic: The Cases of Woodstock and Bayreuth." *Iconic Power: Materiality and Meaning in Social Life*. Ed. Jeffrey C. Alexander et al. (London: Palgrave) 171–86.

Smith, Laurajane (2006). *Uses of Heritage* (London: Routledge).

Sollors, Werner (1986). *Beyond Ethnicity: Consent and Descent in American Culture* (Oxford: Oxford UP).

Stedman, Edmund C. (1885). *Poets of America* (Boston: Houghton Mifflin).

Steiner, George (1975). *After Babel: Aspects of Language and Translation* (Oxford: Oxford UP).

Taylor, Charles (1985). "What is Human Agency?" *Human Agency and Language* (Cambridge: Cambridge UP). 15–44.

Taylor, Charles (1989). *Sources of the Self: The Making of the Modern Identity* (Cambridge, MA: Harvard UP).

Taylor, Charles (2011). *Dilemmas and Connections: Selected Essays* (Cambridge, MA: Harvard UP).

Thomas, Suzie, Vesa-Pekka Herva, Oula Seitsonen, and Eerika Koskinen-Koivisto (2019). "Dark Heritage." *Encyclopedia of Global Archaeology*. Ed. C. Smith (Zurich: Springer).

Tompkins, Jane (1985). *Sensational Designs: The Cultural Work of American Fiction, 1790–1860* (Oxford: Oxford UP).

Truscott, Lucian (2020). "I'm a Direct Descendant of Thomas Jefferson. Take Down His Memorial." *New York Times*, July 6, https://www.nytimes.com/2020/07/06/opinion/thomas-jefferson-memorial-truscott.html. Accessed: August 12, 2020.

Valéry, Paul (1937). "Leçon inaugurale du cours de poétique du Collège de France." *Œuvres*. Ed. Michel Jarrety. 3 vols. (Paris: Le Livre de Poche, 2016) 3: 952–74.

Valéry, Paul (1923). "Le problème des musées." *Œuvres* (Paris: Gallimard, 1960) 1290–3.

Vessey, David (2009). "Gadamer and the Fusion of Horizons." *International Journal of Philosophical Studies* 17.4: 531–42.

Weber, Max (1972). *Wirtschaft und Gesellschaft* (Tübingen: Mohr-Siebeck).

Wendell, Barrett (1900). *A Literary History of America* (NY: Scribner's).

Williams, Bernard (1981). *Moral Luck* (Cambridge: Cambridge UP).

Willis, Lloyd (2006). "Henry Wadsworth Longfellow, United States National Literature, and the Canonical Erasure of Material Nature." *American Transcendental Quarterly* 20.4 (December): 629–46.

Young, Robert C. (1995). *Colonial Desire: Hybridity in Theory, Culture and Race* (London: Routledge).

Zhang, Dora (2018). "Notes on Atmosphere." *Qui Parle* 27.1: 121–55.

List of Contributors

MANFRED BERG is the Curt Engelhorn Professor of American History at Heidelberg University. His work focuses on the history of the African-American civil rights movement, race relations, popular violence, and U.S. political history. He is the author and editor of numerous books, including *The Ticket to Freedom: The NAACP and the Struggle for Black Political Integration* (2005); *Popular Justice: A History of Lynching in America* (2011). In 2006 Berg received the David Thelen Award from the Organization of American Historians and in 2016 the Distinguished Historian's Award from the Society of Historians of the Gilded Age and the Progressive Era. Since 2019, Manfred Berg has been a member of the Heidelberg Academy of Science.

FLORIAN BÖLLER is an Assistant Professor of International Relations at the University of Kaiserslautern, Germany. Between 2017 and 2019, he was postdoctoral researcher at the Graduiertenkolleg *Authority and Trust in American Culture and Society* at the Heidelberg Center for American Studies. His research interests include US foreign policy, transatlantic relations, and parliamentary control of security policy. He published several books and articles in journals, such as *British Journal of Politics and International Relations*, *European Political Science Review*, and *Contemporary Security Policy*.

ULRIKE GERHARD is a professor of Human Geography of North America at the Institute of Geography and the Heidelberg Center for American Studies (HCA) at Heidelberg University. Her research examines how recent political, social, ecological, and economic restructuring shapes urban space, often from an interdisciplinary perspective. She has edited and authored several books, among them *Kulturgeographie der USA: Eine Nation begreifen* (2017), *Inequalities in Creative Cities* (2017), and *Die Stadt von morgen* (2020), and published theoretical and empirical papers in international journals such as *Geographica Helvetica* (2014), *Historical Social Research* (2015), and *Geographische Zeitschrift* (2019).

SEBASTIAN HARNISCH, Professor for International Relations and Foreign Policy, is Executive Director of the Institute for Political Science at Heidelberg University and a member of the Board of Directors of the Heidelberg Center for American Studies (HCA). His main research areas include comparative foreign and security policy, international relations theories, cybersecurity, non-proliferation of weapons of mass destruction, and climate change policy issues. Sebastian Harnisch is co-editor of the series *Foreign Policy and International Order* (Nomos Verl.) and the *Oxford Research Encyclopedia for Foreign Policy Analysis* (Oxford University Press). He has published numerous books, edited volumes, and articles in renowned journals.

CLAUDIA JETTER is a doctoral candidate in American Religious History at the Faculty of Theology at Heidelberg University. Her dissertation investigates charismatization and scripturalization processes in the new religious movements of nineteenth-century America. She is a member of the Graduiertenkolleg *Authority and Trust in American Culture and Society* at the Heidelberg Center for American Studies, and of its graduate council. She has delivered conference papers at such venues as the Ecclesiastical History Society, the Methodist Studies Seminar and the American Society for Church History, and has been a visiting scholar at the Neal A. Maxwell Institute for Religious Scholarship at Brigham Young University.

JUDITH KELLER is a doctoral student in the Graduiertenkolleg *Authority and Trust in American Culture and Society* at the Heidelberg Center for American Studies. In her research she applies trust theory to urban spaces and focuses on housing in major cities. In particular, she looks into how the loss of homes due to changing urban environments and policies affect the trust relationships of urban residents.

GÜNTER LEYPOLDT is a Professor of American Literature and Culture at Heidelberg University, and speaker of the Graduiertenkolleg *Authority and Trust in American Culture and Society* at the Heidelberg Center for American Studies. He is the author of *Cultural Authority in the Age of Whitman: A Transatlantic Perspective* (2009), editor of *Intellectual Authority and Literary Culture in the US, 1790-1900* (2013), and co-editor of *American Cultural Icons* (2010) and *Reading*

Practices (2015). His essays appeared in such journals as *American Literary History*, *Modern Language Quarterly*, *New Literary History*, *American Journal of Cultural Sociology*, *Critical Quarterly*, *Contemporary Literature*, and *Post45*.

MARGIT PETERFY is a Senior Research Lecturer in American Studies at Heidelberg University. She is the author of a book on the reception of William Carlos Williams in Germany, and a forthcoming study on the poetry of H.W. Longfellow and J.G. Whittier. She has also written articles on American popular culture and on intermediality. Her most recent publication is the co-authored volume *Key Concepts for the Study of Culture* (2020). Within the Heidelberg Graduiertenkolleg on *Authority and Trust in American Culture and Society*, her research focuses on the intellectual history of trust relationships in US-American urban fiction.

DIETMAR SCHLOSS teaches American literature and culture at Heidelberg University. He holds a Ph.D. from Northwestern University (Evanston, IL) and a postdoctoral degree from Heidelberg. He is the author of *Die tugendhafte Republik*: *Politische Ideologie und Literatur in der amerikanischen Gründerzeit* (2003), which examines the political visions of American writers during the founding period of the United States, and the editor of *Civilizing America: Manners and Civility in American Literature and Culture* (2009).

TIM SOMMER is a lecturer and postdoctoral researcher at Heidelberg University. He has been a Visiting Fellow at Harvard University and an Academic Visitor at the University of Cambridge. His work on Anglo-American literary and cultural exchange during the long nineteenth century has appeared in journals such as *The New England Quarterly*, the *Harvard Library Bulletin*, and the *Wordsworth Circle.* He is currently completing the manuscript of his first monograph, which reads Thomas Carlyle and Ralph Waldo Emerson against the background of transatlantic struggles for cultural authority.

JAN STIEVERMANN is a Professor of the History of Christianity in the U.S. at Heidelberg University, and director of the Jonathan Edwards Center Germany. He has written books and essays on a broad range of topics in the fields of American religious history and American literature, including a comprehensive study of the theology and aesthetics of Ralph Waldo Emerson (Schöningh, 2007) and *Prophecy, Piety, and the Problem of Historicity: Interpreting the Hebrew Scriptures in Cotton Mather's* Biblia Americana (Mohr Siebeck, 2016). He serves as executive editor for the scholarly edition of the *Biblia Americana* manuscript, of which he edits volumes 5 (2010) and 10 (forthcoming in 2021). Among other multi-authored volumes, he co-edited *A Peculiar Mixture: German-Language Cultures and Identities in Eighteenth-Century North America* (Pennsylvania State UP, 2013), *Religion and the Marketplace in the United States* (Oxford UP, 2014) and the forthcoming *Oxford Handbook of Jonathan Edwards*.

MARTIN THUMERT is Senior Research Lecturer for Political Science at the Heidelberg Center for American Studies (HCA). His research interests are North American political studies, especially the US presidency, think tanks, interest groups and policy advisory organizations. He holds a doctoral degree from the University of Hamburg and held research fellowships at Harvard University's Center for European Studies, McGill University, Canada, and the University of Southampton, UK. He also worked as a committee staff member for the late U.S. Senator Edward M. Kennedy. Since 2007, Thunert has been Research Coordinator for Canada, Chile, Mexico and the U.S. in the Bertelsmann Foundation project *Sustainable Governance Indicators*. Recent publications include *Muster der Politikberatung* (2019); "What the Trump-Administration Means for Canada" (2018); *Entzauberung: Skizzen und Ansichten zu den USA in der Ära Obama* (2016, with D. Stasiak and G. Friedrichs); and *Disenchantment: Sketches and Views on the US in the Obama Era* (with T. Endler).

COSIMA WERNER is a doctoral student at the Department of Human Geography at Heidelberg University. In 2017, she joined the Graduiertenkolleg *Authority and Trust in American Culture and Society* at the Heidelberg Center for American Studies. In her dissertation project, she explores the importance of convenience stores in marginalized US-American neighborhoods in Detroit and Chicago, focusing on how convenience stores are constituted as social spaces in impoverished all-black-communities.

Cultural Studies

Gabriele Klein
Pina Bausch's Dance Theater
Company, Artistic Practices and Reception

May 2020, 440 p., pb., col. ill.
29,99 € (DE), 978-3-8376-5055-6
E-Book:
PDF: 29,99 € (DE), ISBN 978-3-8394-5055-0

Elisa Ganivet
Border Wall Aesthetics
Artworks in Border Spaces

2019, 250 p., hardcover, ill.
79,99 € (DE), 978-3-8376-4777-8
E-Book:
PDF: 79,99 € (DE), ISBN 978-3-8394-4777-2

Jocelyne Porcher, Jean Estebanez (eds.)
Animal Labor
A New Perspective on Human-Animal Relations

2019, 182 p., hardcover
99,99 € (DE), 978-3-8376-4364-0
E-Book: 99,99 € (DE), ISBN 978-3-8394-4364-4

Cultural Studies

Andreas Sudmann (ed.)
The Democratization of Artificial Intelligence
Net Politics in the Era of Learning Algorithms

2019, 334 p., pb., col. ill.
49,99 € (DE), 978-3-8376-4719-8
E-Book: available as free open access publication
PDF: ISBN 978-3-8394-4719-2

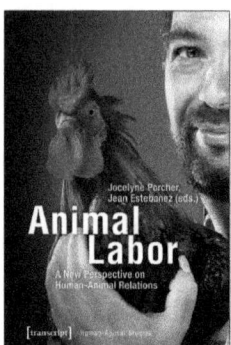

Jocelyne Porcher, Jean Estebanez (eds.)
Animal Labor
A New Perspective on Human-Animal Relations

2019, 182 p., hardcover
99,99 € (DE), 978-3-8376-4364-0
E-Book:
PDF: 99,99 € (DE), ISBN 978-3-8394-4364-4

Ramón Reichert, Mathias Fuchs,
Pablo Abend, Annika Richterich, Karin Wenz (eds.)
Digital Culture & Society (DCS)
Vol. 4, Issue 1/2018 – Rethinking AI: Neural Networks,
Biometrics and the New Artificial Intelligence

2018, 244 p., pb., ill.
29,99 € (DE), 978-3-8376-4266-7
E-Book:
PDF: 29,99 € (DE), ISBN 978-3-8394-4266-1

**All print, e-book and open access versions of the titles in our list
are available in our online shop www.transcript-publishing.com**

GPSR Authorized Representative: Easy Access System Europe, Mustamäe tee 50, 10621 Tallinn, Estonia, gpsr.requests@easproject.com